The Bloody Circus

to be returned before

THE BLOODY CIRCUS
The *Daily Herald* and the Left

HUW RICHARDS

Pluto **Press**
LONDON • CHICAGO, IL.

First published 1997 by Pluto Press
345 Archway Road, London N6 5AA
and 1436 West Randolph,
Chicago, Illinois 60607, USA

British Library Cataloguing in Publication Data
A catalogue record for this book is available from the British Library

ISBN 0 7453 1117 2 hbk

Library of Congress Cataloging in Publication Data
Richards, Huw.
    The Bloody Circus: the Daily Herald and the left/Huw Richards.
        p.   cm.
    ISBN 0–7453–1117–2
    1. Press and politics—Great Britain. 2. Labour Party (Great
Britain) 3. Trade Union Congress. I. Daily Herald (London,
England) II. Title.
PN5129.L7D286   1997
072'.1—dc21   97–14416
                                                              CIP

Designed and Produced for Pluto Press by
Chase Production Services, Chadlington, OX7 3LN
Typeset from disk by Stanford DTP Services, Northampton
Printed in the EC by The Cromwell Press

Contents

List of Illustrations

1. 'A Fantasy (Labour Leaders at their Devotions)' by Will Dyson, *Daily Herald*, 3 December 1913 (reproduced by permission).
2. 'The only way left open to them'; Poplar councillors Susan Lawrence, Nellie Cressall and Jennie Mackay on their way to Holloway jail, September 1921 (photo: Tower Hamlets Libraries, local history collection).
3. Rite of passage: dockers marching during their 1923 strike (photo: Tower Hamlets Libraries, local history collection).
4. 'The great leader who made the *Daily Herald*'; George Lansbury (centre), editor and proprietor 1913–22, waiting to be arrested during the 1921 Poplar dispute. Behind Lansbury's left shoulder is former *Herald* journalist John Scurr (photo: Tower Hamlets Libraries, local history collection).
5. 'They always did what he told them to do'; Ernest Bevin, painting by Thomas Cantrell Dugdale, 1945 (National Portrait Gallery).
6. 'Keeping a level head in the midst of great difficulty'; William Mellor, *Herald* editor 1926–30 (photo: NMPFT/Science & Society Picture Library).
7. 'Election fever'; *Daily Herald* front page, 11 May 1929.
8. 'A keen willingness to identity himself'; Prime Minister Ramsay MacDonald starts rotary machines in the new *Daily Herald* building, March 1930.
9. Never knowingly understated; the new *Daily Herald* hails its first official one million-plus sales certificate, 8 April 1930.

Acknowledgements

Any project which – with some long hiatuses – lasts 17 years from conception to publication accumulates numerous debts to be acknowledged.

First among these is to James Curran, for personal and intellectual generosity far beyond the demands of doctoral supervision. He has given freely of his deep knowledge of the British media and of the Labour movement and been an invaluable friend and adviser at every stage from the early stages of research through to final publication.

A somewhat chequered academic history means that several other people played vital roles in the original research on which this book is based. David Butler and Martin Ceadel nursed its initial stages, Tony Aldgate was a reliable guide through the Open University system and John Rowett offered both free access to his immense knowledge of Labour in the interwar years and perceptive thought on early drafts. Deian Hopkin offered invaluable advice which sustained the project in its early stages and assisted immensely in researching the pre-1912 chapter. Gary McCulloch first planted the idea of researching the history of the *Daily Herald* with a chance remark over a drink.

Other experts have offered advice and assistance. Adrian Smith's notes and conference paper on the *Herald* after 1930 greatly aided the chapter on that period, while John Shepherd drew for my benefit on his unmatched knowledge of George Lansbury. Thanks also to Jamie Belich, Ray Boston, Brian Brivati, Peter Catterall, Richard Cockett, David Englander, Brian Harrison, Peter Hennessy, Steve Howe, David Howell, Ben Pimlott, John Ritchie, Richard Saville, Len Scott and the late Philip Williams.

Four former members of *Herald*/Odhams Press staff – the late Lord Leatherland, Lord Jay and Sir Tom Hopkinson, and Geoffrey Goodman, whose reminiscences of the 1950s were especially helpful – generously gave me interviews. Michael Foot, Richard Hall and Stuart Marshall also provided anecdotes about the paper and its staff.

Several archives, libraries and their staff provided invaluable assistance. Rosie Stone and the filing department of the Trades Union Congress and Stephen Bird, archivist at the Labour Party,

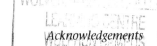

facilitated access to these key institutional archives. Dr Richard Storey of the Modern Records Office, Warwick University and the Transport and General Workers Union permitted access to the Ernest Bevin papers and thanks are also due to Harry Cox, formerly librarian to the Mirror Group, the staffs of the manuscript room at the British Library of Political and Economic Science at the London School of Economics, the South Wales Miners' Library, the Public Record Office and the John Rylands Library. Thanks also to Amanda Kendall of the *Morning Star* and Melanie Aspey of the *Times* archive.

The *Daily Herald* and other newspapers were read at the National Newspaper Library, Colindale – where Geoff Smith was unfailingly helpful – the Bodleian Library, Oxford, Nuffield College, Oxford and the research department of the National Union of Journalists. Help with illustrations was provided by Venita Paul, John Jensen and Peter Rich of the Local History Library, London Borough of Tower Hamlets.

The Society for the Study of Labour History, the Institute of Historical Research Media History and Modern British History seminars, the Institute for Contemporary British History and the University of Wales, Aberystwyth history society all provided with the opportunity to present and clarify ideas through conference and seminar papers.

Friends who have provided practical assistance include Catherine Hastings, Martin Ince, Simon Targett, Steve Pinder, Rob Steen, Paul Anderson and the then (1992) staff of *Tribune*, Mark McDonald, Peter Raikes and Bridget Osborne, Steve Howe and Daphna Vardi, Jane Arms and Brian Matthews, and Rob and Alyson Bell. Jane Elvin lived with the project for several years.

The completion of the first stage of this book, the doctoral research, was greatly assisted by a term as a member of the Oxford Journalism Fellowship Programme at Queen Elizabeth House. Thanks are due to Neville Maxwell, director of the programme, to the Leverhulme Foundation for funding my place, to the fellowship colleagues – particularly Ken Guggenheim, John Nicol, Connie Sage and Aura Triana – who created a pleasurable and productive working environment and to my employers, Times Supplements Ltd for not only granting me leave but continuing to pay my salary.

The second stage was the revised version which forms this book. For this thanks are due to the staff and management of the Hotel Leonor de Aquitania, Cuenca and the Patio de la Cartuja, Seville for providing ideal writing environments.

But the main thanks must be to people directly concerned with the book. At Pluto Press Anne Beech and Robert Webb have provided the mix of enthusiasm, encouragement, long-suffering humour and firmness over deadlines that any author needs in their publisher, while Aleks Sierz brought a sharp, sympathetic eye to copy editing and Ray Addicott to production. James Curran, Mike Marqusee and Paul Melly showed generosity beyond the demands of friendship in reading the final manuscript and offering invaluable insights and suggestions drawn from varied personal perspectives – likewise Kate Green, who took on the singularly thankless task of proof-reading.

Final thanks are to three groups of people who have, largely unwittingly, contributed greatly. Reporting the affairs of Fulham Rugby League Club provided an unparalleled training in the problems afflicting cash-strapped institutions which inspire deep devotion in a few and utter indifference in the majority. Collegues on a variety of newspapers, particularly the *Times Higher Education Supplement*, have been a constant source of insight into the way newspapers and journalists work, or do not work. And my parents, Stan and Sheila Richards, who both grew up in *Daily Herald* – reading homes, passed on the best of its values and an interest in history and have been an unfailing source of support and encouragement, both practical and emotional. This book is dedicated to them.

Introduction

If you cannot ride two horses at once, you have no right to be in the bloody circus.

James Maxton

The 52-year career of the *Daily Herald* is one of the great, largely untold, stories of twentieth-century British journalism. More than 30 years after its closure, it is being gradually forgotten – not so rapidly as the apparently unmourned *Daily Sketch*, yet lacking the ability of the *News Chronicle*, victim four years before the *Herald* of Fleet Street's inexorable competitive pressures, to evoke nostalgia among the liberal-minded middle-aged. It deserves better. The history of the British press is littered with short-lived victims. The careers, in the last decade alone, of *Today*, *The Sunday Correspondent* and *News on Sunday* are a reminder of this. The difficulties faced by so initially impressive and successful a newcomer as the *Independent*, in particular its incorporation into an established press empire, shows how ferociously competitive the market is. Of the five current national popular dailies, the *Mail*, *Express* and *Mirror* were all founded between 1896 and 1903, the *Star* is an offshoot of the *Express* and the *Sun* was built not from scratch, but from the ruins of a previous going concern. The *Herald*, starting with only £300 and a vision of a better world, managed to survive more than half a century.

From its first issue, on 15 April 1912, to its last, on 14 September 1964, the *Herald* was a challenge to the norms and assumptions of the British press. The rhetoric of the national press proclaims that it is an industry characterised by individualism and diversity. In practice, driven by competitive pressures and fear of failure, it tends to conformity and convergence, ever vulnerable to the latest gimmick, craze or means of sales promotion for fear of losing a march on rivals. The *Daily Herald* was different. Where other Fleet Street papers were essentially commercial in motivation, the *Herald* was overtly political. Fleet Street's ideology was capitalist, but the *Herald* espoused anti-capitalism. Other papers were created and owned by wealthy proprietors – the *Herald* was first the creation of part of the labour movement and then the property of the whole of it.

The *Herald* is significant not only in the history of the press, but also in that of the labour movement. Its pages provide an unparalleled account of the movement's development and fortunes over half a century. Labour has always been convinced, with good reason, that the mass of the national press is firmly against it. That maverick press barons have been a constant source of worry for Conservative Party leaders is of no consequence, there being little doubt which side they would choose in the defining conflict between capital and labour. The *Herald* was much the most significant, sustained attempt to redress the balance. By creating a national daily newspaper, labour challenged capital on its own ground, seeking to compete in one of the toughest capitalist markets. The *Herald*'s aspirations, challenges and dilemmas parallel and provide insight into those of the wider movement as it sought to transform British society.

The paper's history was marked by three distinct incarnations. Each recasting shifted it further from its origins, becoming more like the competitors whose values it aspired to defeat, but never so completely that it could be said the *Herald* was no different to other papers. The paper's first decade following its foundation by a committee of trade union activists in 1912 was marked by a freewheeling, independent radicalism, its dominant figure the extraordinary George Lansbury, MP, council leader, poor-law reformer, pacifist, suffragist and Christian. Historian A.J.P. Taylor reckoned that he was 'the most beloved figure in modern British politics'.[1] The labour intellectual Harold Laski said Lansbury had 'far from the clearest mind in the Labour movement, but a heart that reaches to the stars'.[2] In 1922 the paper passed into the reluctant hands of the Trades Union Congress and the Labour Party. They ran it as an official movement organ until 1929, when it was effectively privatised by the TUC's entry into partnership with commercial publishers Odhams Press. That partnership, aimed at producing a paper mixing official labour politics with the editorial and promotional attractions offered by other popular dailies, persisted until the paper's demise in 1964.

Francis Williams, a *Herald* journalist of the early 1920s who returned to become City editor, then editor, in the 1930s, called his memoirs *Nothing So Strange*.[3] There is little stranger than the mix of oddity, paradox and idiosyncracy that crowds the *Herald*'s story. It is admittedly coincidental that its date of birth, 15 April 1912, should also have been that of the North Korean dictator Kim Il Sung, who unfortunately showed greater endurance and instinct for power, but there was nothing fortuitous about the end of its existence. A paper whose *raison d'être* was serving the labour movement, it closed only weeks before the party regained power in 1964, after 13 years in opposition. The 1920s and early 1930s were particularly rich in oddity. The *Herald*'s fervent backing for the rights and interests of trade unions and trade unionists dated back to its origins, yet in 1923 it attempted to blackmail the TUC through the agency of its children's cartoon strip 'Bobby Bear'. In the same year it was the focus for a confrontation between the print unions and its management, hardly unusual in Fleet Street, but it was the unions who demanded job cuts and the *Daily Herald* management who resisted them. The following year found the Labour Party in office and the *Daily Herald* in profit, both unprecedented and short-lived phenomena. The *Herald* had spent much of the previous two years loudly proclaiming the virtues of Labour leader James Ramsay MacDonald. At the end of his period in office he blamed the paper for his defeat. Then, in the early 1930s, this daily paper devoted to the propagation of socialist ideology helped to provoke the most ferocious outbreak of unbridled capitalist competition yet seen in the history of the national press. These incidents are more than just oddities. Each reflected the pressures piled upon the *Herald* as it attempted to fulfil a multiplicity of objectives. The journalist and press historian Matthew Engel has rightly compared the fiendish difficulties facing any popular paper in fulfilling its mix of commercial and journalistic aims with 'lining up the three bells on a fruit machine'.[4]

The *Herald*'s objectives may have been political, but the pressures upon it were as much commercial and financial. The movement leaders who sat on the *Herald* board throughout its history could have echoed the famous words of the maverick Conservative proprietor of the *Daily Express*, Lord Beaverbrook, giving evidence to the 1947 Royal Commission on the Press: 'I ran the paper purely for propaganda, and for no other purpose.'[5] That striking and mischievous remark is invariably quoted whenever the political activities of press proprietors are discussed. Much less has been made of his subsequent, equally significant comment: 'In order to make the propaganda effective, the paper had to be successful. No paper is any good at all for propaganda unless it has a thoroughly good financial position.'[6]

The British national press is an industry which imposes extremely high entry and maintenance costs. London-based, but nationally circulating, papers have dominated the twentieth century, a hegemony epitomised by the decision of the last great exception, the *Manchester Guardian,* to drop the city name from its title and move to the capital in 1961.[7] It is polarised between mass-market titles and what successive *Sun* editors, echoing 1950s *Herald* deputy editor Harold Hutchinson, have delighted in calling the 'unpopular press'.[8] Survival at the popular end of the market means producing and distributing a paper capable of attracting a large audience all across the country. This is not just a matter of providing decent journalism. Throughout the century the popular press has supplemented its journalistic appeal with other inducements. Bingo was to the 1980s what insurance schemes, backed by door-to-door canvassing and with a powerful natural appeal for working-class readers in the days before universal National Insurance, were to the 1930s. In addition the paper has to appeal to advertisers.

No national paper this century has been able to break even on sales income alone. Advertising money is an integral part of the newspaper economy. The 'unpopulars', with their high concentrations of high earners, can survive on relatively small circulations. For popular papers a mass circulation is essential.

Costs have risen consistently. Between 1790 and 1820, it was estimated that £2,000–5,000 was sufficient to launch a London daily.[9] In the 1870s Edward Lloyd spent £180,000 on buying the *Clerkenwell News* and turning it into the *Daily Chronicle*.[10] Rising costs continued through £300,000 poured abortively into *Tribune* in 1906–08, £750,000 put into trying to transform the *Westminster Gazette* in the 1920s and the £8.5m raised by Eddie Shah for *Today* in the mid 1980s.[11] Not having enough money is a certain guarantee of failure, but expenditure does not bring with it assured success – the last three papers in the above list failed. The paper has also to be attractive in itself. The *Herald*'s dilemma in attempting to devise a style of journalism with mass appeal paralleled that of the Labour Party in seeking votes. Both, in seeking a transformation of British society, faced the choice defined by Robert Kennedy: 'Some men see things as they are and say "Why?" I dream of things that never were and say "Why Not?"'[12] But while pursuing the world as it might be, you have to deal with it as it is. How far to compromise is the eternal conundrum, and disagreements on this fundamental question define many of the important debates and divisions within the movement and the *Herald*. In broad terms counterculturalists argue for the creation of alternatives to existing attitudes and structures, while mainstreamers opt to work within those structures and accept some of the attitudes in the hope of changing them. To the mainstreamer, the counterculturalist can appear unrealistically utopian and doomed to remain in a minority. The counterculturalist argues that the mainstreamer accepts incorporation by the society and values they are supposed to be overthrowing.

Philip Snowden, a Labour leader who was conspicuously uninvolved in the *Herald*, pointed to the competitive difficulties that attempting to be different imposed on the left-wing press in the 1919 edition of *Sell's World Press*:

A Labour Newspaper is at a disadvantage from the point of view of establishing a circulation by feeling under an obligation to maintain a higher moral standard than that observed by ordinary newspapers. The directors of a Labour newspaper regard it as inconsistent with their principles to give prominence to sensational news ... [they] have a mission to carry out. They have a gospel to preach. To them a newspaper is primarily a medium for propogating their ideas. The ordinary newspaper is conducted on entirely different lines. It is primarily a commercial venture. It has no scruples which are allowed to interfere with the success of its appeal for popular support.[13]

Tensions between the moral and political aspiration to be different and the pragmatic desire to compete were faithfully reflected within the *Herald*. Should it carry more human-interest news at the possible expense of the politically significant? Should it insist on conformity to Labour and TUC policy at all times? Should it run racing tips? Should it have an insurance scheme? Could it afford one in any case?

An official relationship with organised labour created further demands upon the *Herald*. These were neatly summarised in 1925 by Ethel Bentham, a director of the paper: 'The difficulty of the *Herald* is that a small paper with limited resources has to fulfil two different functions – that of the ordinary daily newspaper and that of the organ of the movement.'[14] It was easy enough to say that the *Herald* was the labour movement's paper, harder to decide what that implied about its position and outlook. Was it to be a paper in which leaders spoke to the led or vice versa? Was it to reflect only an official party line or to act as a forum for debate on that line? What was the party line anyway?

Party papers are pulled in a number of directions. Leaders want the official view to predominate, and may be able to reinforce personal authority with the power implicit in control of movement subsidies. Many activists will want debate, and scope for dissent; journalists dislike saying the same thing day after day. The paper is a major prize in intra-party battles, control carrying with it the opportunity to set the terms of much debate and, perhaps more importantly, to do what James Curran has called 'policing the boundaries of legitimate dissent'.[15]

Party papers divide into three broad types. These are tendencies rather than clear-cut differences or mutually exclusive distinctions. Newspapers are assembled rapidly by a large number of people, so ragged edges inevitably occur, whatever the intentions of the editor or management. One tendency is the top-down conduit. This hands down and expounds the official viewpoint, rejecting all criticism and acting as loyal follower to the leadership of the moment. Dissent is rarely recognised as legitimate. The appeal of this style for party leaders and officialdom is self-evident, but its besetting difficulty is that it lacks what Francis Williams called 'the priceless journalistic gift of surprise'.[16] The other end of the scale is the paper which operates as an independent political actor. It sets its own agenda and develops its own line, even if this conflicts with official viewpoints. Legitimate dissent is its stock-in-trade. The greater appeal of this to journalists and party activists, particularly those out of sympathy with the leadership, is equally clear. In between is the 'candid friend' approach. This gives broad support to the leadership. It reserves the right to occasional criticism and permits debate and dissent within carefully defined limits. But it will always defend the movement or its leaders against attack from the outside.

All three tendencies predominate at different times during the *Herald's* 52-year existence. This book is concerned with the entire story, but its chief focus is on the middle period of direct Labour–TUC proprietorship in the 1920s. Previous accounts of the *Herald* have tended to concentrate either on its rip-roaring radicalism under Lansbury or on its role – brandishing insurance schemes, free knives and forks and, most famously of all, cut-price sets of the works of Charles Dickens – in the circulation battles of the early 1930s. Yet the 1920s were the decisive period in the paper's history. The *Herald* of 1920 – radical, largely independent, Lansbury-edited – had much more in common with its predecessor of 1912 than it did with the *Herald* of 1930. That in its turn had more in common with the last *Herald* of 1964, an official politico-commercial hybrid, than with its predecessor of 1920. The link between them is the second incarnation, the Labour–TUC paper of 1922 to 1929.

At a superficial level this is a two-step shift accomplished by the Trades Union Congresses of 1922 and 1929. The reality is that it was a long drawn out transition, as the TUC and the Labour Party underwent progressive disillusionment with the role of press proprietor. That transition accompanied one of the most exciting periods in the movement's history, incorporating post-war industrial militancy, the first two Labour governments and the General Strike of 1926. Direct movement control meant that men like Arthur Henderson, Ernest Bevin, George Lansbury and A.J. Cook, who had decisive roles in those events, were also closely concerned with the *Herald*. To look at the fortunes of the *Daily Herald* in this period is to have an insight into the ambitions, problems and limitations of both the paper and the wider movement. The 1920s is also the period best provided with sources. There are a number of complete runs of the *Herald*, but other documents are in short supply. The papers of the Lansbury *Herald* are long lost. The Odhams Press archive appears to have been lost when the *Herald's* successor paper, the *Sun*, was sold to Rupert Murdoch in 1969 and moved from London's Long Acre, home to the *Herald* from 1930, to join the *News of the World* in Bouverie Street.[17]

But the archives of both the Trades Union Congress (now held at the Modern Records Centre, Warwick University) and the Labour Party (now held by the National Museum of Labour History, Manchester) retain some records from their period as joint proprietors. They are incomplete and unsatisfactory. It is for instance desperately frustrating, as a journalist, to be able to say so little about the men and women who worked on the *Daily Herald*, but they are the only papers we have. The other major source is the *Daily Herald* itself. Analysing content raises considerable difficulties. The historian of public policy can, subject to the weeding process, read copious Public Record Office files to examine the gestation, organisation and presentation of a single decision – a mass of input in relation to the output. The press historian, particularly when archives are as limited as those of the *Herald*, faces a mass of output in the form of the papers, backed by very little input. The sheer bulk of material is daunting. As the American press historian Joel Wiener has said: 'Everything in a newspaper, however insignificant, is potentially of interest, which complicates the matter.'[18] A loose, conservative estimate of the word-count in the *Herald* in the seven years between the crucial TUCs of 1922 and 1929 suggests that it is around 25 million words – or more than 300 times the length of this book. This makes decisions on how to analyse content vital. This book's structure is chronological. While all life is by definition lived chronologically, there are few activities where this is as important as journalism, dominated by the weekly or daily routine of production. A chronological approach provides the best means of examining a paper and how it changes in response to commercial, journalistic and political pressures. A subjective, interpretative approach has been adopted in preference to quantitative analysis. This is heavily reliant on the judgement of the individual historian – although quantitative approaches have problems with categorisation – but more effective in charting a paper's changing worldview. Personal judgement and interpretation dictate what is emphasised amid a mass of material.

Newspapers are complex, sensitive mechanisms subject to an immense range of influences and pressures. They are put together in a hurry. Editors are important, but cannot write or edit every item that appears. Much rests on decisions taken by other members of staff – writers, subeditors, picture editors and others – under the pressure of deadlines. Because of these pressures and the dependence of newspapers on unpredictable external events for their material, much of what appears is fortuitous. It would be rash to make much of a run of the mill news story appearing at the bottom of page five. It may reflect some crucial political subtext. But it is far more likely that it was selected at the last moment from a mass of agency copy by a subeditor desperate for something the right length.

But some elements are not fortuitous. Lead news stories are not chosen without forethought. Their selection represents the considered view of the editor and other senior staff that this is the most important item available to the paper and its readers on that day. Similarly the choice and content of leader articles, particularly in an explicitly political paper such as the *Herald*, and of the main features, most of which will have been commissioned or selected in advance, will reflect forethought rather than reflex. These elements are emphasised, but this does not mean dismissing the fortuitous. Much selection of stories may be reflex, but it is conditioned reflex, responding to the journalists' assumptions about the sort of story that is required. Conditioned reflex under deadline pressure will, if the conditioning is strong enough, lead to consistency of decision-making. News coverage has been examined on the 'once is coincidence, twice is suspicious, three times is enemy action' principle, although once is occasionally worthy of note along the lines of the 'exception proving the rule'. This reflects the complexity of the pressures and demands placed upon the *Herald*. Any estimate of its performance must take them into account. But it explicitly set itself the task of competing as a mass-market national newspaper, and must largely be judged on its success or otherwise in matching those aspirations. It laboured under immense handicaps in hugely competitive markets. It can be argued that it never stood any real chance in a grossly unfair world, but the essential unfairness of the world was, after all, the *Herald*'s motivating premise.

1
The First *Daily Herald*, 1912–21

> What should I do? ... Start an Owenite profit-sharing factory
> perhaps. Or a new Socialist paper. We want a new Socialist paper.
>
> H.G. Wells, *Kipps*

'It was called the *Daily Herald* for some reason or other which
everybody has forgotten.'[1] Thus veteran diplomatic editor W.N. Ewer,
looking back from the late 1940s, recalled the paper's very earliest days.
Lord Northcliffe had considered the same name for his halfpenny
daily in 1896, before settling on *Daily Mail*.[2] The attraction of a name
implying that the paper was a harbinger of progress and better times
to come is clear.

There was nothing new about the idea of a radical daily. Received
images portray the Victorian age as one of oppressive respectability in
which everyone was born Conservative or Liberal. The reality was
livelier and more complex, particularly in the first half of the period.
The 1830s saw the growth of the unstamped press and Feargus
O'Connor's *Northern Star,* a Chartist national paper whose function as
a forum for debate anticipated the early *Herald* by three-quarters of a
century.[3] The middle of the century saw the rise of rumbustious mass-
circulation Sunday newspapers such as *Reynolds News*, whose vigorous
relish of scandal had a political edge.[4] It produced a paper whose 15-
year career anticipated that of the *Herald*. Launched in 1861, the
Beehive had its roots in a building workers' strike. Growing from
London roots – it was run at first by the London Trades Council – into
a national role, it was ultimately forced into conformity with the
moderate views of the dominant union leaders of the day and was sold
to a proprietor outside the labour movement, a Liberal MP.[5] *Reynolds*
was similarly deradicalised as it pushed upmarket in pursuit of a
middle-class readership which would attract advertisers.[6] James Curran
has argued that the press of the 1860s, which had just escaped from
the government control of newspapers by means of stamps, was
considerably more radical than that of 50 years later, by which time
the modern commercial model, dependent on advertising income,
predominated.[7]

Fresh left-wing impetus came late in the century with the push for
separate labour representation. The Independent Labour Party,

9

founded in 1893, could muster around 100 papers by 1914, with the Marxist Social Democratic Federation counting a further 15, the trade unions around 30 and syndicalists and anarchists a further 20. The bulk were small, local and short-lived. But there were exceptions – Robert Blatchford's weekly *Clarion* was selling 74,000 copies by 1906 with a mix of sharp editorial comment, humour and non-political features such as short stories and cycling columns. Keir Hardie's *Labour Leader*, more explicitly political, emphasised the exposé: 'A means to an end, the target chosen because of its political significance', according to historian Deian Hopkin.[8]

Journalism provided an extension of the public platform and a source of income for Labour leaders. Historian Alan Lee argues that, without extra income from writing, it is possible that there would have been no Labour or Irish Nationalist MPs before the introduction of parliamentary salaries in 1911.[9] Robert Williams, the dockers' leader who would become general manager of the *Herald* in 1925, had been a major contributor to the labour press in Swansea, while textile worker Ben Turner, who chaired the *Herald* in the 1920s, said of *Yorkshire Factory Times* that 'it made our union proper'.[10]

They could also look abroad to the vigorous left press in other countries. In the United States *The Appeal to Reason* claimed a 200,000 national sale in 1902, while the French Socialist Party had four daily papers by 1914 including *L'Humanité* with a readership estimated at 200,000.[11] The German Social Democrats (SPD) constructed an even more impressive press machine. In 1914 there were 90 SPD papers, almost all dailies, with a total sale of 1.465 million. *Vörwarts* alone sold 175,000 while the weekly cultural and entertainment paper *Neue Welt* sold 550,000. Historian Alex Hall points to their early recognition that general news was as necessary as political information in capturing readers – a service facilitated by the creation of a central party press bureau in 1908.[12] They encountered problems readily recognisable to the British left. Party journalists were ill-paid and factional, with tension between the moderates who staffed *Vörwarts* and the radicals of the *Leipziger Volkszeitung*, and the SPD's ability to win electoral support was not always reflected in the sales of the party press. But British enthusiasts, notably dockers' leader Ben Tillett, whose lecture on the glories of the SPD press would become an annual feature of TUC debates on the *Herald* in the 1920s, naturally enough saw the benefits of so sizeable a press machine when compared to their own.[13]

Changes in the British national press also underlined the case for a labour daily. Thirteen new dailies were started in London between 1890 and 1914.[14] Among them were the trio, still published today, which represented the foundation of the modern popular press and would dominate the market in turn. Lord Northcliffe's *Daily Mail* was followed in 1900 by Arthur Pearson's *Daily Express* and in 1903 by a fresh Northcliffe creation, the *Daily Mirror*. While all sales figures from this period have to be treated with caution, there is no doubt that they attained circulations undreamt of by previous best-sellers such as *The Times* and *Daily Telegraph*.[15] Where earlier papers sought influence among the political elite, the *Mail* and its imitators aimed for financial success through sales and advertising. The two are not mutually exclusive – press barons have always been motivated by both money and the power that comes inevitably with a large daily sale. But commercial success came first. The difference was epitomised by an exchange between *Westminster Gazette* editor J.A. Spender and a mass-circulation proprietor. When he asked the press baron to justify a recently introduced policy, the proprieter replied by pointing to increased sales since its introduction. 'I found it impossible to persuade him that there was any gap in his reasoning,' recalled Spender.[16]

The historian Collingwood noted with distaste that the *Mail* was 'the first English newspaper for which the word "news" lost its old meaning of facts which a reader ought to know if he was to vote intelligently'.[17] Its success inspired imitators and, in D.L. LeMahieu's words, 'Journalism divorced itself from prevailing notions of historical significance. News no longer concentrated exclusively on the public lives of powerful elites. The everyday life of the common man acquired more importance.'[18] Out went the huge parliamentary reports which were to the press of the Victorian age what the three-volume novel was to its literature. In its place as the defining element was the human interest story which, says LeMahieu, 'engaged their readers because they drew upon the emotions of private life'.[19] Research in the 1930s showed that political stories appealed to only a section of the national audience, heavily skewed to men and the higher social classes. Human interest stories had uniformly high appeal across the entire population. Subsequent studies have produced similar results and there is no reason to suppose that findings would have been any different in the first third of the century.[20]

Accompanying this shift in content was a sharp change in technique. In place of the orotundities of the Victorian press came a new style. R.D. Blumenfeld, editor of the *Daily Express* from 1904 to 1932, called for 'Simplicity, accuracy, conciseness and purity of style' expressed in sentences that were 'short, sharp and clear-cut', using 'short words in preference to long ones' and 'emphatic words like must and will'. He introduced the streamer headline, running across more than one column but less than a page and encouraged five or six-deck headlines which conveyed the gist of a story in telegraphic style.[21] The effect, as LeMahieu has noted, was to draw the reader into the drama of events while a paper like *The Times* distanced itself from any emotive reaction.[22] The old style retained its adherents. J.L. Garvin, editor of the *Observer* from 1908 to 1942, declared: 'I mean to give the public what it does not want.'[23] Ernest Bevin, who would be both the dominant union leader of the interwar period and a key *Herald* influence, put a strikingly moral spin on his rejection in 1919 of the capitalist press:

> We may be certain that there is such a growing working-class consciousness that a large clientele is awaiting serious literature. Labour's press must be a real educational factor, provoking thought and stimulating ideas. In addition it must not be full of the caprices of princes, the lubricities of courts and the sensationalism produced by display of the sordid. All these things are but passing phases and are the products of an evil system which is rotten at the base.[24]

Contemplating the burgeoning sales of papers like the *Mail*, the labour movement recognised a genuine threat. It did not entirely understand it. One of the *Herald's* enduring weaknesses would be that it saw its rivals in purely political terms and failed to understand the popular appeal of human-interest news. But the movement was painfully aware that none of the new mass-circulation papers supported Labour or was likely to. Few doubted that if Labour was ever to make an impact as a political force, it must have its own voice capable of reaching millions. It was no coincidence that one of the most vigorous voices calling for the creation of a separate labour press was Keir Hardie, the pioneer of independent political representation for the movement.[25]

That belief found voice at the successive conferences of the Independent Labour Party and the Trades Union Congress. The issue turned up regularly on the TUC agenda from 1903. By 1907 it had passed a resolution to start a daily paper and a special conference in February 1908 backed the creation of a paper called the *Morning Herald*.[26] Labour finally got its daily press in 1912 in a manner recalling the old joke about London buses – after a long wait, two came along almost at once. (The weekly *New Statesman*, initially Liberal but soon to be an influential Labour organ was also in gestation during that year, its first issue coming out in April 1913).[27] The two daily papers were a reflection of rival tendencies within the movement. Independent Labour politics were still something of a novelty and the Labour Party, founded in 1900, was a federation of affiliates with no individual membership. Allied to Asquith's Liberal government, it was dependent on agreements with it for the bulk of the 40 seats won at the October 1910 election.[28] 'Lib–Labism' – respectable, moderate and reformist – predominated among party and union leaders. The Miners Federation, the largest union, had moved its MPs from Liberal to Labour as recently as 1909.[29] This cautiously conformist tendency found its voice with the

creation in October 1912 of the *Daily Citizen*, an official paper backed
by a consortium of the Labour Party, TUC and the Independent Labour
Party.[30] But Labour's vigorous minority counterculture, not content
merely to make the best of the existing system, but set on radical
change, got there first on 15 April 1912. The *Daily Herald*'s outstanding
characteristics were established from its first issue. It was financially
and organisationally anarchic and politically disinclined to take orders
from anybody. While the first board of directors included moderate
authority figures like veteran TUC secretary C.W. Bowerman, this was
a reflection of its origins in trade union activism rather than an
indicator of its political stance.[31]

The *Herald* was the direct successor to the paper of the same name
started during the London printers' dispute of January 1911. The first
Daily Herald appeared on 25 January 1911, putting the case for a 48-
hour week in the trade and replying to the attacks of employers.[32]
Within days, encouraged by their initial success and a sale of around
25,000, the printers broadened coverage to include general as well as
strike news and began to talk seriously of keeping the paper
permanently.[33] Its closure on 28 April was accompanied by a
commitment to relaunch as a permanent paper as soon as sufficient
funding had been raised.[34]

A committee chaired by David Walls of the Association of Correctors
of the Press, and dominated by London trade unionists such as Tommy
Naylor of the compositors and dockers' leader Ben Tillett, spent the
next year appealing for funds. They promised 'a Labour organ ...
conducted on the broadest and most democratic lines' whose policy
would be 'one of inclusion and not exclusion'.[35] It was to 'contain all
the usual features of a general newspaper but its home and foreign
news will not be written and coloured against the interests of Labour'.
Its pictures would depict 'mainly the incidents occurring in the Labour
world and not merely the frivolous doings of the idle rich' and it
promised that 'a special feature will be the attention paid to trade
disputes'.[36] The committee believed that it could attain an 80,000 daily
sale. This should ensure £7,500 a year in advertising income and
financial stability. Initially appealing for £10,000 in start-up capital,
they then adjusted their sights to £5,000 in 5-shilling shares, saying
they would not start until they received 20,000 applications.[37] The
paper would have a mixed record on promises about content. This
promise on money was blatantly broken.

The *Herald* started life with £300.[38] All logic suggested that it was
doomed before it started. The *New Statesman*, launched the following
year into the less financially demanding weekly magazine market,
raised £5,000 and found that insufficient.[39] Even arch-optimist George
Lansbury, recruited to the committee by Ben Tillett, admitted that the
failure to raise capital 'knocked all optimism and faith out of me and

left me speechless'.[40] Raymond Postgate, a member of staff after the First World War, recalled that the decision to start was precipitated by the closure of the *Morning Leader*, swallowed by the Liberal *Daily News*.[41] The *Herald* committee will also have been conscious of the advantage of getting their paper out before the launch of the *Daily Citizen*.

Early organisation was scarcely more encouraging than the finances. George Slocombe, a stalwart of the early days recalled: 'The staff was the best that could be found in a Fleet Street suspicious of new enterprises and definitely anti-Labour and anti-Socialist.' [42] Among those founders was Rowland Kenney, hired for £5 per week as labour editor. In the days before the launch, his main contact was freelance journalist W.H. Seed, secretary of the *Herald* committee.

> In my conversation with Seed, I had tried to get some clear idea of the organisation of the editorial side of the paper, but each explanation required another explanation to explain it, and he ended up with the qualification that such and such was their 'intention or hope'.
> 'Who was editor?'
> 'The committee,' I was told.
> 'But the committee can't edit a paper.'
> 'Oh well, they had him as secretary,' suggested Seed.
> 'What did they mean by a "Labour Editor"? One would think that on a labour newspaper the Labour Editor would have practically all the "editing" to do.'
> Here again there was no clear idea anywhere; so I could only hope that someone, somewhere, somehow would wave a magic wand and bring this newspaper, to be started under such fantastic auspices, into being.[43]

Within four days of his appointment, Kenney was at work. The first day in the office at Victoria House in Tudor Street, just off Fleet Street, was hardly more encouraging:

> That one room was the Editorial Department. It contained either two or three tables, two chairs and a telephone on the floor in one corner and the day's newspapers. There was not a piece of copy paper or a pencil, blue or otherwise; nothing. So on my suggestion Seed slipped out and bought a parcel of scribbling pads and other material. Then we began to discuss our 'news service'![44]

Collective editorship was predictably unsuccessful. The first appointed editor was Sheridan Jones, who in Kenney's words, 'Wrote the odd leader or two, was obviously the wrong man for the job, and was soon dismissed'.[45] Slocombe recalls that one early editor left when the staff revolted over his decision to lead the front page with a royal wedding. He does not say who, but all the evidence points to Jones.[46] It certainly would not have been either of his two immediate successors, Kenney or Charles Lapworth. If Lansbury and Tillett had had their way, Jones's successor in June 1912 might have been Frank Harris. But the *Herald* committee was less convinced than its leading members by his proposal for a policy of 'applied christianity'. Harris did not consider his brush with the paper worth noting in his extensive, imaginative and famously pornographic memoirs.[47] Instead the decision lay between two founders – Kenney and W.P. Ryan – poet, veteran Irish radical journalist and, in his rival's words, 'calm as a rock in the midst of our storms'. Each agreed to serve under the other. Ryan's deep-rooted commitment was to be proved over the next two decades as he spent long periods as acting editor, was assistant editor into the 1920s and libel catcher into the 1930s. But Kenney got the nod, before he in turn was ousted in favour of Lapworth in late 1912.[48]

Lapworth's sponsor was Charles Granville, a publisher who had promised to put £4,000 into the paper.[49] While the paper's policy was that no financial backer should take control, it was in no position to be fussy. If its organisation was chaotic, its finances were a triumph of optimism and faith over logic. In spite of backing from sympathisers like the Prudential Assurance heir H.D. Harben, who eventually guaranteed the paper for six months, the suffragist and pacifist Baroness de la Warr, chemical millionaire Joseph Fels and the clergymen W.H. Paine and Jocelyn Buxton, it teetered constantly on the verge of closure.[50] Slocombe recalled:

> The paper had little or no advertising and no capital. It lived literally from day to day. The most fantastic resources, not all of them strictly legal, were exhausted in order to bring the daily quota of paper to the hungry machines … the several hundred pounds required each night to pay for paper were somehow obtained, usually at the last minute.[51]

Lansbury gives credit to general manager Hayward – a member of the original *Herald* committee – as 'a perfect genius at getting money from the clouds' and also acknowledges the generosity of Victoria House and paper suppliers Bowaters.[52] Even so Raymond Postgate, in his analysis of the *Herald*'s early years, points to crises in June, August and October 1912. On 23 October 1912 it announced: 'We may come out again or we may not.' They did because a man turned up in the office at the last moment with £150.[53] On another occasion the decision was taken to close the paper and Lansbury left to address meetings in Hanley and Crewe. On the following morning he was able to buy a *Herald* at Crewe station. The printing staff had begged some part reels of paper and old outsize reels from Drew, the manager of the Victoria House Printing Company, and improvised a paper that was 'all sorts of shapes and sizes'.[54] Three issues were produced with brokers' men on the premises – on the third day Lansbury, Tillett and transport unionist Bob Williams blocked the doorway while money was found to buy back the tables, desks and chairs.[55]

Staff lived an uncertain existence. Kenney recalled: 'When pay-day came the staff had an apprehensive time. Sometimes there were funds, sometimes there were not.'[56] Ryan told Postgate of one occasion when after two consecutive payless weeks, the staff were invited to divide up the contents of the cash box – receiving a grand total of 1s 6d each.[57] Yet amid the chaos the paper established a distinctive character, offering a mix of news, debate, polemic and biting satire in its crowded pages. Within a week of the first issue Ben Tillett was writing in its columns that British politics had entered 'an entirely new and revolutionary phase'.[58] The *Herald* was happy to aid in this process. Its viewpoint was consistently countercultural – a rebel outsider implacably opposed to the dominant forces in British society. Postgate recorded that 'It printed anything that the libel laws would permit (and at least five times what they would not). To get into its columns a writer had only to be a rebel; he had to be an enemy of the existing capitalist system, and what he was in favour of mattered less.'[59] This inclusive quality, redeeming promises in the circulars of 1911, led to accusations of inconsistency. Lansbury was unconcerned: 'A newspaper such as ours should always allow its columns to be open for the expression of views, whether these are in accord with the editor or not.'[60] In a time of intellectual flux on the left, the *Herald* provided a forum for polemic among and between proponents of guild socialism, syndicalism, christian socialism and even the distributivism of Hilaire Belloc and G.K. Chesterton. Women's suffrage and the independence movements of Ireland and India also found consistent support.[61]

News coverage reflected the vigorous industrial militancy of the period. Lansbury's summary holds true for the *Herald*'s first decade: 'It could with truth be said of us that wherever a strike took place there we were in the midst.'[62] The second issue, on 16 April 1912, featured coverage of strikes at the Earl's Court exhibition and the Great Northern Railway. It did not matter that the railwaymen were not being backed by their union.[63] As Lansbury said: 'The policy of the paper was not merely unofficial, it was avowedly anti-official.'[64] The early headline 'Strike and strike hard' might have served as the paper's motto.[65]

The *Herald*'s first week of publication was favoured by any new paper's dream – a major news story particularly amenable to its particular style of coverage. Considerately going down on the very day when the *Herald* was first published, the *Titanic* provoked fierce class-based polemics both against the disproportionate death rate among steerage passengers – 'Women and children last' was the headline on W.J. Titterton's story – and the conduct of the owners, the White Star Line.[66]

While Titterton was given the first big story, other figures from the early days were to have much longer *Herald* careers. Kenney recruited Charles Langdon Everard and George Slocombe. Everard, brought in to provide a lighter touch, did so to great effect over the next two decades as house humourist 'Gadfly' while Slocombe, employed at 18 as Kenney's secretary, would be a noted Paris correspondent and chronicler of international conferences in the postwar decade. Immediately after the war, Slocombe was news editor and Everard chief subeditor.[67] While less pertinent to the *Herald*'s political progress, boxing writer Jimmy Butler was also a long-term survivor. His experiences included refereeing an office punch-up while his work as 'Pollux' injected expertise and enthusiasm into the otherwise perfunctory sports pages.[68]

Granville's takeover was shortlived, as he failed to fulfil his promises. Kenney reports that years later he was charged with bigamy and fraudulent conversion.[69] But he left his mark through the appointment of Lapworth and the recruitment of Australian cartoonist Will Dyson, described by *Guardian* journalist and historian of editorial cartooning Martin Walker as 'one of the angriest and most ferocious cartoonists ever to sketch a line'.[70] Treating Labour's moderate leaders as savagely as opponents like Asquith, his drawings, if not their rather convoluted captions, were a radical break with the genteel pattern of the Victorian political cartoon.[71] Appearing from September 1912, his brutal caricatures were rapidly recognised as the *Herald*'s greatest asset. Entire front pages were devoted to his cartoons, and collections issued in booklet form.[72] Walker records that when the Hearst press attempted to lure him away with a massive salary, a special fund was created, allowing the payment of £20 per week, a large salary by any pre-1914 standards, let alone those of the impoverished *Herald*.[73] Dyson's cartoons provided the leitmotif for the editorship of Lapworth, subsequently the first British director of Metro Goldwyn films. Lansbury, Postgate and Slocombe all agree that the *Herald*'s ferocity peaked during this period, when it was said that 'The *Daily Herald* contains the noblest aspirations and the basest adjectives in the English language'.[74]

Herald invective was trained not only on political enemies, but on nominal allies as well. Ewer recalled: 'It lambasted with cheerful impartiality Tory employers, the Liberal Government and the official leaders of the Labour Party and the Trades Union Congress.'[75] Postgate

Figure 1 'A Fantasy (Labour Leaders at their Devotions)' by Will Dyson, *Daily Herald*, 3 December 1913 (reproduced by permission).

notes: 'Lapworth and his colleagues were not content to attack the system, but denounced everyone who compromised with it.'[76] *Herald* priorities were seen in the denunciation of parliament as 'The House of Pretence' while industrial news was headlined 'The war that really matters'.[77] The movement's leadership were warned: 'Lead on you Labour leaders, if you do not want to be run over'.[78] This style peaked with the famous 'Hurrah for the rebels' issue of 20 September 1913, vigorously supporting unofficial strikers, the bitterly-fought Dublin strikes led by James Larkin and syndicalism – a theory which rejected parliamentarism and called for a 'social general strike' to bring organised labour to power in place of capitalism.[79]

Never stronger than during this period, the *Herald*'s 'independent actor' identity was carried to its logical conclusion after October 1912 by the formation of its own activist organisation, the Herald League. The League was set up as an attempt to counter the paper's chronic insolvency by creating a supporters' network for fundraising. But these activities rapidly extended to political education, propaganda and the running of unofficial Labour candidates at four pre-1914 by-elections where official Labour had declined to stand.[80]

Dyson was not Lapworth's only notable recruit. A group of left-wing intellectuals destined for longer, if less spectacular, continuous *Herald* careers made their first appearances at this time. Francis Meynell contributed *joie de vivre* and a specialised knowledge of typefaces to the *Herald*'s affairs until 1920.[81] Poet and ex-academic Gerald Gould would be one of the key figures of the period until the official takeover in 1922.[82] William Mellor and Norman Ewer would have still longer and more significant *Herald* careers. Mellor, described by Slocombe as 'a tall, black, grim young man' and by Beatrice Webb as 'a very determined rebel' who 'if he does not produce light, produces heat' was, with G.D.H. Cole the main intellectual proponent of Guild Socialism.[83] Remembered by Margaret Cole as 'a forceful personality, commanding if not always wise', he would bring those characteristics to bear after the war as successively industrial editor, assistant editor and editor.[84] Ewer made less initial impression after first coming to the paper as a go-between for the financial contributions of the Liberal MP Baron de Forest, but his career would be as long as that of the *Herald* itself – he finally retired in 1964 when the paper closed.[85]

Lapworth's spell in charge ended late in 1913. Lansbury was by now the proprietor, having bought the *Herald* from the Official Receiver for £100 earlier in the year, cheerfully renaming the publishing company The Limit in tribute to Lloyd George, who described *Herald* questions about the Marconi scandal – which threatened to end his career – as 'the limit'.[86] Due to go to the United States for a long trip at the end of the year, he concluded that Lapworth's violence of opinion and expression made him too risky in his absence, so he dismissed Lapworth and took over himself, leaving Gould and Ryan in charge while he was away.[87] Slocombe recalled: 'The paper lost some of its fighting quality. It became less mordant, less cynical, less irreverent ... and more sentimental'.[88] Beatrice Webb was less convinced, feeling that Lansbury exercised an emotional, paternal influence but had little real control over 'a team of clever and intellectually unscrupulous journalists with Will Dyson at their head'.[89]

What was not in doubt was that the *Herald* was still very different from the *Daily Citizen*. The difference was epitomised by the coincidence of its October 1912 launch date with that of the Herald League. The *Citizen* would no more have supported independent candidates than it would have published nude pin-ups. Its answer to the vigorously activist League was local circulation committees. These were passive follower bodies, run by local Labour organisations purely as a means of increasing sales and with no element of debate.[90] The *Citizen* was, in the words of its historian, 'an official organ of the Parliamentary Labour Party financed by the Trade Unions'.[91] The Independent Labour Party, more radical than the PLP, was also a partner, but at best a marginalised minority. The *Citizen* was both more palatable to moderate officialdom than the *Herald*, and a warning of what might happen should the *Herald* ever fall into official hands. While its initial capitalisation was not quite as ludicrously inadequate as the *Herald*'s, the £85,000 it raised was still well short of its £150,000 target and it was always undercapitalised.[92] Deian Hopkin underlines one of the eternal difficulties facing organised Labour in competing with Fleet Street capitalism by noting that the amount raised, 'while impressive by the standards of the Labour Movement, was inadequate by those of Fleet Street'.[93] The *Citizen* recruited conventional pressmen rather than *Herald*-style activist-journalists. Editor Frank Dilnot and news editor Stanley Bishop both came from the *Daily Mail* and the first issue carried good-luck messages from Lord Northcliffe and leading Liberal editor Robert Donald.[94] Historian Bob Holton points to a desire 'to model the *Citizen* as far as possible upon existing mass-circulation dailies'.[95] Kenney, receiving a dummy issue, was unimpressed:

> It simply could not be true. This attempt was too poor to be believed. With all the resources of the Labour Party behind them, with good paper and excellent printing, they were going to turn out a paper that was as dull and lifeless as any other journal that is smothered in 'thou shalt nots', doubt and hesitancy and the constant need for political opportunism.[96]

Beatrice Webb would subsequently describe it as 'smug, common and ultra-official'.[97] For while the *Herald*'s voice was that of the militant activist, the *Citizen* spoke for the moderate centre. Holton argues:

> In practice the presentation of representative 'voices' in the paper was severely restricted to orthodox opinion centred on Labour Party pragmatism ... Editorial initiative was narrowly based and came from above. It was geared to the incorporation of Labour unrest into conciliatory forms of protest and pressure, harmonising relations between labour and capital, and re-directing energies towards the Parliamentary area.[98]

This emphasis was reflected in the decision to launch at the start of the parliamentary session. Company secretary Clifford Allen argued that: 'Interest in politics and everything serious lags during the summer months'.[99] This was in spite of unrest involving miners and transport workers in the months up to the launch.[100] While the *Herald* was cheering unofficial strikers, Holton records that in the *Citizen*: 'At all times the authority of union leaders was upheld over unofficial or spontaneous outbreaks of rank-and-file discontent.'[101] That contrast was particularly marked during the 1914 London builders lockout when, in the not entirely objective view of Lansbury, the *Herald* 'pitched its strength against the official *Daily Citizen* which cried "Yield!", and won'.[102] Union agreements were invariably endorsed by the *Citizen*. The *Herald* view was summed up in the headline 'Agreements made under coercion are never morally binding'.[103]

The *Herald* cheerfully satirised its staid rival as the *'Daily Gamp'*.[104] Contrasting as they were, the papers had problems in common. Holton estimates that *Herald* sales oscillated between 50,000 and 150,000, peaking during strikes, in a pattern that was to continue into the 1920s. The *Citizen* ran at 130,000 to 200,000. Given the limited resources of both, neither was a poor result, but at the same time the *Express* was selling around 300,000, the *News* 350,000–400,000 and the *Mail* around 750,000.[105] Mid 1914 found the *Herald* towards the bottom of its range – printing between 52,000 and 59,000 – and with Beatrice Webb complaining that neither Labour paper had any influence.[106] Webb was never knowingly under-acerbic, but her analysis was supported years later by Ewer: 'The *Daily Herald* of 1914 was a miracle of survival, but its influence was negligible.'[107] Within four years it would be, also in Ewer's words: 'Almost a national institution, a political force. Its circulation ... was now nearer a quarter of a million'.[108]

The outbreak of the First World War in August 1914 split Labour, as it split other European socialist parties. A mainstream majority, led by trade union-based figures such as Arthur Henderson and J.R. Clynes, took a pro-war line, but a substantial vocal minority, including party leader Ramsay MacDonald, who resigned the post, Keir Hardie, Philip Snowden and Lansbury, opposed the war. The two Labour papers reflected this division. The *Citizen* was patriotic from the start and by January 1915 was enthusiastically printing glowing accounts of action in the trenches.[109] The *Herald* greeted the declaration of war with a debate between Lansbury and G.K. Chesterton, but by the end of 1914 was clearly anti-war.[110] Meynell's pacifist article in the Christmas 1914 issue was the first of many.[111]

Both papers suffered financially. The *Citizen*, founded on orthodox political, journalistic and business assumptions, was the one that failed to survive, appearing for the last time on 5 June 1915. Labour Party secretary Arthur Henderson's epitaph would be horribly recognisable to subsequent *Herald* fundraisers:

> If resolutions could have saved the *Daily Citizen*, it would have had a long life. So far as the National Committees of the movement are concerned, I think every practical step has been taken to ensure the continuance of the paper. The plain, blunt fact is that the Labour Movement does not want a daily newspaper and is not prepared to regard such a weapon as necessary in the Labour fight.[112]

The *Herald* might easily have gone the same way – its entire staff was on notice of dismissal by 1 September 1914.[113] But it was more used to surviving on its wits and enthusiasm. Recognising that it could not survive as a daily, it went weekly from 6 September and prospered both editorially and financially.[114] With fewer strikes to champion, it turned its attention to the treatment of war resisters and the fight against conscription.[115] November 1917 brought a classic journalistic stunt as Meynell and a female companion were despatched to the Ritz to consume the most elaborate meal possible after 39 months of war and a submarine blockade. Coincidentally or not, the publication of 'How they starve at the Ritz', was rapidly followed by the introduction of food rationing.[116]

The same year brought the *Herald* a second major cause to supplement that of war resistance, as the British press's most enthusiastic proponent of the Russian Revolution, which in turn brought its greatest scoop as it published the secret treaties between the Great Powers, found in the Russian imperial archives by the Bolsheviks.[117] Coverage was not uncritically pro-Bolshevik since *Herald* foreign affairs columnist Noel Brailsford, though an enthusiastic supporter of the Revolution, was an early left sceptic about some of their methods.[118] War resistance was always a minority cause and the extent of mass British support for the Russian revolution is unclear, but a sizeable group adhered to one or other cause, and in the absence of alternatives they naturally gravitated to the *Herald*. A conventional commercial publisher, noting the journalistic success, growth in sales and relative financial stability attained during the war, might have concluded that they were on to a winner and stayed as a weekly. 'Financially it was our easiest time. We were very successful as a weekly, and although we did not actually pay our way, the losses were manageable and fairly easy to meet,' recalled Lansbury.[119] Nor would conventional publishers have been found sponsoring sell-out Albert Hall meetings in support of the Russian Revolution, as the *Herald* did in March 1918, or calling on trade-union muscle to threaten to pull the plug on the November Victory Ball unless the hall authorities withdrew their attempts to cancel a subsequent *Herald* rally.[120]

But financial means were always subordinate to political ends for the Lansbury *Herald*. Numerous promises had been given that the daily would return after the war, and there were political battles to be fought. The *Daily Herald* returned on 31 March 1919, complete with a spectacular sales campaign, which identified it with the intellectual as much as the political avant-garde, and based on the 'Soaring to success' poster by the vorticist MacKnight Kauffer.[121] Optimism was an ingrained habit, but it looked on this occasion as though the paper might live up to the promise of the poster. Sales, reflecting a persistent tendency to rise in times of political or industrial excitement, had been 200,000 at the relaunch, but rapidly passed 300,000 and topped 400,000 during the 1919 Rail Strike, when the *Herald* would spend £14,000 it could ill-afford on ensuring that the paper was still distributed.[122] Lansbury wrote to Ernest Bevin, leader of the Dockers' Union and soon to be general secretary of the Transport and General Workers, that: 'We were quite unable to cope with the huge demands made upon us and there seems no limit to the power and usefulness of the paper.' But to achieve its purposes the *Herald*, still exclusively London-based, had to be able to print in a northern centre.[123] Thus one of the dominant themes of the 1920s was introduced. Bevin, not easily convinced of anything, was impressed. He wrote in the *Herald* that a one-million circulation was possible within a year if it were given the right machinery, including a Northern edition.[124]

Lansbury continued as editor, with Gould as associate editor. Decision-making structures remained as before. Lansbury recorded: 'We decided to continue on the same lines as before: editing and management should be co-operative, always leaving me, as editor, the last word in case of disagreement. We were a very lively band indeed. Our discussions, which at times were prolonged and heated, were, I think, viewed with dismay by experienced newspaper friends like Norman Angell [Formerly manager of the Continental *Daily Mail*], who occasionally came along to see us.'[125] Whatever the formal titles were, Gould seems to have been in charge from day to day. Literary staff member S.K. Ratcliffe's recall a decade later of having been recruited by 'editor Gerald Gould' might be dismissed as a slip of the memory were it not that, in reply to a complaint from Miners Federation secretary (and *Herald* director) Frank Hodges about a leaked document in March 1921, Lansbury explained: 'It just happens that I personally made the decision in the matter, as Gould has been away for the last week.'[126]

A fresh influx of recruits, several of whom remained throughout the 1920s, reinforced the veterans of the prewar days. Parliamentary correspondent S.V. Bracher, literary subeditor Arnold Dawson and industrial correspondent Vivian Brodzky were to be mainstays of the *Herald* for the next decade.[127] Raymond Postgate, war resister, Oxford intellectual and Lansbury's son-in-law, joined as a foreign subeditor.[128] Asked later to recall the atmosphere on the paper, he wrote that his memories were:

> Not mostly of dramatic events. These are fewer than people imagine; hardly ever does – or did – anyone rush in shouting 'Hold everything for a replate!' or anything like that. The picture I keep with me is, in fact, one of silence – a period almost of rest when I could think about what I was doing, because it was the gap between two editions. I can see the long sub-editors' rooms in Tudor Street, with immensely tall windows, shining black and blank because the bare electric lights inside are so strong. The chief sub-editor Sam Everard, is about to go out for a drink at the White Swan, the door opens and one overhears a reporter cursing and swearing mechanically into a telephone.[129]

The location was evidently functional rather than stylish. W.J. Ryan's volume of poetry *Fleet Street in Starlight* included the simile 'Drab as Tudor Street'.[130]

Where the prewar *Herald* had been preoccupied with British events, its successor of 1919 was distinctly international in coverage as well as ideological outlook, campaigning against western intervention in Russia, chronicling reactionary repression in Hungary and laying mercilessly into the statesmen assembled to settle with defeated Germany at Versailles.[131] The peace negotiations prompted the most famous of all Dyson cartoons. 'Curious, I seem to hear a child crying' was the caption to his drawing of puzzled-looking Lloyd George, Clemenceau and associates juxtaposed with a child labelled, with uncanny prescience, as 'Class of 1940'.[132] A strong team of foreign correspondents was assembled: Vernon Bartlett wrote from Paris, former *Manchester Guardian* correspondent Morgan Philips Price from Berlin and Noel Brailsford, possibly the oustanding left-wing journalist of the time, from Central and Eastern Europe.[133] Hannen Swaffer, who would be the *Herald's* star columnist of the 1930s and after, was sent to the USA as a special correspondent.[134] Lansbury, hailed by Beatrice Webb as 'the chartered revolutionary of the world', spent weeks in Russia in 1920,[135] while Gould's literary connections reinforced the *Herald's* relationship with the intellectual and literary left. Siegfried Sassoon was literary editor for a while and other writers and reviewers included Havelock Ellis, Israel Zangwill, Alec Waugh, Rebecca West, E.M. Forster, Robert Graves and Osbert Sitwell, who contributed a memorable leader in verse when War Minister Winston Churchill ordered the burning of copies of the *Herald*.[136]

The virulent prewar spirit had to some extent departed. The *Herald* was still trenchant in criticisms of the existing order, but attacks on moderate labour leaders had ceased. Lansbury was conscious of the responsibility of running the only labour paper and aimed to extend his inclusive policy across the whole movement: 'This paper belongs not to the right or left, but to the whole of the Labour movement.'[137] This owed much to memories of the divisions of 1914–18. Lansbury said: 'Both the policy and expression of policy was much more moderate than in the days preceding August 1914 ... it was felt that if both sides sat down and indulged in recriminations, only the possessing classes would triumph.'[138] That distinction was lost, however, on the outside world. In the fevered political atmosphere that followed the war and the Russian Revolution, with industrial disputes close to the spectacular prewar levels, the *Herald* looked like subversion made print.[139] Hamilton Fyfe, who was to succeed Lansbury as *Herald* editor in 1922, retold the anecdote of a railwayman sorting through discarded papers on a train: '*Daily Mail*, all lies, *Daily Express*, all lies, *Daily Herald*, all trouble.'[140] *Herald* journalist Evelyn Sharp recalled that: 'These were the days when universal revolution seemed more imminent than subsequent events proved it to be in this country.'[141] Christopher Andrew, historian of Britain's secret services, records the government view that: 'Men who would subsidize the *Daily Herald* were in their view men who would stop at nothing' and points to considerable surveillance of the paper.[142]

Even if it lacked its pre-1914 savagery, the *Herald* was, with Labour still a relatively ineffective minority force in Parliament, more interested in industrial than party-political news. Postgate recalled that 'it never incited strikes (as it certainly used to) but it came directly to the help of any union on strike.[143] The doctrine of 'direct action', using union power for political ends, was in among the left fashion after 1919. Miners' leader Robert Smillie said that the moderate Labour Party executive 'feared more than anything else what had come to be seen as direct action', while the conservative historian Maurice Cowling has said that direct action 'would have left little mark without the part played by the *Daily Herald* in systematising its insights and publicising its intentions. Under Lansbury, Ewer, Brailsford, Meynell, Williams and Mellor ... it presented a fundamental challenge.'[144] Enthusiasm for direct action led the *Herald* not only into enthusiastic support for the police strikes of 1918 and 1919, but misleadingly bullish reporting of the prospects for the ill-fated dispute. The historians of the strikes call this 'the least admirable chapter in the long and often gallant story of the *Daily Herald*'.[145]

Direct action culminated in 1920 by combining with another *Herald* enthusiasm, the campaign against intervention in Russia. In May dockers, cheered on by the paper, blocked the loading of arms intended for use against the Bolshevik government.[146] The *Herald* campaigned against intervention throughout the year, with a special Sunday edition on 8 October proclaiming 'Not a man, not a gun, not a sou'.[147] Some historians have suggested that resistance to intervention was founded more on war-weariness than class solidarity.[148] Direct action proved to be a transient phenomenon, effectively killed off by the collapse of the Triple Alliance of the three most powerful unions, the miners, railwaymen and transport workers. This formidable-looking grouping failed its first test on Black Friday in April 1921 as the miners' allies refused to support them. Postgate argues that this effectively ended independent policy in the *Herald,* depriving it of its distinctive policy.[149] Cowling says that its political achievement was essentially negative, frightening Britain's rulers so much that they were galvanised into effective anti-Labour action.[150] The elegiac tone of Gerald Gould's leader on Black Friday, a valediction for the *Herald*'s days of rebellion, supports Postgate's analysis:

> Yesterday was the heaviest defeat that has befallen the Labour Movement within the memory of man. It is no use trying to minimise it. It is no use pretending that it is other than it is. We on this paper have said throughout that if the organised workers stood together they would win. They have not stood together and they have reaped the reward.

The leader went on to state: 'What we need is a new machinery and a new spirit. The old machinery has frankly, in the hour of emergency, failed.'[151]

This was a recapitulation of a developing *Herald* theme, the need for a powerful central coordinating 'General Staff' of labour to ensure that the movement's collective strength was deployed to maximum effect against capital and government.[152] But it also reflected another issue preoccupying Gould – the *Herald*'s mounting and intractable financial problems. The independence not just of *Herald* policy, but of the paper itself, was all but finished. The high hopes of 1919 had started the process. The capital developments Bevin said were essential for the one-million sale would have cost an estimated £400,000, much more than any individual backer could afford.[153] Lansbury was not prepared to entertain a commercial offer, although several were made: 'Our one answer to everybody was that the *Daily Herald* would never pass voluntarily from our control except as it now passed to the Labour Movement. We would prefer the paper die a glorious death rather than see it become the property of the Liberal Party, masquerading as friends of Labour.'[154] This left only one option – mobilising the organised movement. Lansbury said: 'We knew that our fate as an independent paper was settled'.[155] He subsequently conceded that it was a mistake not to go directly to the TUC and the Labour Party and ask them to take the paper over. But there was no guarantee that they would have been willing to do so in 1920 – although that year's conference accepted unanimously the Chorley constituency party motion for a takeover.[156] Instead, they called on their friends within the movement, mobilising a trade union committee to call for a debenture issue. Of the committee members, Ernest Bevin, Ben Turner, Robert Williams and Labour Party general secretary Arthur Henderson would have important *Herald* roles throughout the 1920s. The debentures were offered in blocks of £500, to institutions only.[157] The committee hoped for £400,000 but had to settle for around £100,000, of which the miners subscribed more than £42,000.[158] It was not enough, but the principle of movement-wide involvement was established. From now on Lansbury kept Henderson fully informed about the paper's finances.[159]

True to its tradition of doing things differently, the *Herald* became a victim of its own success. In October 1920 its daily sale was certified at 329,869 – well ahead of any pre-1914 estimate and a respectable figure by most national daily standards.[160] In 1921, by comparison, the *Daily News* was selling 300,000, the *Express* 579,000 and the *Daily Chronicle* 661,000.[161] Lansbury recorded: 'By the calculations of 1918 330,000 sales should have established it comfortably.'[162] But, unlike its rivals, the *Herald* could not assume that increased sales would lead to increased advertising income. The implicit political and social bias of the advertising industry's conventional wisdom loaded the scales against it. It was not listed in *Newspaper World*'s monthly 'space barometer' and subjective analysis still held sway in the industry. A standard text, Freer's *Inner Side of Advertising*, asserted that 'you can not afford to place your advertisement in a paper which is solely read by the down at heels who buy it to scan the "Situations Vacant" column'. Just in case anyone missed the point, Freer added: 'The Socialist press has a following of people who cannot persuade the world to share its wealth with them.'[163] Industry leader Thomas Russell believed that the sobriety of *The Times* induced readers to order goods through tradesmen, while the *Daily Mail's* vivacity was good for direct mail order.[164] His psychological nostrums were typical of a world where conventional advertising analysis was dominated by such subjective elements as 'atmosphere', 'force of impression', 'pulling power', 'confidence factor'.[165] A paper associated with Red Revolution could hardly be regarded as a promising medium. The later 1920s would bring more sophisticated quantitative research and the replacement of 'wealth' by 'disposable income' as the key concept. This would benefit the *Herald*: a 1928 survey showed a previously unsuspected lower middle-class readership.[166]

But such future developments were no help in 1920. Postgate records that *Advertising World* admitted that there was a political boycott of the paper.[167] Advertising manager Poyser had no doubt that: 'the only reason that the *Daily Herald* has not received its share of advertisement business is because advertisers have allowed political prejudice to influence their judgment'.[168] His view was supported by a letter to *Newspaper World* quoting 'a well-known man of business' saying: 'If you can prove to me that the *Daily Herald* would produce more orders than any other paper, and at a lower cost even, I would not give them an advertisement, because they support a policy intended to bring about the downfall of independent businessmen such as myself.'[169]

If increased sales do not lead to extra advertising income, their only commercial consequence is higher production costs. The price of newsprint in 1920–21 was six times what it had been in 1914 and distribution costs, on Lord Beaverbrook's reckoning, three to four times what they had been before the war.[170] Here too the *Herald* faced a boycott, this time from the paper suppliers, although this was rapidly called off after Williams threatened Lord Burnham of the Newspaper Proprietors Association with a general press strike.[171] The higher *Herald* sales went, the closer financial disaster came. Extra sales may have meant increased political influence, but they posed a fresh threat to the paper's independence. Losses reached unprecedented levels – running at £1,400 to £2,400 per week by November 1919 and amounting to £113,661 for 1920.[172]

The paper was also beset with allegations about its sources of funding. A document of apparently official provenance suggested that the Bolsheviks were funding the *Herald* via 'Chinese bonds', although it was never specified what these were.[173] The *Herald's* humorous versifier Eleanor Farjeon (best remembered nowadays for writing *Morning Has Broken*), in the guise of 'Tomfool', cheerfully sent up the idea:

Chinese Bonds, Chinese Bonds
With which Lansbury absconds;
Chinese Bonds, Chinese Bonds,
Smuggled by Peroxide Blondes;
Tightly packed by Spiers and Ponds;
Chinese Bonds, Chinese Bonds,
                                    CHINESE BONDS![174]

Lansbury countered the allegations by publishing the entire list of share and debenture holders.[175] His openness was timely, and would be necessary again within weeks as life imitated 'Chinese Bond' art and the *Herald* received a genuine offer of Bolshevik assistance. Director Francis Meynell, acting on his own initiative and with breathtaking ill-judgement, met Soviet representative Maxim Litvinov and secured a £75,000 subsidy. Meynell and Postgate both insist that there were no strings attached and that the Bolsheviks merely wished to support a rare friendly voice in the overseas press.[176] Meynell's account of how he got the money to Britain in the form of two strings of pearls, which were concealed inside a box of chocolates and then put on the market by Lansbury's son Edgar, a jeweller and founder member of the Communist Party had, as Postgate wrote, the makings of a first-class film comedy,[177] but the possible consequences for the *Herald* were anything but funny. Realising that news was leaking, Lansbury again opted for openness. The *Herald* of 10 September 1920 led with the question 'Shall we accept £75,000 of Russian money?'. Appended was the comment that, as internationalists, the paper had no objections to accepting the offer, but the propriety of taking money from so devastated a country was doubtful.[178] Postgate reports that the readers were in favour of acceptance,[179] but debenture holders, staff and directors were against – the board, according to Meynell, unanimously against.[180] Meynell resigned and the rest of the British press, happy to see their accusations given weighty supporting evidence, enjoyed themselves hugely at the expense of the *Herald*'s apparent complicity in a red plot.[181]

There was now no escape from the financial necessity of a price increase, a move taken reluctantly by newspapers at any time in history, and particularly disadvantageous when the standard price was 1d. In the same month as the news of Soviet funding broke the *Herald* went up to 2d. A quarter of a century later, Ewer would recall this as the origin of the 'Miracle of Fleet Street' label, after Lord Northcliffe's reaction to its ability to retain circulation at 2d.[182] Northcliffe said: 'I thought I knew everything there was to know about the newspaper business, but these fellows have something I do not understand.'[183] His reasoning, suggests Ewer, was that 'if he had raised the price of the *Mail* to twopence, it would have died in a week'.[184] The *Herald's* ability to hang on to the bulk of its sale under these circumstances was indeed remarkable, but with circulation falling to 210,512 by September 1921, and with losses at around £1,000 per week and sales dropping rapidly its fate looked likely to differ only in speed.[185] Trade paper *Newspaper World* commented: 'At twopence per issue the *Daily Herald* suffers naturally by comparison with some of its contemporaries – I might add almost all of them. The other dailies so priced give a larger sheet and more pages and it is a difficult proposition for the industrial classes who buy the *Herald* to pay double the price asked by contemporaries.'[186]

It was a bad time to be uncompetitive. The 1920s would be characterised by increasingly expensive and sophisticated sales promotion, dominated by reader insurance schemes backed by intensive canvassing. Accident insurance had a ready appeal for working-class readers before comprehensive national insurance. Colin Seymour-Ure credits the idea to the *Daily Chronicle*, which in 1915 offered readers insurance against spectacular and frightening, if largely innocuous, German Zeppelin raids.[187] Initially intended as a means of stabilising sales – readers had to be registered with papers to qualify for benefits – insurance was by the early 1920s being promoted aggressively as a sales inducement. Neither the National Union of Journalists nor *Newspaper World* expected insurance to last.[188] For a start, it was extremely expensive – the *Mail* had paid out £100,000 in claims by August 1922, rising to £1m by 1928.[189] But the attractions of insurance for working-class readers were confirmed by sales figures. The *Daily News* rose from 336,609 in October 1921 to 635,934 in November 1922.[190] The *Mail*, selling 1,295,807 in February 1921, reached 1,532,709 by the end of the following January and was brandishing a sales certificate for 1,817,947 by mid-July.[191] The *Express*, entering on a decade of steady progress that would make it the first serious challenger to the *Mail's* generation-old sales primacy, was up 200,000 to 825,000 in the four months to June 1922 and topped a million in August, shortly after the *Chronicle* had done the same.[192] The *Herald's* contrasting loss of sales, falling to 185,889 by November 1921, was not acceptable to a paper whose basic purpose was political proselytisation.[193] A return to the 1d price was essential, but the financially-straitened *Herald* would have to find extra income to bridge the gap until sales rose to cut losses. It reckoned that £100,000 would be needed to bring the paper to a self-sustaining circulation of 500,000, an aspiration that was to echo unattainably throughout the 1920s.[194]

There was only one place left to go – to its loyal readers. On 6 September the board voted to go back to a penny per issue, financing the move by a new issue of £5 and £1 debentures aimed at individual supporters.[195] The campaign was launched by the TUC chairman,

R.B. Walker of the Agricultural Workers. His exasperation with the reading choices of trade unionists would recur as often as the cry for a half-million sale: 'I am amazed when I reflect on the success of Labour papers abroad and watch the struggles of our own. Is it that Labour people in other countries have grit, enthusiasm and loyalty which we lack? If so, the sooner we get some "vim" among the *Daily Herald* readers the better.'[196] This was unfair to *Herald* readers. The problem was not them, but several million trade unionists who chose other newspapers. Still, the belief that the workers owed them a living was a recurrent *Herald* theme in propaganda. In November Lansbury wrote: 'People often say to me "You are always begging for the *Daily Herald*". That is true, but the trouble is you never give what we asked for in the first place. We asked for £400,000 in order to develop the paper, and you gave us less than £200,000. Had we got what we asked for at the start we would not be begging today.'[197]

He was to be disappointed again. For all his celebration of the paper's relationship with its readership – 'Since we made our appeal you have sent in, mainly in sums of £1, a total of £8,000. What capitalist newspaper could raise that amount from its readers, not one!' – the brutal fact remained that £8,000 was not remotely enough to achieve the *Herald*'s objectives.[198] Lansbury wanted to keep the *Herald* independent, arguing that 'movements such as this need the stimulus which independent thought and expression alone can give. Officialdom always dries up initiative and expression', but independence depended on commercial viability, and its loss was the inevitable consequence of annual deficits of £113,000. Lansbury was to say: 'It is the money question, and the money question alone which had placed the *Daily Herald* under the control of the Labour movement'.[199] With conventional commercial proprietors ruled out, massive losses made movement control the only conceivable means of survival.

2
The First Transition, 1921–22

'Why, certainly', said Brandon, with deep irony.
'Apart from circulation and advertisements we are almost too blatantly and indecently prosperous!'

Philip Gibbs, *The Street of Adventure*

Lansbury could not attend the launch of the second debenture issue on 6 September 1921, but his excuse was impeccable. He was in Brixton jail, and for once his problems had nothing to do with the *Herald*. His reason for being there gave the paper its last great campaign before it passed into official ownership. Lansbury was *de facto* leader of 30 Labour councillors from Poplar, a poverty-stricken borough in the East End of London, who were jailed for defying a court order. Since taking control in 1919 Labour had been in constant confrontation with the authorities as they raised council pay, improved conditions for the unemployed and demanded a system of equalisation payments to relieve the burden on poor, low-rated boroughs with high rates of unemployment.[1] It was a divisive issue for Labour – moderate council leaders such as Herbert Morrison of Hackney feared 'Poplarism' would damage the party's chances of national success.[2] The confrontation was highly personal for both Lansbury and the *Herald*. His son Edgar, daughter-in-law Minnie and former *Herald* journalist John Scurr also went to jail on 3 September 1921.[3] In any case this was a quintessential *Herald* story, with Labour people carrying their struggle for justice against uncaring and overbearing authority to dramatic and self-sacrificing lengths. The paper's coverage of Poplar epitomised its priorities and outlook.

The *Herald* gave the Poplar story consistent attention as it developed during 1921, culminating in the eight consecutive issues around the time of the arrests when it commanded the prime front-page left-hand column news space.[4] News coverage was supplemented by leader comments and signed articles by Lansbury.[5] He wrote that the scenes accompanying the arrests – journalist John Scurr had tired of waiting and gone out for a walk while the Lansbury family parrot accompanied his arrest with interjections of 'Chuck, chuck, pretty, pretty!' – would have made 'a screamingly funny farce'.[6] But a powerfully-written account in the issue of 1 September, the most Poplar-dominated of all, of the pre-arrest meeting at the Town Hall was more Eisenstein than Keystone Cops:

> The men and women of Poplar gathered in imposing force to prove to the Councillors, whose last night of liberty they generally believed it to be, that they recognised to the full the sacrifice which these 30 men and women were making on their behalf and that the community as a whole was solidly behind its representatives ... The big building was crowded, until it was literally impossible for another person to gain admission ... Impressive as was the crowd within the hall, it dwindled into insignficance when compared with the huge overflow concourse outside ... There was nothing pessimistic about the huge gathering, no note of misgiving in the fighting speeches of the Councillors. Every speaker was greeted with loud applause, and at times, speakers could not continue until the tumult of enthusiasm subsided.[7]

Those images of resolution were reinforced by a leader rooted firmly in an ethical critique of the system the councillors were fighting. That it was wasteful mattered, particularly in the context of attacks made on Poplar on these grounds, but far more important was its concept of justice – that the system was inhumane, had different rules for rich and poor and was underpinned by 'the wickedness of capitalism'. The *Herald* said of the councillors:

> They are going, not with any display of martyrdom or in any mood save that of the simple resolve to see justice done. They are going because it is the only way left open to them of making an effective protest against injustice ... To keep children at an insufficient standard of life because their parents – through no fault of either parents or childen – are out of work is, anyway the act of a blackguardly system. But it is also the most monstrous form of squandermania ... the rich unemployed do not want work, but insist on getting money out of the pockets of the workers for no refund at all, whereas the unemployed men and women of the working class do want work, ask nothing better than work at a reasonable wage and are denied it by the folly and wickedness of capitalist society and a capitalist government.[8]

The final element in that day's comprehensive treatment of the issue was a front-page article by Lansbury. If leader-column polemic was the official voice of the *Herald,* his was the personal voice, lacking the polish of the professional journalist but with a sermon-like quality that spoke directly to the reader as a fellow participant in the struggle. He concluded:

Today with my colleagues I await arrest. Putting us in prison may suit Sir Alfred Mond and the Government. They are drawing dragon's teeth. When the prison door closes its clang will resound throughout England, bringing a note of good cheer to the poor, the sick and the unemployed. For in prison by our very silence we shall be smashing down the theory that the beastly system which dooms the workless to poverty must continue. I repeat: our call, comrade, will be to you, and you must organise to ensure that victory shall see the end of our imprisonment.[9]

This implied assumption that the reader was a fellow-activist was maintained, albeit in polemical rather than conversational tone, after the councillors had been imprisoned. An article on 3 September responded to the imprisonments themselves and the way the prison authorities placed male prisoners in a category which, among other deprivations, stopped Lansbury editing the paper. It was on a news page, headlined 'Workers and workless: back up Poplar!'. It concluded:

Figure 2 'The only way left open to them'; Poplar councillors Susan Lawrence, Nellie Cressall and Jennie Mackay on their way to Holloway jail, September 1921 (photo: Tower Hamlets Libraries, local history collection).

Pass Resolutions! Flood the Home Office! ORGANISE! Demonstrate!
But don't stop demanding first class treatment! DEMAND RELEASE!
AGITATE NOW!
What agitation has done, agitation can do. If Stead could edit the
'Pall Mall Gazette' from prison, why should not George Lansbury edit
the *Daily Herald* from prison? The imprisonment has been
deliberately delayed until Parliament is not sitting. But there are
other ways of approaching and influencing the Government.
Already demonstrations and protest meetings are being organised.
ROLL UP AND KEEP IT UP![10]

When news stories have this tone and approach, the simultaneous
printing of a leader in the same issue appears somewhat superfluous.

The paper recognised that the issue was London-wide as well as local,
and extended its campaigning efforts accordingly, encouraging groups
of the unemployed to besiege meetings of local Poor Law Guardians
with demands for work or adequate maintenance. It reported that 'The
Daily Herald slogan "Go To The Guardians" is acting as a fiery cross',
a popular *Herald* image dating back to the days of James Larkin's
Dublin transport strikes. Demonstrations were reported from
Shoreditch, Woolwich, St Pancras, Hackney and even suburban
Bromley.[11]

Lansbury, however, was never allowed to be a prison editor. His
article on the subject linked his fate to the tradition of John Wilkes,
revealingly assuming that *Herald* readers would have sufficient
historical and political knowledge to understand an unexplained
reference to an eighteenth-century radical. He couched his thoughts
in familiar conversational style: 'Now we are in. YOUR work becomes
more and more intensified. We shall all be content to leave you to
decide whether a no-rent strike is the best way to help, or whatever
efforts you should adopt. We are only anxious that the agitation
should be kept going.'[12] It was, in the *Herald* at least – aided by the
concession of daily meetings between Lansbury and a representative
from the paper – until their release on 12 October could be greeted with
a front-page headline running across all six columns, a three-column
news story and a message of thanks from the Mayor, Sam March.[13]
Enthusiasm was justified. The councillors had held out against
imprisonment, government and labour sceptics. The Minister of
Health, Sir Alfred Mond, whose personal wealth and role in the affair
guaranteed a prominent place in the *Herald*'s populous demonology,
was forced to introduce equalisation.[14] The *Herald* concluded
triumphantly: 'They have fought a great fight, not only for Poplar, but
for all the poor and all the unemployed of the country. They have
forced things to a crisis.'[15]

Asked about their prison experiences, Lansbury and Scurr might have replied that the *Herald* had accustomed them to confinement and constriction. The paper was being produced in quarters as cramped as their financial circumstances. The office was recalled vividly by Francis Williams, then an aspiring freelance: 'Its offices were up a flight of stairs in Carmelite Street, not many yards from the great mass of the *Daily Mail* building and its reporters' room a tiny den hardly enough for half a dozen people.'[16] The paper was similarly overcrowded, an eight-page six-column broadsheet crammed with as much information as possible. Every other daily except the *Express* was still carrying advertisements on the front, but the *Herald*, which would have struggled to muster a page of adverts on most days, carried news. General news pages might carry as many as 25 stories, the bulk of it agency copy, and a single-column story could run to as many as 170 lines of newsprint. Concerned with content rather than presentation, the *Herald* made few concessions to visual variety – there were very few pictures, mainly half-column mugshots. The pages had a distinctly up-and-down feel with headlines predominantly single-column, although standfirsts (short summaries in larger type) and multiple-bank headlines often conveyed the gist of stories. News by-lines were rare with the main correspondents identified by function – diplomatic (Ewer), industrial (Brodzky) and political (Bracher).

While the *Herald's* identikit reader was never as specific as the family from the backstreets of Derby who informed Arthur Christiansen's winning formula for the 1930s *Express*, it is clear who the paper was calculated to appeal to – a serious-minded, well-informed and possibly highbrow trade unionist and political activist with more interest in the latest news from the Genoa conference or a strike than in the most lurid murder or court case.[17] The 1921–22 period was a vintage one for murder trials – the case of Hay-on-Wye solicitor Herbert Armstrong would be cited as a classic by George Orwell in 'The Decline of the English Murder'.[18] Such stories got on to the front page, but rarely displaced the political lead stories. Where 'human interest' was splashed, there was invariably a political angle such as the fraud trial of maverick journalist and MP Horatio Bottomley, or a pit disaster costing 18 lives in Tipton, used to illustrate the carelessness and brutality of capitalism.[19] Assumptions about activism occasionally reached bizarre levels – had a substantial section of the readership taken up the idea implicit in the headline 'Your summer holiday' on a story about a TUC summer school, the 45 places available might have been seriously oversubscribed.[20]

There is a strong sense of the *Herald* and its readers being a family headed by Lansbury. This was epitomised by the death of Minnie Lansbury less than three months after leaving prison. Although this would have been newsworthy for any Labour paper, a Herald front-page news column plus funeral arrangement announcements on the following two days showed the importance of the Lansbury–Poplar axis.[21] So too did half a column on a dinner for 10,000 children in Bow and Bromley and a warm obituary notice for borough clerk Charles Skeggs.[22] The family feel was reinforced by the gently conversational style of Lansbury's Saturday column, speaking for instance of 'All that matters to you and me'.[23] It was shown most of all in the way *Herald* stories often failed to explain who key participants were: here was a world in which everyone knew everyone else. So a reporter visiting the Cornish tin-mining communities could write: 'I interviewed Dan Hillman on the way back' without feeling any need to explain that he was a district secretary of the Dock, Wharf, Riverside and General Workers Union.[24] Similar treatment was extended to Leonid Krassin, the Soviet representative in London, former explorer Fridtjof Nansen and Labour MPs Arthur Henderson and J.H. Thomas.[25] Lansbury was frequently described simply as 'G.L.'.[26]

Similarly indicative of confidence in its relationship with readers was the copious use of irony, often a journalistic boomerang. Faith that they shared its worldview underpinned dry observation in a news report on the 1922 Honours List: 'A whole host of Mr Lloyd George's political friends will in future be able to point with pride to their names in Debrett.'[27] Anyone who did not understand the *Herald*'s conviction that there were different rules for rich and poor might have mistaken their juxtaposition of a massive will from the Wills tobacco family with Lord Tredegar's announcement that he had been forced by financial pressures to give up fox-hunting for an escaped cutting from the ultra-reactionary *Morning Post*:

> The world is full of oddities, as everyone knows. While some have made millions out of puffs of smoke, the exercise of that truly Christian virtue – the self-sacrifice of a pack of hounds – is harshly imposed on a wealthy Welsh peer who owns land by the thousand acres.[28]

Irony was also the stock-in-trade of in-house humourist 'Gadfly', the (still-youthful veteran Everard), and of the 'Way of the World' diary column. Both would be disliked by former *Citizen* general manager Clifford Allen when he joined the *Herald* board later in the 1920s. He argued that 'Way of the World' was 'much too highbrow and clever' and implied strongly that Everard was a drinker and a bad influence.[29] But the column's mix of quirks and oddities survived fundamentally unchanged until 1930 while 'Gadfly's' status as the *Herald*'s star attraction was underlined by his pay, second only to that of the editor, and by the normally acidulous Hamilton Fyfe's comment that 'he did not think they could improve' on 'Gadfly'.[30] 'Way of the World' scavenged other sources – the *Morning Post* was a particular favourite – for items amenable to mock-horror treatment:

> 'An appalling picture of the morals and conditions of the rising generation in Russia', I read in a Sunday paper, 'is drawn by Professor Amfiteatroff, a well-known Russian writer living in Prague. Under the Bolshevist principles of equality all classes mingle in the schools and boys and girls study together'. I got no farther. It was too dreadful. I don't think the newspapers ought to tell us these horrors, do you? Not at this time of year.[31]

'Gadfly's' favourite technique was seeking out the wilder fringes of the far right and undermining them with the pretence that he really sympathised. A characteristic sketch examined the incontestably colourful Conservative candidate at the Motherwell by-election:

> Some Tory candidates are content to take their inspiration from Conservative Central Office, with particularly ghastly results. Not so Bailie Ferguson of Motherwell. The Bible is good enough for him. 'It is', he says conservatively, 'the Old Book that has taught one the menace of the Irish Romanists and Socialists' ... It is a pity considering how dull Westminster is nowadays that 15,000 of his neighbours turned him down with a thud in 1918.[32]

Lansbury's stated policy was that the paper should be 'an open platform for the expression of opinion by all sections of the movement'.[33] A distinct oddity was that little of this function was fulfilled by letters. Many issues carried only a single letter, often from an organisation rather than an individual and frequently more of a news story than a contribution to debate. A typical example was from the secretary of the St Pancras Unemployed Committee, complaining that a demonstrator had been unfairly convicted of striking a policeman.[34] Without by-lines or a record of contributors it is impossible to establish whether the paper's function as a popular platform was fulfilled by direct contributions, but this appears to have been an underdeveloped area. Lansbury protested that 'this paper belongs not to the right or the left, but the whole of the Labour movement'. But the left – pro-Russian, anti-war, internationalist and still placing greater hopes on trade unionism than on a 57-strong Parliamentary Labour Party whose impact was as moderate as its political line – still predominated.[35] His 'open platform' credo concluded with the view that it 'should at all times be a pioneer that should lead the movement rather than lag behind'.[36]

One clear dividing line was the dedicated 'constitutionalism' of the right. The *Herald* followed its Poplar line of showing much less respect for constitutionalist moderation than for the historical knowledge of its readership in calling on Labour to refuse to recognise the reformed House of Lords planned by Lloyd George:

> Such action would be technically 'unconstitutional'. What of it? In such an issue there could be no place for pedantries. The future of the country is more than the niceties of the 'constitution'. Labour would turn from the quibblings of lawyers to the bold commonsense of the men who created the constitution itself by breaking through the meshes of legalism. The precedents of 1640 and 1688 would become valid.[37]

The *Herald* continued to emphasise industrial more than parliamentary matters: union conferences mattered more than Commons sessions, hunger marches and strikes more than by-elections. Labour candidates received noisily partisan support, but the preference for industrial stories was shown in March 1921. An 11,000 Conservative majority was turned into into a 5,000-vote Labour by-election win at Leicester, but the front-page lead 'Industrial warfare spreading' focused on a chemical industry dispute.[38] Headlines made up in partisan bite what they lacked in size. London transport employers were the target of 'Men who sleep in the bus: hardships of London busmen; heartless combine'. The Asquithian Liberals were dismissed with 'Wee Frees in Labour; ridiculous mouse produced'.[39] A partisan spin might be put on innocuous stories. A brief, descriptive account of a Lords and Commons v Westminster School cricket match acquired fresh dimensions of ironic contempt from the headline: 'NOVEL SPECTACLE: Coalition members try to play cricket: low scores'. Yet the parliamentarians scored nearly 200 and had the better of a draw.[40]

While the language of the *Herald*'s political and industrial reporting drew on the ethical, moralistic tradition of which Lansbury was an exemplar, the paper's analysis showed signs of the influence of then-Marxist staff members like Mellor and Postgate. The underlying thesis was that the state was no more than the instrument of capitalism, and that Big Business (habitually capitalised for emphasis) would always try to drive living standards down to a minimum. At the start of 1922 a leader argued:

> A year ago we prophesied a co-ordinated development of the attack on wages. We do not claim to have foreseen – no-one could have foreseen – how rapid that development would be, or how successful.
>
> The government has worked in with the employers. Unemployment has been their weapon.
>
> The employers were to cut wages to a point at which it was reckoned that the spirit of the men would be broken by sheer

starvation. If the men refused such wages, the Goverment was to declare that this was 'War on the community' and place all its strike-breaking resources at the service of the employers.

At the same time, the unemployed were to be refused adequate maintenance, and were to be thus coerced by starvation into becoming blacklegs and being willing to do any work at any stage.[41]

The *Herald* placed the Federation of British Industry (now CBI) at the centre of this conspiracy. It endorsed the claim by George Hicks, left-wing secretary of the Amalgamated Building Workers, that the FBI was 'the most ruthless combination of capitalist interests the war of classes has yet to produce' and blamed the the preponderance of businessmen on the Geddes committee on public expenditure for a report calling for £75m cuts, including £18m from education.[42] This reasoning also fuelled continuing support for wider powers for the TUC General Council to counterbalance the FBI.[43] As historian Richard Price has pointed out, the belief that capitalist manipulation determined government policy was at least a more sophisticated view of the relationship between political and economic power than that of moderate leaders like MacDonald who assumed that winning power in Parliament was sufficient.[44]

One consequence was that Health Minister Sir Alfred Mond rather than Premier Lloyd George was its Public Enemy Number One. Not that Lloyd George escaped criticism. Lansbury would describe him as 'the greatest failure of all time, and this because of his constitutional inability to either see or speak straight'.[45] Mond's role in Poplar's battles – as health minister he was responsible for poor relief – gave attacks a personal edge. But combining this with the wealth and influence derived from his chemical combine made him the ideal symbol of social inequality, organ-grinder to Lloyd George's monkey. It made no difference that both, although leading members of a coalition government dominated numerically by Conservatives, were nominally Liberals. All capitalist parties were enemies. The Liberals were in one sense more dangerous, as they might be mistaken for friends. The only battle that mattered, said a March 1922 leader, was 'Between the Old Gang, who oppose the interests of the people in the interests of their own class and Labour, whose cause is the people's'.[46] In the same article as his attack on Lloyd George, Lansbury – his powers of invective in excellent order – devoted much more space to a definitive polemic against Mond and the conspiracy:

Sir A Mond, well fed, and with a bank balance supplied from the sweat and toil of thousands of workers, asks, with a sneer: 'Is anyone starving?' What a question coming from the Minister of Health, whose idea of sufficiency is derived from the miserable standard of life he has set up for the unemployed of 25s, plus 3s for coal per week, for a man and wife, while he himself accepts a salary of £96 per week from the pockets of the poor, in addition to his enormous private income, also derived from the labour of the workers ...

This rich, contented, happy Sir Alfred Mond ... has commenced to practise economy, not of course in connection with his own salary or income, but vicariously by robbing little children of the milk they need, and nursing and expectant mothers of food and nourishment. He has also taken in hand the task of cutting down the provision of clinics for the treatment of consumption and bad teeth ...

Sir Alfred Mond, representing the school of employers known as the Federation of British Industries, is endeavouring to drive the workers down to the wretched level which existed from the inception of the 'New Poor Law' in 1834. I beg every reader of the *Daily Herald* to watch Mond and all his works. He is in one of the key positions for beating down the workers' standard of life.[47]

The capitalist plot was similarly pervasive in the *Herald*'s analysis of foreign affairs, which saw much of the manoeuvring of the time as a plot against the Soviet Union. Andrew Williams points to a 'love – hate' relationship between Labour and the Soviet Union, with even moderates like Ramsay MacDonald and Philip Snowden prepared to argue for 'fair play' – a powerful concept in the ethical tradition – as a reason for not isolating the Soviet Union.[48] The *Herald* was unquestionably at the affectionate end of the love–hate axis and diplomatic editor Ewer's communist sympathies were a constant worry to the Labour leadership.[49] Lansbury's account of his meeting with Lenin – 'I shall always esteem it the greatest event of my life' – has the awestruck tone of a middle-class patriot meeting the Queen.[50] A consortium – excluding Russia – to open up European trade, was greeted as 'a new move against the Socialist Republic of Russia, and its main motive is to prevent the spread of Socialism'.[51] The Russians, claimed the *Herald*, only 'demand for themselves the toleration and peace they extend for others'.[52] The *Herald*'s recognition of the Soviet Union and communism as part of the socialist brotherhood was signalled on May Day when messages from Arthur MacManus of the Communist International and Grigory Zinoviev stood alongside those from Henderson, Friedrich Adler of the Socialist International and American socialist Eugene Debs. Lenin's message arrived too late for publication.[53]

International conferences were frequently treated as part of the plot against Russia. The paper announced 'Soviet delegation refuses to betray workers' as the Genoa conference deadlocked.[54] They were extensively covered with a mix of world-weary cynicism and outright hostility. The abrasive Raymond Poincaré – greeted on his accession as French Premier in January 1922 with the headline 'Poincaré's plans for war' – attained full-dress villain status by first threatening to occupy the Ruhr industrial region of Germany, then insisting that restored property rights be built into demands on Russia.[55]

Even so, doubts that the Soviet Union might not be the socialist paradise were beginning to creep in. The trial of the Social Revolutionary Party leaders in June 1922 produced reporting of both sides that was straight and even-handed – always a sure sign of discomfort.[56] The same phenomenon was seen when civil war broke out in the newly-independent Irish Free State. The *Herald*'s longstanding support for Home Rule had previously been expressed through comparisons between bloodshed in Northern Ireland – 'Orange savagery' in the headlines – and 'Sinn Fein Ireland ... at the moment peaceful and progressive and asks only to remain so'.[57] Irish leader Michael Collins was described in terms that readers could hardly fail to contrast with devious British premiers and murderous Orangemen: 'The most friendly and obliging of men ... he has all an Irishman's quick-wittedness ... a charm which is quite impossible to get into print.'[58] But amid the preponderance of political coverage, there were concessions to other interests. The 'Home Rulings' women's section including illustrated dress tips, cookery and advice, generally shared page seven with the children's cartoon strip 'Bobby Bear' – whose anthropomorphic adventures in verse had been around for longer than those of the *Express*'s better-known Rupert. The weekly book reviews, also on page seven, made few such concessions. As Ross McKibbin has pointed out, self-educated activists, the core of the *Herald* audience, assumed that there was 'A body of culture that people ought to know. The culture was very largely grounded on the classic texts of British literature, and it is surprising the extent to which they were known.'[59]

That outlook and aspiration, so fervently expressed in Bevin's comments in 1919, suffused the *Herald*. It was reflected in the allusions of 'Way of the World', in feature-page reflections and short stories by writers like Ivor Brown and Evelyn Sharp, and above all in book reviews – a formidable mix of politics and demanding literature contributed by heavyweight reviewers. A typical week saw a feature on Milton, Wyndham Lewis reviewing Clive Bell's *Since Cezanne* and Ewer lacerating a volume on *Europe in Convalescence*.[60] A month later G.D.H. Cole was reviewing Harold Laski's tome on *Foundations of Sovereignty* while R.H. Tawney discussed Marion Phillips' study of workers' educational needs and a Labour Party publication on secondary education policy.[61] There were compromises in sports coverage. Racing tips were a constant plague to the socialist conscience which loathed gambling in principle but recognised racing coverage could be a circulation-builder among working-class readers, including the politically minded. An excellent tipster was later credited with boosting the otherwise derisory sales of the Communist *Daily Worker*.[62] The Independent Labour Party made the exclusion of tips a condition of its support for the *Daily Citizen,* and the decision to carry them in 1914 provoked Arthur Henderson's resignation from the Board.[63] Lansbury dropped racing from the *Herald* when he became editor in 1913, but was persuaded to reinstate it when the daily returned in 1919.[64] Postgate remembered racing journalist Taylor – whose Templegate by-line still survives in the *Sun* – telling Lansbury:

'Well, G.L., we had five winners yesterday' and being answered 'That's fine brother, I'm very glad' in a tone of great dejection; and these two excellent men looking at each other in distress, each respecting the other, anxious to avoid hurting the other's feelings, desiring nothing so much as the success of the paper, yet aware of the high fence of misunderstanding between them that nothing could overlap.[65]

Sports coverage was conventional and uninspired, offering readers prosaic match reports and previews, heavily factual rather than imaginatively written. Little, the occasional National Union of Railwaymen Football League result apart, reflected the paper's distinctive character until a campaign to cut Football League match admission prices was launched at the start of the 1922–23 season.[66]

In the same week as sports coverage took this rare enterprising turn, the *Herald* was undergoing a compromise with external values far more fundamental than printing racing tips – the acceptance of official movement control. Whatever the excitements provided by the Soviet Union, capitalist plots or Poplar there is no doubt that the *Herald's* best story in the 1921–23 period was itself – containing all its preferred elements of political commitment and uphill struggle, and maintaining the paper's traditions of uncertainty, galloping insolvency and resistance to financial logic. Residual hopes of independence dissolved with the failure of the September 1921 debenture issue. Four issues now confronted the paper and its prospective owners, the Labour Party and the TUC. Four were strategic: did they want the *Herald*?; how would they fund it?; what sort of paper did they want? how would they control it? These decisions took most of 1922, but any impression of a leisurely, thought-out process is misleading. The reasons for this were rooted in question five – how to keep the *Herald* going while massive losses were threatening its existence. That short-term imperative defined the atmosphere in which all the other decisions were taken. As Ross McKibbin has noted, the national bodies were reluctant proprietors, but 'each step taken to assist the *Herald* made it more difficult for the movement to extricate itself'.[67]

By Christmas 1921 both the *Herald* board and the debenture holders had declared themselves unable to maintain the paper, and offered it to the Labour Party and TUC,[68] who reacted in the time-honoured manner of either group when confronted by an issue with wide-ranging implications – they set up a joint sub-committee.[69] The group's composition showed that they took the issue seriously. Henderson, MacDonald and Tom Shaw of the Textile Workers represented the party, while the TUC nominated its chairman – R.B. Walker of the Agricultural Workers – Arthur Pugh of the Iron and Steel Trades Federation and Findlay of the Engineering and Shipbuilding Trades Federation.[70] Their first task was to disentangle the paper's finances, which even *Herald* director Frank Hodges admitted confused him. A report from chartered accountants W.A. Scott found chronic insolvency. Liabilities exceeded assets by £159,741, and a further £50,000 would be needed for the next year if the price was restored to 1d. At current sales of 185,889, the price cut would lead to weekly losses of £2,200. The one bright point was the solvency of the associated Victoria House Printing Company, which would be thrown in with the *Herald*.[71]

Not all of the leadership wanted the *Herald*. Unemployment was up, which meant that union and party membership was down. Experience of the *Citizen* forewarned them that a national newspaper could be an expensive commitment, despite the fact that there would be a general election within, at most, two years. The *Herald* was far from the ideal cherished by a largely moderate leadership, but as McKibbin has pointed out: 'The *Herald* had one indispensable quality, it was the only paper Labour had got.'[72] Henderson's reasoning outweighed all opposition: 'It would be nothing short of a disaster were the Movement without a daily paper to express a definitely working-class point of view on questions affecting the workers as customers, citizens and producers.'[73] He carried the sub-committee, and a joint meeting of the national bodies which declared: 'The time has now arrived when the Labour Movement should take over the *Daily Herald* and the Victoria House Printing Company, so as to provide the Movement with a daily Labour paper.'[74] Question one had been answered.

Thus committed, the two national bodies took a step further, accepting a sub-committee recommendation to return to 1d from 23 January, a move aimed at improving sales, but certain to lead to large short-term losses. Each put £5,000 into *Herald* funds, a sum which together with the same sum from the paper's own resources was expected to sustain it for three months.[75] The *Herald* trailed the price cut with a daily front-page feature, while the national bodies circularised affiliates with the claim that a one-million sale could be obtained if every member at once ordered the paper. Belief in the efficacy of appeals from leaders was still deep-rooted, although they recognised the attraction of modern circulation methods by promising, in place of 'free insurance schemes of doubtful validity', a 'real insurance scheme', meaning Labour's policies against ill-health and poverty.[76]

The headlines on 24 January were triumphant: 'Unanimous cry of "Sold Out": big demand for penny DH: now for the million.'[77] But this announcement of triumph was wildly premature. The sale of 290,000 – up 127,000 on the last week at 2d – was a peak rather than a first step. By 15 February they were back to 213,345, hard evidence that leadership exhortation would not work by itself. Losses on the first fortnight were £4,217 19s 6d, threatening to exhaust the subsidy in a little over seven weeks. Advertising was up, but only just.[78] The directors, who said that the *Herald* would break even at a sale of 375,000 and be self-supporting at 500,000, estimated that £50,000 would have to be spent to make it competitive. They suggested a levy on the movement to provide the necessary breathing-space and a development fund. The sub-committee agreed, telling the TUC General Council that a halfpenny per member levy was the only alternative to closure.[79] The General Council agreed and asked unions to reply by 31 March.[80]

Lansbury, desperate to settle the future of the *Herald*, had been appealing since January for the appointment of movement trustees.[81] On 2 March he switched to direct action. The board resigned en bloc, electing in their place Lansbury, Henderson, TUC secretary Charles Bowerman and staff representatives.[82] It was an imaginative, but doomed, gambit. The national committees were not to be railroaded and told him firmly that the takeover would not be completed until finance and policy arrangements had been finalised.[83] Both his anxiety and their reluctance were understandable. On 18 March the *Herald* launched its latest distress signal. An appeal for £25,000 was promised, like many, to be the paper's last.[84] It would raise £4,786 by 12 April.[85] The levy failed as well, cumbersomely dependent on individual union procedures when the *Herald* needed instant action. By 12 May – six weeks after the target date – only 27 out of 194 unions had said yes. The 27, including the Miners and Transport and General, had 2.35 million members, but total promises of £4,970 were little compared to the paper's 1922 losses of £80,485.[86] Lansbury records, without giving a specific date, that a £3,000 loan from the London Society of Compositors was needed to save the paper in early 1922.[87]

Individual appeals had failed. Now decisive, united central action was needed. On 9 May the Labour executive and TUC General Council, 39 in all, met the *Herald* board and staff members who promised between them £8,000 – about £1 15s each per week – over the next six months, if the national bodies would pay the balance. The meeting considered the options – staying at 1d, reverting to 2d or becoming a

Sunday paper. After a three-hour debate they accepted Henderson's proposal that the national bodies take financial responsibility, guaranteeing up to £500 per week for the next six months and a subsidy from annual affiliation fees as part of the movement's propaganda operation.[88] A long-term decision dictated by short-term survival needs, this was the decisive step in the takeover. There is no more fundamental assumption of responsibility than agreeing to sign the cheques. Both national conferences had still to ratify the decision, but with question two answered the rest was mere mopping up.

The *Herald*, though forced to return to 2d, was exultant, devoting half its front page to a report headlined '*Daily Herald*'s future now assured', which explained that it would become 'the mouthpiece of organised Labour'.[89] Sales were down to 160,000 by the end of June,[90] but by then management and finance issues had been settled. An 11-man board chaired by Henderson, including five from the TUC, four from Labour, Lansbury and a representative of the debenture holders, was elected on 21 May and in operation by August. The 21 May meeting also organised the levy. Each union belonging to the TUC would increase its annual affiliation fee from 1d to 3d, while Labour was to pay an annual block grant of £10,000. The levy would be binding on unions, who could only escape by disaffiliating.[91] The National Union of Journalists did disaffiliate, saying it was unfair to ask members on other papers to subsidise the *Herald*.[92] Even the ever-supportive Miners pointed out that it would take half of their income.[93] The first of many failed attempts to bring in the Co-operative movement, to the *Herald* what some elusive giant fish is to an angler, took place in June but the Labour conference at the end of the month proved more tractable, endorsing their executive's actions and pledging collective and individual efforts to raise daily sales to half a million.[94]

Now came questions three and four. One suggestion was a policy committee consisting of five leading movement figures ex-officio. It never met, possibly because all of them were already directors and it was easier to leave policy to the board.[95] The key to policy was the editorship. Lansbury wanted to go, recognising that his determined radicalism made him an unsuitable editor for an official paper.[96] He signalled his departure in the *Herald* of 29 July in terms calculated to help the new owners: 'My resignation is perfectly voluntary. I desire the new owners to be perfectly free to appoint who they please.' He pointed out that any political body would expect to control the policy of its own paper.[97]

Chosen instrument of that control was Henry Hamilton Fyfe, at 53 an established star of the mainstream press, more in the *Citizen* than in the *Herald* tradition. He was first of all a professional journalist, his political views more a consequence of, than the catalyst for, his journalism, and he had edited the *Mirror* and the *Morning Advertiser* before spending years as *Mail* special correspondent, becoming a socialist during the war.[98] The initial approach was made by Henderson, and Fyfe had agreed to take the post by the end of July. He told Lansbury he was confident the paper would succeed if the TUC kept its financial promises, though there was an early warning of a fraught relationship when he added: 'I was a little amused by the attitude of several of the directors, and a little puzzled, though not discouraged.'[99] The announcement had to wait until the TUC met in September and the secret was remarkably well kept. *Newspaper World* did not get wind of it until the end of August, and then only as unconfirmed rumour.[100] As the TUC opened in Southport on 4 September, the return to 1d was announced. After further attrition during four months at 2d, Fyfe's inheritance would be a circulation of 142,000, very low compared to 330,000 in 1920 and 210,000 in September 1921.[101]

The *Herald* debate, disguised as a General Council motion to amend standing orders and increase the levy, was uneventful. Support from Ben Turner and Frank Hodges on the left and John Clynes and James Sexton on the right showed the leadership consensus. The only outright opposition came from left-wing engineer Brownlie, who said the levy was unenforceable, and Weston of the Shipwrights, who said the standing orders device concealed an important issue. Possibly the most effective display of scepticism came from the seconder of the resolution, J.H. Thomas, whose exposition of the 'Yes, but' position betrayed continuing doubts about the *Herald*, warning that if it did not do better 'you had better stop providing the workers with something they do not want'. The motion passed by 4.057 million to 916,000. Meeting after the vote the *Herald* board formally appointed Fyfe from 11 September.[102] Both vote and appointment were front-page news in the following day's *Herald*.[103]

Fyfe, invited to address Congress, was optimistic: 'I think we can produce a good newspaper which will stand with all the rest and be better than the rest. We do not want a subsidised newspaper, but one that will pay.' Its fate, he said, was in the movement's hands: 'Good wishes this morning have touched me deeply, but do not think I say it ungraciously when I say that good wishes are not enough.'[104] It was left to Lansbury, summoned by acclamation, to strike a note of true exuberance while reinforcing Fyfe's message: 'Only one thing ... will make this thing successful and that is if you are going to be co-operators ... if you are going to join yourselves to us on the paper by seeing that it is bought ... Six or seven million trade unionists! You ought to have a circulation of 5,000,000, not 500,000.'[105] His enthusiasm, after nine years of unremitting struggle, was understandable, but the future would not be that simple. The *Herald* of

1920–22 had been afflicted by an inadequate financial base, aggressive sales promotion by rivals who could offer larger, more varied papers, rising unemployment which hit the purchasing power of working-class readers and the passing of the immediate postwar mood of militancy. Past experience had shown the sales limitations of appeals to solidarity in the face of such handicaps. Official status would change neither that nor an awesome capacity for losing money. If anyone thought its troubles were over, the next year was to prove them spectacularly wrong.

3
The Second *Daily Herald*: On the Edge, 1922–23

Nothing is more dangerous than trying to cross a chasm in two leaps.

David Lloyd George

Any hopes that official ownership would bring stability were rapidly dashed. The *Herald*'s first year under movement control recalls nothing more than a movie-serial heroine, left tied to the rails or hanging by her fingertips at the end of each episode, although *Herald* readers were disappointingly disinclined to tune in for the next instalment. A fresh threat emerged within weeks, in spite of the sales boost provided by the November General Election. Going back to 1d had been disastrous financially. Losses rose to more than £2,200 per week. Higher sales, most lost rapidly after polling day, were more than offset by the cost of large election issues.[1] A distress signal was hoisted in the issue of 23 November. But it lacked the Lansbury touch, substituting union circularese and conference rhetoric for his gentle exhortation: 'The moment is critical. Only by a united and determined effort can the great and growing party of the Workers keep its one and only daily organ in existence to put its point of view and give news of its MPs doings; this preventing the rest of the Press misrepresenting and ignoring them. We cannot believe that our appeal will be disregarded, seeing how vital is our need.'[2]

The General Council agreed to plug the gap, while an appeal was made to the rank and file.[3] Lansbury and Henderson's call for another 150,000 readers again conveyed the exasperated belief that the movement owed the *Herald* a living: 'Surely you will add your voice and energy to ours and together by word and deed declare the DAILY HERALD SHALL LIVE or Five Million Trade Unionists and Labour men and women will hold their heads in shame and declare before the world their unfitness to stand in the shoes of the heroes and prophets who made the Movement possible.'[4]

The paper did not get the 150,000 extra sales, but there was sufficient response to convince the national committee that perseverance would pay. Circulation rose 60,000 to 260,000 by the New Year,[5] but losses were still intolerably high at £1,700 to £2,000 per week. A fresh sub committee, led by Pugh, concluded that a higher circulation was the only way forward. At current levels the *Herald* was consuming money much faster than the levy would raise it – with only £6,800 of the 1923 levy left by 24 January, cost-cutting would bring only marginal benefits. They concluded that 'to satisfactorily establish a national daily Labour paper must involve a subsidy for some few years at least' and asked unions to pledge their 1924–25 contributions now to support a vigorous sales push.[6] The national committee considered the report, in the *Herald*'s words, 'determined that the thought of letting the paper close could not be entertained', and predictably appointed another sub-committee.[7] This group had two differences. It was concerned with longer-term strategy as a means of circumventing the short-term problems which had preoccupied previous inquiries, and the leadership repertory company was supplemented by two party members with extensive newspaper experience. Norman Angell had managed the Continental *Daily Mail* while Clifford Allen, treasurer of the Independent Labour Party, had been general manager of the *Citizen* and would be a major influence on the *Herald* for the rest of the 1920s.[8]

This was a decisive point in the paper's development. The activists on the board found trade unionists buying other papers inexplicable – Angell and Allen saw this as a logical response to their superior news and features plus insurance. They proposed that the *Herald* should match them with a 12-page paper plus a 'simple and not very extravagant' insurance scheme.[9] The board rejected insurance but accepted the bigger paper together with Norman Angell's Pledge Scheme, an ingenious attempt to capitalise on the movement's mass following.[10] Under it, members would 'Pledge to Take the Labour Daily First'. Not necessarily to take the *Herald* or eschew its rivals, but simply that if they did take a paper, the *Herald* would be first choice. Hailed as 'A method and a field of advertising which is closed to competitors', it was expected to bring in two million promises and the dreamed-of 500,000 sale.[11] This would be accompanied by a capital development plan under which unions would pay levies five years in advance, freeing the paper from recurrent crises by generating a £150,000 development fund. Of this, £120,000 would be spent over the next year to reach a self-supporting circulation of 450,000.[12] Fighting off a faction which argued that the paper was doing fine as it was – sales had reached 275,000 – the *Herald* unveiled its plans in late April, promising to 'appeal to everybody, whether they are interested in the politics of the Labour Movement or not; and while it will deal very fully with politics its first cause will be to see that the *Herald* is a complete newspaper, giving each day the full history of yesterday'.[13]

The newly expanded paper appeared on 1 May. The following day's issue headlined 'Instant success of twelve pages', apologised to those unable to find a copy and claimed a sale of close to 400,000. It boasted a milestone in labour history: 'The May Day on which it became evident that the Trade Unions and the Labour Party succesfully ran a fully-equipped modern newspaper.'[14].

The paper had already undergone a partial transformation under Fyfe's editorship. Fyfe's memoirs record a warm reception from the *Herald* staff, with the news editor saying: 'We're sick and tired of having people over us who don't know their own minds', while *Newspaper World* reported 'the happiest results among the staff' who regarded him with 'full confidence and loyalty'.[15] But Postgate, a subeditor, Lansbury's son-in-law and card-carrying leftist, points instead to staff discontent at Fyfe's changes of tone, make-up and policy: 'Discontent was particularly bitter in the journalists' chapel.' Lansbury sympathised with the critics, but loyally kept quiet.[16]

Transforming a daily newspaper is a formidable task. Every issue is a consequence of thousands of rapidly taken decisions. The editor can only take or reverse so many, so change is inevitably gradual. Fyfe's most significant area of influence was the leader column, a key element in a party paper. Change here was immediate, with the column shifted from page four to the front and labelled 'From the workers' point of view'.[17] The Fettes-schooled Fyfe was an implausible conduit for any worker's point of view and the new title lasted only until 1 May, but the change in subject matter reflected an intention to broaden the paper's appeal. Lansbury and Gould's leaders had almost invariably been political. Fyfe began to leaven the mix, frequently balancing one political piece with one lighter leader. For example, on 23 November he rejected the Irish Civil War, the Lausanne conference and an unemployed march as possible second leader subjects in favour of a boy being fined 10s for shouting 'Beaver'.[18] Four days later he quoted a barber arranging wireless concerts for his customers and speculated whether they would soon want to dictate letters and eat and drink as they were shaved.[19]

Style changed. In place of Lansbury's excitably exhortatory rhetoric, Fyfe's editorials were measured, detached and a trifle didactic, reflecting the personality of which an exasperated Walter Citrine once remarked: 'You're not advanced, you're remote.'[20] A typical effort attacked France's hard-line policy on German reparations in a mannered style, speaking at the reader, citing capitalist authorities and using the epithet 'anti-British' in a way that Lansbury – for all that he might have enjoyed the sideswipe at the pro-French *Daily Mail* – would never have contemplated:

All serious financial and economic authorities now know that Germany has not the power to pay. The Association of British Chambers of Commerce said so plainly last week. Lloyds Bank, in its current monthly circular, rubs it in. Yet many credulous people are still deluded by the anti-British propaganda of the London edition of the Paris *Daily Mail.*

Ha! You begin to see the light?[21]

Political policy became much more reformist and deferential to the party leadership. When communist Robin Page Arnot attacked Labour policy it said the party need not be 'anxious about its moderation. There is little chance of that happening as long as the present spirit of our Parliament keeps up.'[22] Extravagant praise was heaped on John Clynes – the Lancastrian union leader who gave the Parliamentary Labour Party competent but uninspired leadership in 1918–22 – when he responded to a magazine invitation to name the 'Seven Wonders of Britain' by naming industrial sites as well as conventional beauty spots: 'He has done a great service by forcing reflection upon the prosperous, comfortable and mostly self-centred folk who read the shilling magazines. That is the work of a real leader, boldly to keep the end he seeks always fully in the national view.'[23]

The rightward shift in the *Herald*'s politics was apparent when Labour elected its leader after the 1922 General Election, a divisive moment for any party paper. Labour had risen from 57 seats to 142, becoming the official opposition to Bonar Law's Conservative government. The incumbent was the archetypally Clynes, who had supported the war, and his challenger was Ramsay MacDonald, returning to Parliament after losing his seat in 1918. He was no leftist, but his anti-war and ILP credentials made him by default the candidate of the left. The *Herald* called for an uncontested election, implicitly endorsing the status quo.[24] MacDonald won. This was backing the wrong horse with a vengeance. MacDonald's biographer, David Marquand, records that he never forgave the paper for trying to block him.[25]

On his first day in office Fyfe issued an order to exclude comment from stories and headlines.[26] But mixing commentary with reporting was deep-rooted, with the irony seen in the description of ex-Premier Lloyd George's claim to be a 'poor man' on £40 a week as 'a heartrending yet dignified protest' under the headline 'Ex-premier's pitiful plight', a taste of the old *Herald.*[27] As Fyfe would tell the directors in 1925: 'Habits are difficult to break, and this was the habit of the *Herald* for a long time.'[28] Decisions on which story to run and with how much prominence are more readily influenced. Even so Fyfe's impact was less than might have been expected. Lead news stories continued to be chosen for political importance rather than any human-interest conception of newsworthiness. A.G. Gardiner, who spoke with authority on combining politics with mass-market appeal after 17 years as editor of the Liberal *Daily News*, would say in September 1923: 'The carpenter, the cotton operative and the shipwright buy a newspaper to be interested and entertained and not primarily for the purposes of propaganda ... this elementary consideration has, I think been ignored.'[29] Resistance to conventional news values remained strong. The *Herald* did not simply refrain from the heavy coverage given by most papers to the salacious details of the Russell divorce in early 1923, it made a loudly proclaimed virtue of its divergence, saying: 'The *Daily Herald* has not printed, and will not print, the sordid details of such cases.'[30]

There was, however, a small shift from exclusively political emphasis when Fyfe accorded the trial and execution for murder of Edith Thompson and her lover Frederick Bywater the lead coverage Lansbury had denied cases such as Armstrong's. But it was not treated as pure human interest. A leader and a letter from MacDonald emphasised a political campaign against the death penalty.[31] The heaviest coverage, on the day of Mrs Thompson's execution, came complete with a banner headline conveying both story and editorial policy.

> Shall not this end capital punishment?
> Scenes of horror and shame
> Woman carried
> to scaffold
> Pitiful condition of
> Mrs Thompson
> Report of screams.[32]

The other concession to breadth was greater interest in scientific and technological progress. This also had a political dimension as a reflection of Labour's modernising self-image. Scientific progress was backed as a means of improving humanity's lot, but with a wary eye on potential destructive uses. Advances in flight were a particular focus for these interests in the 1920s, February 1923 bringing a neat juxtaposition of both themes as talk of 12-hour flights to New York coincided with Air Ministry concern about the state of Britain's defences: 'Shall our conquest of the air bring war and doom or peace and friendship', asked the headline.[33] More straightforward enthusiasm was accorded a new British air speed record in August, which was the lead story complete with large picture in spite of news competition from a docks strike.[34]

Within political coverage, there was also a heavy shift in emphasis to Parliament. Coverage of the 1922 election was robustly propagandist, with the *Herald* concerned to extol old adversaries such as Snowden, Clynes and Thomas as much as favourites such as Lansbury and Fred Jowett. In devoting considerable space to Labour's key policy of the Capital Levy to pay off war debt it was both propagandist and a provider of ammunition to speakers and canvassers. It offered a reassurance to the middle classes unlikely to have occurred to the old *Herald*. 'Only those will be affected who earn more than £5,000. Up to £20,000 the contribution will be small and the gain from lowered income tax will be considerable. It is those who boast a vast superfluity of wealth, a great deal of it land wealth, who will bear the brunt of the capital levy.'[35]

MacDonald may not have liked *Herald* coverage of the leadership contest, but he could hardly complain of its parliamentary reporting, which Postgate reckoned was two to three times as extensive as it had been. This reflected both Labour's greater prominence at Westminster and a shift towards *Citizen*-style priorities.[36] The paper clearly believed that parliamentary coverage was a winner, on one occasion publishing comparative figures – which showed that it had run more than 2,500 words from eight Labour speeches in one Commons debate against the 350 or fewer words run by its competitors – with the comment: 'The capitalist press itself provided an effective illustration of the importance of the *DAILY HERALD*.'[37] Change was reflected in tone as well as bulk, with parliamentary reporter S.V. Bracher striking a constant note of loyal followership. A characteristic comment was that 'no previous opposition so short in numbers has in so short a time attained so great an influence'.[38] Labour members were profiled serially and flatteringly under headlines such as 'A teacher who has suffered for his principles' (Morgan Jones – Caerphilly) while copious praise was heaped on MacDonald: 'The House is his true sphere ... was Mr MacDonald made for Parliament ... or was Parliament for Mr MacDonald?' and other leaders such as Snowden: 'The work of a master mind and he revealed also his great gift of touching human hearts.'[39]

But the really decisive shift was in industrial coverage. The *Herald* still gave a far higher proportion of space to industrial stories than any of its rivals.[40] There was still some leeway for the individual reporter – coverage of the strongly communist-influenced National Union of Unemployed Workers continued to be fulsome. But the influence of official status could also be seen clearly. Postgate singled out the weekly union matters column by Vivian Brodzky as 'confined to innocuous platitudes'.[41] The 1923 Docks Strike was a decisive rite-of-passage for the paper which had once proclaimed that 'Agreements made under coercion are not morally binding'.[42] There is no doubt that the old *Herald* would have backed the strike. The dockers were ill-paid and many came from Poplar, where George Lansbury's son Edgar was chair of the local Guardians and ensured that strikers were paid during the dispute.[43] They were contesting a pay-cut, but the cut was imposed as part of an agreement concluded by the Transport and General Workers Union. To the union leaders on the *Herald* board,

Figure 3 Rite of passage: dockers marching during their 1923 strike
(photo: Tower Hamlets Libraries, local history collection).

agreements were sacrosanct. A battle between the paper's heart and its
head ensued. Emotionally it was drawn to the strikers, with reports
emphasising their courage and determination. Brodzky described 'the
solemn ceremony of 1,500 dock strikers standing beneath the hot
sun with bared heads' in respect for Tid Marsh, a picket killed by a
motor lorry, and noted the solidarity implicit in their references to
miners killed in recent disasters.[44] A leader juxtaposed the jollifications
of Henley Regatta and the incomprehension of the 'Thoroughly
Comfortable', capitalised like all abstract *Herald* villains, with the
reality of the lives of low-paid workers. It questioned the calculations
on which the pay cut had been based.[45] As the breach grew between
the union and the strikers, the *Herald* resorted to BBC-style even-
handedness, giving scrupulously even length to both strikers and
union whenever possible.[46] But if its heart was with the workers, its
head and leading articles increasingly followed the officials. A warning
was seen in the same leader as the Henley comparison: 'We do not
claim that the dockers are acting wisely. They would do better to face
this situation calmly and follow men whom they have chosen to
negotiate for them.'[47]

The logic of that view was followed through fully on 7 July 1923 when the leader 'Don't sell the pass' signalled decisively the burial of the *Herald* as the militants' paper. It started:

What would be said of members of a Trade Union who refused to down tools when their union proclaimed a strike?

They would be called renegades, traitors to the workers cause, short-sighted and stiff-necked obstacles in the struggle for better conditions of life.

What the union decides is held in such a case to be binding upon all its members ...

But now let us put the position the other way round. When a Union executive decides there shall be no strike, when it calls for work as usual, are not all the members equally bound to show a united front?

It is all very well to shout, as a strike sheet does 'To hell with all agreements!'. But what does that really mean?

It really means:

To hell with Trade Unions!

To hell with the Labour Movement!

To hell with the workers chance of better ages, more leisure, decent homes, decent opportunities for children!

To hell with the Socialist Commonwealth which is so nearly within our reach!

At this moment to break up the united front would be to sell the pass and let the enemy overwhelm us to our utter confusion and despair.

It concluded: 'We have said that we have the greatest sympathy with the dockers. We can understand their behaviour. But to understand all is not to pardon all when the interests of millions of other people are liable to be very grievously injured.'[48]

Fyfe had expanded the letters column, but when real controversy blew up he ran letters on the news page as stories in their own right. This was just such a case, with the overwhelming majority attacking the paper. C. Abbott of Walworth said their policy should be 'The workers are right', no matter what agreement is made: 'I have been a reader of the *Daily Herald* since its inception, but can now see that it stands for capitalism and not for socialism.'[49] Another reader, G.H. Richards, from that unlikely centre of revolutionary fervour Bridgnorth, Shropshire, said the *Herald* was 'more and more the mouthpiece of reactionary officialdom'.[50] A.J. Horton of King's Heath echoed the old *Herald* spirit by arguing that the agreement was a form of economic slavery.[51] These reactions can hardly have come as a surprise. The paper's position was restated in a leader.[52] Resentment of *Herald* policy was justified when a striker claimed that the paper had failed to cover their case.[53] The *Herald* chronicled every twist and turn of the dispute until the men, who had decided to break away from the T and G, returned to work on 21 August.[54] Even so, a clear signal had been given to the movement's rank and file, one clearly recognised by strikers, as Brodzky found on visiting one meeting: 'I was quickly recognised as a *Daily Herald* representative and a strong attack on the policy of the paper in connection with the strike was made, and received with applause.' As if to reinforce the point, he noted that the same meeting cheered when Lansbury was mentioned.[55]

Yet the readers should not perhaps have been so surprised. Fair warning had been given of the *Herald*'s changed style in the paper's treatment of Mussolini's coup in Italy in October 1922. The *Herald* had spent the last few years denouncing his 'White Terror' and comparing him to the Black and Tans – potent comparisons given the paper's Russian and Irish policies.[56] Fyfe, in a signed article, acknowledged violence towards the Italian left, but said: 'It is impossible not to feel a certain amount of admiration for this man who has organised what he calls a bloodless revolution, even though the aims of it appear to be entirely opposed to those which the workers of this country set before them' and equated Fascism with Bolshevism as a creed based on violence: 'Nothing lasting, nothing useful, is achieved by violence.'[57] That comparison was revolutionary in *Herald* terms. Enthusiasm for Il Duce as a modernising man of action, his dynamism contrasted with Premier Bonar Law's somnolence, was again apparent when he visited Britain in December. The report, headlined 'Signor Mussolini disturbs Mr Law's tranquillity; getting down to realities', said that Mussolini 'believes in and practises Direct Action. He brought the conference at once down to realities'.[58] It appears to have taken the Italian occupation of Corfu in the summer of 1923 to persuade Fyfe that no good would come of Fascism.[59] Fyfe's reaction was more one of curiosity than outright sympathy with Fascism, but the episode is notable for two reasons – one is the early indication that he saw himself in part as an independent operator with a right to his own views, rather than simply as a passive servant of the movement. The other is that there were no critical letters from readers or none, at least, were published. Maybe readers were distracted by the General Election, or perhaps they saw it as an elaborate hoax.

Fyfe was not the only newcomer in the pages of the *Herald* in this period. Among the lapsed traditions of the paper was cartooning, save for Lance Mattison's efforts on the sports page. Editorial cartoons used in the late Lansbury period were largely from the continental socialist press. This may have been for cost reasons. Top cartoonists were highly expensive – by 1928 David Low of the *Evening Standard* would be on £4,500, four and a half times as much as the editor of the

Herald.[60] This gap was filled to some extent from early 1923 by Henry Dubb, a strip cartoon based on the stock worker-figure created by *The Call*, a New York Labour journal.[61] 'Gadfly' and 'Way of the World' used him as an imagined audience for their commentaries, reflecting usage by such figures as Tawney and Shaw.[62] The name regularly appears to this day among the regular donors to *Tribune*.[63] Henry Dubb was the visual doppelganger to the hapless painters of Robert Tressell's *The Ragged Trousered Philanthropists*, the ordinary decent working man whose uncomplaining and unthinking acceptance of the capitalist system helps to underpin it. The frustrated activist's image of his non-political workmate, he epitomised for the *Herald* the people who should have been reading it, but were not. His appearance – cloth cap, drooping moustache, check jacket, painful thinness and the unease of the perpetual supplicant – was established in an anonymous appearance in January 1923.[64] The first Henry Dubb cartoon saw him flatten an MP who was complaining about hunger marchers, but he was rarely so assertive.[65] Usually, Henry was the hapless everyman – trusting, decent and honest with rulers, employers and his betters – outmanoeuvred through naive good nature, and seeing the light when it is too late. Thus, accompanied by a son also clad in cloth cap and check jacket, he is cheated of his savings by 'George and Law', who invest the money in war in Mesopotamia and return only a few coins marked 'dole'.[66] On Budget Day he is left wearing a barrel as Chancellor Stanley Baldwin runs off to give his money to industrialists and landowners.[67] Taken into his employer's confidence, he listens contentedly to the fat, complacent magnate until he discovers that his part will be lower wages and longer hours.[68]

Stuart MacIntyre argues that Henry Dubb 'consoled the elect in their conviction that they were right and their audience manifestly dim-witted'.[69] As such he provided the perfect symbol for *Herald* frustration at working-class sales resistance. A pledge campaign advertisement used an imagined, extremely stilted, conversation at a union branch meeting concluding with the words: 'I notice that our brother Henry Dubb is not present – *We will pay him a special visit. He is injuring us all by giving preference to the newspapers run by our opponents.*'[70] When the paper ran into serious problems in the autumn, Henry Dubb was first shown outside a *Herald* office bearing the legend 'Closing down owing to the indifference of Henry Dubb', then a few days later he was seen discovering that he is in fact the owner of the paper, derided by a capitalist who taunts him: 'So you can't make your paper pay Mr Dubb ha! ha!'[71] Opinions of Henry Dubb varied. Clifford Allen would argue in 1925 that the cartoon was 'insulting to the worker' in the same way as later middle-class radicals would object to Tressell's *The Ragged Trousered Philanthropists*.[72] The *Herald*'s trade union directors and working-class readers do not appear to have felt insulted. One reader wrote to say that a previously anti-labour friend, impervious to socialist tracts, had been converted by the cartoons: 'He appreciated the Dubb cartoons and said it was quite true ... he reads the *Daily Herald* every day and says what a mug he has been. The Dubb cartoons may not reach the high artistic standard desired by our highbrow friends, but they get home.'[73]

The highbrow friends were in any case still well catered for on the books page, which continued in its serious way, its sole gesture to populism a half-column of short reviews called 'The pick of the shelf'. Other running features were 'For the workers bookshelf' including such heavyweight works as the reissued *Fabian Essays* and 'Books we all pretend to have read' which raised heavy letters-page controversy with an irreverent reading of the Bible: 'A free translation by a Jacobean clergyman of a Greek text of doubtful authenticity and multiple ownership. The Bible is as divinely inspired as Shakespeare or Milton or Anatole France.'[74] It has to be questioned how many *Daily Herald* readers really were given to claiming that they had read Plato's *Republic*.[75] H.G. Wells felt compelled to question the extensive coverage of poetry and literary criticism, accusing the paper of 'review after review of the work of little poetlets of whom nobody wants to hear'. He argued, and on this the review page editors evidently agreed, that 'the readers of the *Daily Herald* are the intellectual cream of our population, a bookbuying public'.[76]

The problem was that, whatever their personal or intellectual virtues, there were not enough of them. May Day euphoria chilled rapidly. The last eight-pager had sold 278,300 and the much-vaunted 12-page May Day issue 351,400. Within a week, however, the daily print run was back to 300,000.[77] Losses doubled to £2,800 per week, a rate which would exhaust the promised £120,000 in ten months. Nor did the twin pillars of the relaunch, the pledge and the levy, produce the hoped-for results. Nearly four million pledge cards were dispatched, but only 83,316 had been returned by August.[78] The failure of capitalisation was equally decisive, confirming the fears of a union leader who told Fyfe: 'The unions will promise anything, but they won't pay up.'[79] It was a bad time to ask, with membership down by a third in two years and most unions in deficit because of heavy demand for benefits.[80] The appeal fell nearly £50,000 short, bringing in just over £70,000 by late August. The *Herald* recorded: 'We have had this sum provided in small sums week by week, instead of finding ourselves with a large sum in the bank for development purposes, and there is no prospect of the sum being raised.'[81]

The failure of the pledge scheme ended any illusion that simple loyalty to the movement was sufficient to win readers, and the attempt to make the paper competitive by increasing its size merely generated hugely increased costs with little improvement in circulation in return. Liabilities of £81,000 were accumulated in four months, far more than the movement could afford.[82] In January it had been argued that it was politically inconceivable that the *Herald* should die – by the summer there was weary acceptance that whatever the political cost, the financial one had become insupportable. In late June Henderson warned the Labour conference that closure might be weeks away.[83] Yet another sub-committee – Pugh, Lansbury and Allen – was appointed in July and on 9 August the paper's doom was signalled. A meeting between the trio, the *Herald* directors and the TUC Finance Committee agreed to recommend closure to the TUC, to be held in Plymouth in early September.[84] The decision was ratified by the two national committees, with a combined vote of 47 to 3, on 23 August.[85] They considered a report from Lansbury and Pugh showing that the *Herald* could look forward to £125,638 over the next five years – scarcely enough for a paper that at eight pages would need a further £20,000 to get to the end of 1923. Fee capitalisation had depleted future income, and had reached the limits of its support for the paper. Sales had risen, but there was no likelihood of finding the funds needed to make the paper self-supporting.

There were alternatives. Lansbury argued for a eight-page paper for one year, but even this would cost £60,000. Other options were a daily paper with eight half-size pages, a midweek 16-pager or weeklies in Manchester, Cardiff and Newcastle as an extension of the Labour Press Service. The national committees saw no future in these.[86] Lansbury told *Herald* readers: 'The decision came to us in a quiet uneventful sort of fashion which told, as no words can ever tell, that parleying, reasoning, was of no avail, because, in the judgment of the joint meeting ... circumstances were such that no talking could change, and in the judgment of those responsible drastic action was the only course left open to them to follow.'[87] But the decision had still to be confirmed by the Plymouth Congress, and the *Herald* had no intention of going quietly. Whatever its defects as an all-round newspaper, it knew how to campaign. The closure announcement opened a ferocious week-long campaign aimed at decision-makers and delegates: 'We shall write again tomorrow and continue to do so, and day by day fight against the sentence of death being carried out. We shall not stand idly by and see the sweat, toil and sacrifice of years thrown away.'[88] Lansbury wrote of 'this most loved and cherished child our movement has produced'. There were multiple messages of support from MPs and union leaders and constant exhortation to recruit friends and workmates.[89] A story exposing British fascists said that if 'the *Daily Herald* ... did not do this, nobody would'.[90] The endurance of a shipwrecked crew was treated as a lesson in the will to survive.[91]

Even Bobby Bear was mobilised. The normal strip cartoon story was supplemented on 30 August by an item headlined 'If the *Daily Herald* dies: Bobby Bear in an orphanage'. This shameless attempt at manipulation was clearly aimed at Plymouth delegates with young children.

> It was not a cruel place, that Orphanage, and those who were in charge of it were not unkind. I must not be mistaken on that point ...
> There was no room for pranks there, no scope for jolly naughtiness. And what do you think our Bobby would be without his pranks, without any scope for those exasperating lovable tricks and fun to which he is always up, and for which poor Auntie Kitsie has educated us all to look every day when we open our paper?
> Bobby Bear's home was Bear Villa and his playground was the Children's Corner of the *Daily Herald*, but now Bear Villa is let to Henry Dubb and the Children's Corner is gone. Bobby, and of course Maisie and Ruby are in an Orphanage for friendless children.
> It would have broken your heart if you could have seen them standing in a corner of the yard so disconsolate. I hardly recognised Bobby at first, so changed was he.[92]

Bobby's chances of escaping this fate depended on the TUC. A report on the closure recommendation was to be made on the opening day, but the debate was postponed until later in the week – a clear indication both that the General Council still hoped to find a way of avoiding closure and that it expected the important action to take place in the backrooms.[93] Those who stood to lose most were the *Herald*'s 396 staff. They and their unions, represented by the Printing and Kindred Trades Federation, provided the main impetus for rescue. Successive reports had shown that the paper's problem was insufficient sales and advertising income, rather than overspending, but if unpleasant economies were the only alternative to closure, they were prepared to accept them. Both groups had economy plans, and it looked briefly as though the PKTF had made the crucial breakthrough. Their proposal for a three-month stay of execution backed by a £12,500 TUC subsidy while a Committee of Investigation looked into the *Herald*'s finances was accepted by the Finance Committee,[94] but they were overruled by the full General Council, which ruled that 'the situation had not essentially changed'.[95]

The only chance left, reported the *Herald* on the morning of the decisive debate, was that 'delegates may take matters into their own hands'.[96] The PKTF now took that route, formulating their plans as a resolution moved by F.O. Roberts of the Typographical Association. He argued that the *Herald* was 'one of the finest instruments that it is possible to forge. You are going to destroy it wilfully because you do not understand, or because the country is apathetic.' Closure made no economic or political sense and would waste a commercial asset – better to keep the *Herald*'s goodwill even if this meant producing a four-sheet paper.[97] Thomas, for the General Council, said they would welcome the resolution provided the money was also provided: 'You have no right to vote unless you give us the brass. Give us the brass and we will carry on.'[98] He set the tone for the rest of the debate, with immediate support from the print union NATSOPA and the Workers Union and a clear will to give the paper another chance.[99] One speaker suggested an alternative to close or pay up. W.J. Brown of the Civil Service Clerical Association said:

> The paper is within a short distance of becoming a paying proposition ... it may be possible to find a capitalist, or a group of capitalists, who are prepared to regard the *Herald* as a speculative proposition, and to make such arrangments as may, or would, enable the Trade Union Movement to retain a truly Labour policy editorially.[100]

His suggestion was remarkably similar to the deal which would be made with Odhams Press in 1929, but in 1923 it looked like heresy. The movement had several stages of disillusionment to go before it was prepared to entrust the *Herald* to a commercial publisher. Instead, the *Herald*'s ordeal was prolonged still further. Stephen Walsh of the Miners pointed to the impracticality of consulting a 130-strong delegation on the conference floor, and an adjournment to the next day was agreed.[101] A.J. Cook, mercurial general secretary of the Miners Federation, had been pressing the *Herald*'s case so vigorously that Walsh rebuked him publicly for conflating his own viewpoint with union policy. Cook too was ahead of his time, but in his case by only a few hours. The Miners met after the adjournment and decided to switch their votes from closure to keeping the paper open until Christmas.[102] This was the decisive shift – the Miners were just under one fifth of the total Congress and their influence was immense. In his memoirs Fyfe, not overgenerous by nature and no lover of Cook, credits the MFGB secretary with saving the *Herald*.[103] Walsh moved the resolution to provide the £12,500, pending a committee of inquiry and a movement conference to settle policy. It was passed by 3.06 million to 808,000.[104]

The *Herald* had won another stay of execution. Serial melodrama now gave way to black comedy. The next three months were bizarre even by *Herald* standards. Fierce debates over economies were to be expected; that staff and unions should be seeking cuts, and the *Herald* management resisting them, was less predictable. Yet it had a certain logic. The paper's management knew further cuts would damage already limited competitiveness. The unions, part-owners of the paper, wanted to protect their investment and the staff preferred cutting some jobs to possibly losing them all. The emergence of Conservative Prime Minister Stanley Baldwin as the paper's unwitting saviour seems almost natural in such a context.

The Committee of Inquiry could not start work until the £12,500 was raised, which took most of September. By the time it met, the *Herald* management had staged a pre-emptive economy drive. By 19 September £600 per week had been cut, of which £240 came from editorial, a 40 per cent cut sacrificing foreign correspondents and leaving 34 staff journalists. Circulation travellers were cut from 16 to 7 in spite of the protests of manager Le Good who warned that a smaller paper would need more selling.[105] Advertising, down to £300 a week during the crisis, had revived. The committee met for the first time with losses running at £960 per week, just inside the £12,500 limit.[106] While the *Herald*'s managers had argued consistently that staffing was already at a minimum, outside experts like Allen endorsed that view. Cuts had been made reluctantly, in the absence of real alternatives. It was certain that further economy demands would be resented and resisted. So it proved. There were few objections when the staff presentation to the inquiry called for a paper with 38 journalists – the cuts had already gone further.[107] But a proposal to abolish the day production staff induced predictably fierce indignation from them, only defused when printing manager Barrow demolished the calculations on which the proposal was based.[108]

This contretemps served as a warm-up for the PKTF plans, discussed at a series of meetings in October. A systematic department by department assault on the paper's organisation was begun by an analysis of the editorial side by H.M. Richardson, general secretary of the National Union of Journalists. He said, 'The Herald has been and is still very overstaffed ... greater economies than those contemplated by the Management could be effected without injury to the paper.'[109] Richardson called for a staff of 24, with all full-time correspondents paid by the line rather than having regular salaries and the abolition of the post of foreign editor, necessary only 'on very big papers such as *The Times* or *Telegraph*'. He argued that the heavy political emphasis deterred readers.[110] Fyfe's response was roundly contemptuous, alleging that Richardson had relied for advice entirely on his brother, a *Herald* journalist evidently not in editoral favour. His proposal to cut subeditors showed 'surprising ignorance of actual conditions' and his reasoning about the foreign editor was 'antiquated'. The *Herald* had always emphasised foreign coverage and reliance on agency copy would be pointless: 'Why provide a paper at all if we only give what the capitalist papers give?'[111] A similar story was seen in other sections as department heads demolished the PKTF plans as unworkable and ill-conceived.[112] The target was a reduction in losses to £500 per week. The economy drive ground to a halt in late October with sales at 300,000, weekly losses close to £600 and both Lansbury and Fyfe adamant that no further cuts were available.[113] On 7 November the inquiry committee decided that there was no point in asking for a movement subsidy of more than £550 per week, but as Lansbury and Fyfe reaffirmed their position, a fresh clash over costs seemed inevitable.[114]

It was now that Conservative Prime Minister Stanley Baldwin appeared in his unlikely role as the *Herald's deus ex machina*. With a comfortable parliamentary majority and four years of his term to run, he called a General Election, seeking a mandate for a policy of tariff reform. If there ever was a *Herald* miracle this was it. Without it the paper's survival into 1924 would have resulted in a struggling, straitened existence, but elections were always good for it, boosting sales by making politics the priority of a large group of potential readers and reminding the leadership why they were maintaining the paper in the first place. The *Herald* inquiry adjourned for the duration of the election. Before they could return to their duties the political landscape, and the immediate prospects of the *Herald*, had been transformed almost out of recognition.[115]

4
The Second *Daily Herald*: 'Not at All Satisfied', 1923-26

Newspapers, in truth, are always either rising or falling. It is rare for them to remain static.

H.L. Mencken

'From now on the story becomes, by comparison, dull.'[1] So wrote Norman Ewer at roughly this point in his 1949 historical survey of the *Herald*. Not only was this a hostage to fortune, it was also demonstrably wrong. It is true that the excitement of day-to-day threats to the paper's survival ceased, but the next three years offered the paper the challenge of reporting the first Labour government, in office during 1924, its demise at that year's General Election, and the mid-decade crisis of the coal industry, culminating in the General Strike of 1926. The paper's commercial and journalistic fortunes, if more secure, were still linked inextricably to those of the movement it served. If 1924 was epochal for the Labour Party as it took office for the first time following the election precipitated by Baldwin's shift to protectionism, it was scarcely less so for the *Herald*. The change in its fortunes was summed up by Lansbury's simple statement to the 1924 TUC: 'The *Daily Herald* for the first time in its history has for the last six months paid its way.'[2] February had found him once again taking the paper's fortunes as the subject for his Saturday sermon, exulting where so often previously he had been appealing: 'If we are not very careful we shall within a very short time find ourselves in the same position as our worthy competitors – the Rothermeres, Beaverbrooks, Burnhams and Riddells. We shall actually be making money. When this happens you may look out for shocks.'[3]

The December 1923 election might have been designed with the *Herald* in mind. The political excitement of an election in which Labour did unprecedentedly well – winning 192 seats and depriving Baldwin of his majority – was prolonged by seven weeks of tense hiatus, waiting to see if it could also take office. There was also the bonus of a rail strike. Daily sales rose from below 300,000 to over 400,000 for the results issue on 7 December when, *Newspaper World* reported: 'It was almost impossible to pick up a spare copy in small newsagents shops or at the station bookstall.'[4] Sales were back over

400,000 again when MacDonald finally took office in late January.[5] Advertising, so scarce in December that the *Herald* was reduced to making a virtue of it, pointing to the extra editorial space created, was similarly buoyant, more than doubling 1923 figures for the first 15 weeks of 1924 and providing more than 20 per cent of the paper's income against 10 to 12 per cent six months earlier.[6] These benefits accrued to a paper that had just cut costs to the bone to ensure survival.

The psychological benefits can hardly be overstated. The threat of closure was lifted and for a while the *Herald* could regard its front page as more important than the balance sheet. It could fairly claim 1924 as 'the best year in our history'.[7] But such evaluations are relative. If the serial heroine could be untied from the rails, she was still suffering from a degenerative disease. The holy grail of 500,000 sales, self-sustaining growth and Northern edition foreseen by Lansbury in February did not happen.[8] Instead there was steady attrition, condemned by Lansbury as 'a disgrace to the movement', to just over 350,000 in mid-September.[9] The October 1924 General Election, although it was won resoundingly by Stanley Baldwin's Conservatives, brought a fresh surge. It also further underlined the paper's inherent uncompetitiveness. Clifford Allen, by now a director, said: 'The hard fact is that we can't retain circulation even when we temporarily secure it.'[10] The post-election pattern of decline in 1925 would follow that of the previous year with remarkable consistency, albeit at around 10,000 higher. Sales finally stabilised at around 360,000 in the first half of 1926.[11]

Cuts helped save the *Herald* in late 1923, but undermined its subsequent competitiveness. The board report to the 1924 TUC was a reasonable description of the paper at any time between 1923 and 1930:

> The *Herald* is by no means the kind of paper which would be, in every sense of the term, a credit to our movement. The management is restricted in finance, business operations are curtailed and several important developments have been postponed pending the accumulation of the necessary capital for the promotion of new plans and contemplated efforts to secure an improvement in the circulation.[12]

Fyfe put the same argument more graphically to that year's Labour conference:

> What would they think of anybody who saw a ragged man in the street, with his clothes in tatters, unfit to shelter him from the

winds and weather, and who went up to him and said, 'Have you considered buying yourself a nice new suit and a warm overcoat?' Almost every question that had been asked has been as to why they had not done something that would cost a great deal of money.[13]

Losses, renewed in late 1924, grew in 1925 to £11,882.[14] Lansbury warned that amid competitors producing larger papers with Northern editions and insurance schemes, the Ragged Man of Fleet Street was likely to 'lose the opportunity to take its place among the other daily newspapers; it will remain an exotic probably requiring a subsidy again before long.'[15] Several schemes were devised for reviving its fortunes. In August 1924 Fyfe and Lansbury, arguing that 'just paying its way is no good' and that on present progress the paper would take years to reach 500,000 or accumulate the profits needed for investment, suggested taking it out of the Fleet Street jungle and running a controlled circulation paper issued to trade unionists as part of their membership benefits in return for a weekly levy.[16] The idea sank without trace, and there was little more leadership sympathy for the board's proposal in early 1925 – while reaffirming the priority given to a Northern edition – for a Sunday paper.[17]

Fred Bramley, general secretary of the TUC, noted that all *Herald* development proposals assumed increased General Council funding.[18] But with unemployment increasing pressure on union funds and the General Council taking on extended responsibilities after 1924 – a move, ironically, that the *Herald* had long advocated – the money was not there.[19] Indispensable the paper might be, but no more than the General Council and its duties. The TUC Finance and Office committee concluded that the best policy was one of 'consolidating and strengthening the paper as a daily paper, prior to any further extension of liability'.[20] A fresh attempt in 1924 to hook the Co-operative movement was equally unsuccessful.[21]

There was steady growth in advertising income. After the crises of 1923 it could scarcely have fallen much lower, but the persistence of advertising manager Poyser's staff and the advertising industry's gradual discovery of quantitative analysis also played their part.[22] The progress of 1924 was maintained in 1925, with a Lever Brothers account, seen as crucial for credibility, secured in July. A 14 per cent increase in revenue all but doubled annual income within two years to just over £63,000.[23] Welcome as it was, this performance served merely to ease pressure on a paper losing ground and money elsewhere. Early in 1926 Poyser warned that sales attrition was attracting attention from the British Advertising Agents Audit Bureau, who wanted an up to date sales certificate: 'I was able to entertain their secretary, with a few "chestnuts" and can only trust he will be content for an indefinite period.'[24] Such is the lot of all unsuccessful newspapers, but the *Herald* had problems peculiar to itself. Political events provoked cancellations, although these tended to be shortlived. Kruschen Salts, whose hyperactive grandfather, fuelled by their product, was almost as familiar a front-page presence as Ramsay MacDonald, cancelled their account after the 1924 General Election.[25] A little earlier Lansbury had compiled a list of boycotters including Lyons, Quaker Oats, Lever Brothers, Ovaltine, Birds, HP and Huntley and Palmers.[26]

There was further evidence of competitive weakness in December 1925 when an anonymous letter-writter was blamed for the loss of the Anglo-American account.[27] If advertisers thought so little of the *Herald* that they dropped accounts on such flimsy pretexts, it would never be commercially viable. Poyser was also periodically hampered by the *Herald*'s still vigorous anti-capitalism. A critical leader about Boots the Chemists in the last week of 1925 drew a classic howl of fury from him:

> I should be glad if you could discourage editorial attacks on known advertisers ... they only make our task harder and the securing of advertisements for the *Daily Herald*, even at the best of times, is far from easy ... Is there not ample scope for editorial vigour in concentrating on capitalism and its attendant evils, without the necessity of referring to individual advertisers?[28]

Evidently not – he was to complain about further attacks on Boots in the following April.[29]

Political scruples also created problems. The 1925 TUC considered a resolution that the *Herald* refuse adverts from 'firms whose working conditions are known to be unfair', the latest shot in a seven-year-old Upholsterers' Union campaign against H.J. Searle and Co. of Bromley over female labour.[30] The *Herald* had protested that it could not check pay and conditions at every firm before accepting adverts, and directors argued its financial circumstances did not permit picking and choosing advertisers.[31] The TUC, doubtless mindful of its own subsidy, accepted the argument but the Upholsterers continued to press their complaint during 1926 and 1927.[32]

Frustration at the paper's continuing struggles was also doubtless a factor in the internal tensions evident during this period. Lansbury resigned as general manager in January 1925 in order to start his own paper, *Lansbury's Labour Weekly*, a paper initially advertised as the *Weekly Herald* before *Daily Herald* pressure forced a change.[33] Fyfe paid tribute in a leader: 'As long as the *Daily Herald* lives its name will be coupled in thoughts of the workers with the name of the great leader who made it' and records that he pleaded for a continuation of the Saturday column, but was told other commitments would make this impossible.[34]

Figure 4 'The great leader who made the *Daily Herald*'; George Lansbury (centre), editor and proprietor 1913–22, waiting to be arrested during the 1921 Poplar dispute. Behind Lansbury's left shoulder is former *Herald* journalist John Scurr (photo: Tower Hamlets Libraries, local history collection).

This was a decisive symbolic movement in the *Herald*'s shift to the mainstream. While Lansbury had held a key job and went on penning his Saturday sermon, it could reasonably claim kinship with its radical predecessor. The surprise is that he had not gone long before. He was on his own admission unsuited to the disciplines of reporting to a board and constantly at odds with them: 'The board of directors acted as if any proposal coming from me was sure to be wrong.'[35] Accompanied to *LLW* by five members of staff, he would be followed shortly afterwards by another old guard stalwart, company secretary Philip Millwood.[36] But it is possible that the new paper was not the only reason for his departure. The day before Lansbury resigned a TUC committee was told he had informed the Labour executive of a £4,000 General Council payment to the *Herald,* when nothing of the sort had happened. He was to be asked to justify the statement and the matter would be raised at the next directors' meeting.[37]

Lansbury argued that appointing a professional manager as his successor would be too expensive and advocated the part-time appointment of an existing director.[38] Fyfe wanted 'a thoroughly competent man with plenty of experience'.[39] Several candidates met his specifications, but what he got was 'a trade union official who knew nothing about newspaper production' – Robert Williams, General Secretary of the National Transport Workers Federation.[40] This appointment offended the Typographical Association as much as Fyfe, and looks to have had as much to do with trade union rivalries as the needs of the *Herald.*[41] One of the dominant figures in transport trade unionism, Williams was *Herald* director Ernest Bevin's only serious rival for leadership of the sector, making his departure suspiciously convenient.[42] The appointment worsened Fyfe's relationship with his board. He had no regard for chairman Ben Turner, appointed in 1924 when several directors including Henderson left on becoming ministers in the new Labour government. He called Turner 'a figure-head with white whiskers whose method of settling controversy I was told (he never tried it at board meetings where we had no controversy) was to take a bible out of his pocket and read it aloud'.[43] He made his contempt a little too apparent. Bevin's account of Fyfe's attitude was remarkably reminiscent of Lansbury's perception of the board: 'If suggestions are made on the Board for the editor or anyone else, instead of the suggestions being received with an open mind, and examined as to their workability and usefulness, they are met in an entirely wrong spirit.'[44]

Nor was Fyfe's relationship with his staff all it might be. He had never been happy with their quality, while Williams also complained about indiscipline.[45] A breakdown in staff–editor relationships was exposed in 1925. Hicks, a reporter, was sacked for poor work and the National Union of Journalists chapel, appealing to the board, said it had been 'more tolerant than some incidents over a long period have warranted'.[46] The board confirmed the sacking, but was unhappy about the attitude of both chapel and editor, extracting a promise that he recognise the NUJ in future disputes, a surprising request to have to make on a labour paper.[47] A fresh dispute a year later, after a reporter named Fox libelled the *Daily Mail* and venerable libel-catcher W.J. Ryan passed the copy, further eroded relationships.[48] A board sub-committee confirmed Fox's sacking, the NUJ appealed and, in Fyfe's words, 'The directors went back on their promise, arranged an arbitration and allowed the customary compromise to be patched up.'[49] Had the tensions been purely internal, it might not have mattered much. But the general ill-temper affected the movement as a whole. This was, paradoxically, in part because the paper's short-term future was secure. Just as the *Herald* management could for once worry more about its contents than its finances, so could the movement and its leadership. Criticism had been muted of a paper that was visibly struggling for its life, but survival by itself was no longer enough to satisfy. Even Turner, loyal to a fault, conceded to the 1925 TUC that the directors were 'not at all satisfied that we have as good a paper as we ought to have'.[50] He was replying to a debate initiated by the Iron and Steel Trades Confederation, which argued that 'if that is the best effort in Labour journalism, then the sooner the General Council get out of this business and leave it to the amateurs, the better for us'.[51]

When directors were asked in the summer of 1925 to make suggestions on possible editorial improvements, Clifford Allen produced an extraordinarily vituperative seven-page diatribe damning the current style of the paper, its past controllers, present staff and its political fixations. It was, he said, 'ungenerous and unBritish ... littered with Communist and minority dodges' and still working in the spirit of former proprietors, 'who lifted their eyes to heaven with brotherly love on the tips of their tongues and fraternal hate on the tips of their tails'. For Allen, formerly general manager of the conformist *Citizen,* the loyal follower role was the only one permissible for a party paper: 'It is its duty to hearten, not to warn; to inspire confidence, not watchfulness.' The staff should 'give up thinking it is the conscience of the movement' and 'remember that the elected leaders must be allowed to think best what the Movement wants'. Internal movement controversies, giving too much space to minority points of view, should be minimised. Open or 'strategically retired' communists should be removed, in particular Ewer: 'Here has been called on the Movement the biggest bluff I can remember. He should be removed at once.'[52] Little matter that Hamilton Fyfe cast serious doubt on his detailed knowledge by pointing out that one of the design changes he requested had been implemented over a year ago.[53] Allen's views were undoubtedly his own. They reflected his time at the *Citizen* and were doubtless reinforced by his recent defeat by radical Clydesiders for control of the Independent Labour Party, but he was also MacDonald's voice on the board – the attack on Ewer in particular reflected MacDonald's views – and making his contribution in the knowledge that the party leader considered it 'excellent'.[54]

In November 1925 MacDonald told Allen: 'My major objection to the whole paper is that it shows nothing but incapacity from beginning to end, and instead of being a great Party organ giving us spirit and uplift, it is a miserable, cantankerous, narrow-minded and pettifogging propaganda sheet.'[55] Nor were his views a recent development. Early in 1925, reflecting on the reasons for the loss of the 1924 General Election in a strikingly intemperate letter to Turner, he argued: 'For a long time the *Herald* has been a mischievous influence in the party ... Nothing contributed more to our defeat than the policy of the *Herald* and the way it handled our case ... If I did not consider it a duty I should no more think of subscribing to the *Herald* than I would to the *Morning Post*.'[56]

MacDonald was still disappointed at losing office and personally sensitive to the point of paranoia. The *Herald* would have been only too pleased to have been capable of swinging general elections, but could hardly do so with a daily sale of less than 400,000. But however misplaced MacDonald's views were, they reflected relations between paper and government during his short-lived Labour administration of 1924. The challenge for the new government had been summed up by the *Herald* leader welcoming it to office:

> Up to now its political representatives have been critics: they have attacked Tory and Liberal governments for sins of omission and commission: they have told what they would do and what they would avoid if they had the opportunity of governing.
>
> Now they have it: now they are critics no longer; they are become marks for criticism: now the great Movement which they have behind them waits with its leaders to justify the confidence and loyalty that have placed them where they are.[57]

A parallel challenge faced the *Herald*. Opposition as much as penury had shielded it from conflict with the movement's leadership. This was not only the paper's traditional role, but is deeply rooted in journalistic culture. Most journalists are happier in the role of critic and sceptic than those of the loyal follower or cheerleader. Now, however, the compromises, equivocations and hard choices of government would be Labour's lot and the *Herald* had to find a way of supporting it without reducing all coverage to predictable propagandist tedium.

The paper's self-image as the guardian of socialism was made clear by a 1925 leader-page short story by Francis Williams, later to edit the paper. This page's mix of short stories, notes and features might be dismissed as inconsequential had Fyfe not recorded that they were chosen very carefully. He himself read the 30 to 40 sent in each day and would hardly have accepted a piece using the paper's name as a punchline if it had not been in accord with its self-image.[58] The story 'What the Public Likes' told of a pub landlord whose customers liked his beer, not knowing it was watered, because it provided the illusion that they could hold their drink. The narrator's memory went back to a provincial newsroom, telling a news editor of a strike:

> And the News Editor: 'Learn! They're not going to learn. Smooth it down my boy, smooth it down. It's too strong at the moment – goes to folks heads. Smooth it down: they'll like it all the better.'
> 'Water! Water! Why they likes water – only you mustn't let 'em know.'
> I sighed, 'The true philosophy!' I remembered the DAILY HERALD and smiled. 'But just you wait', I said, 'Just wait.'[59]

Whatever a party paper serves up, it is doomed to be accused of adulteration. Fyfe's adoption of the candid friend mode – defending Labour whenever it came under attack from the outside, but prepared both to criticise on occasion and provide a forum for debate for all sections of party opinion – was a sensible journalistic response to the challenge of a Labour government. It was also calculated to maximise criticism, and not only from the leadership. Lansbury illustrated the dilemma in July 1924: 'We also hear from our travellers that we lose circulation because people dissent from our presentation of Labour's case. What are known as the Right Wing disagree because we are said to favour the Left, while those who are Left say we favour the Right.'[60]

Some movement leaders were sympathetic to the *Herald*'s difficulties. Agricultural workers leader R.B. Walker would note in his summer 1925 director's memo that it could not 'speak with any more authority, or any more consistently on any one issue than the movement does. It is notorious that there are divided opinions on many important issues.'[61] Nor was the left any different to the right-wing leadership in demanding unquestioning support. *Herald* industrial columnist Brodzky, taking official status to its logical conclusion, wrote to the left-wing TUC general secretary Fred Bramley seeking advice on appropriate topics.[62] Bramley's reply denied the paper any independent journalistic or critical role:

> This appears to me to be the business of the Council and consisting as it does, in the main of experienced Trade Union officials, and men of national standing with qualifications which justify their position, I think you ought to leave all questions of policy to be dealt with by the national body elected for the purpose ...
>
> I think it would be much better for the writers on the *Herald* to limit their attention to giving publicity to the policies laid down by the people responsible and popularising the objects we have in view as they are made clear and definite from time to time in our circulars and publications.[63]

of God, a city in which there shall be no workless, no wage-slavery, no hungry children and no slums.[77]

It was taken as self-evident that the route to the City of God ran via Westminster. Whether Labour was in government or out, Bracher's parliamentary reports were couched in terms that could have gone straight into election addresses. He argued in 1924 that 'the record of the first Labour Government during its first session is one that reflects the greatest credit on it ... it has passed a budget which is the most popular in living memory ... brought a new atmosphere into foreign affairs', while a year later he found Labour 'mobilised, united and determined – the most formidable opposition of our lifetime'.[78] Major debates invariably commanded front-page lead coverage, while determination to provide detailed reports produced such phenomena as the four-column page two headline 'Sugar Subsidy Bill – 3rd Reading' which can have done little to encourage any wavering *Daily News* reader to switch allegiance.[79]

The breach with MacDonald came during his period as prime minister, rather than at the very beginning as Labour debated whether or not to accept office, if it were offered. The *Herald*, siding with the centre against the left, had no doubt that it should in spite of all the potential difficulties. During the wait it aligned itself firmly with MacDonald's intention to prove that Labour was both safe and respectable.[80] Its leader on the subject was remarkable both for conflating the metropolitan chattering classes with the nation and the absence of any expectation that Labour could accomplish radical change:

It is instructive to notice how quickly people have got used to the idea of a Labour government. At first they were most of them incredulous. They felt alarmed – a few went so far as to put their money into American securities, losing half-a-crown in the pound on the transaction. Now they have become accustomed to the prospect they are sensible enough to see that there is nothing to be alarmed at, they are discussing what Labour will do with a great deal of interest and without excitement or panic.[81]

As premier-designate, MacDonald remained the centre of political coverage. He was pictured on holiday with the wistful caption 'What are his thoughts?' while an article on cabinet-making was headlined 'Secrets that only Mr MacDonald knows'.[82] Taking office was almost as much a challenge for the *Herald* as for the new premier. On the day when Labour took office, Fyfe and his staff had also to cover the rail strike and Lenin's death. Any of the three stories was stronger than those which the paper usually encountered in a month and, thanks to the strike, the issue only had six pages. The *Herald* lobby correspondent reported that he was among the first to greet MacDonald as 'Mr Prime Minister' but this intimate touch contrasted oddly with the routine agency biography of the new premier, dull by comparison with Ewer's vivid obituary of Lenin, carried on page five.[83]

Once MacDonald was in office, the *Herald* continued to play down expectations, presenting the government's modest ambitions as unavoidable in the circumstances: 'A great many among us might have preferred a different kind of ministry, other things being equal. But other things were not equal', carefully not endorsing the frustrations of the left while implying some sympathy with them.[84] Fyfe examined the government's programme from the point of view of the unemployed: 'A Government', they would say 'which deliberately tried to do things at present impossible, in preference to improving the condition of the people, would betray its supporters'.[85] Pragmatism continued to rule when the government, citing public opinion, went back on its own (and the *Herald*'s) declared opposition to higher air force estimates. The *Herald* argued that if ministers were expected to act exclusively in line with their consciences, nobody with a conscience would ever accept office, leaving the job to the unprincipled: 'We should go from bad to worse. As it is we are going from bad to better, but we cannot do it in one great leap.'[86] Direct criticism of the government was ruled out, in the early stages at least. But there are other means by which candid friends convey discontent. One, a fashion still in use today among the Conservative Party's politer dissidents, is to criticise presentation.

However moderate the policy, the *Herald* saw no reason why it should not be prosecuted with conviction and vigour. Thus the Clydesider Minister of Health John Wheatley – credited with showing 'the irresistible value of judiciously bold and vigorous leadership' – and Employment front bencher Margaret Bondfield – 'the best man of the lot' – became favourites.[87] Their efforts were contrasted favourably with the defensiveness shown in important debates by India secretary Lord Olivier, Minister of Labour Tom Shaw and deputy premier Clynes, who was in MacDonald's place when a vote was lost in April: 'The bold front was dropped. A conciliatory, almost apologetic tone was taken.'[88] MacDonald as ever was exempted from criticism. The government's difficulties, it was said, would bring into play 'his exceptional genius for Parliamentary leadership'.[89] This approach might have been tolerated, though hardly welcomed. Real trouble began over the *Herald*'s insistence on printing letters critical of the government. This reflected Fyfe's view of the paper as the property of the movement as a whole, and not just of its current leadership. As he would tell MacDonald: 'It is very important that no section shall feel resentment at not being allowed to express its views in its own newspaper.'[90]

First and most combustible of a succession of letter-page controversies was that over Cabinet ministers wearing court dress, a classic
symbolic issue in which MacDonald's desire to prove Labour's
conformist respectability ran counter to many activists' views that
court dress was the sort of flummery the movement existed to abolish.
The *Herald*'s initial response to MacDonald was mildly indulgent.
'Way of the World' described the garb as a 'penalty of office' and
interpreted his mildly ironic comment that 'I feel like a High Church
elder' as reluctant acceptance of the dress in order to avoid hurting
royal feelings.[91] There were no direct editorial attacks on MacDonald
or other leaders for wearing court dress, but the paper's view was
demonstrated when it sympathised with a minister who refused an
invitation to dine with the Speaker because of dress requirements.
Moderation was fine when it served a practical purpose such as staying
in power, but the *Herald* could see no purpose in court dress or its near
relatives: 'There is no reason, indeed, we can see why politicians
should be expected to change their social habits and to attend
festivities out of their line just because they have accepted great
responsibility as members of the government. This kind of thing
belongs to the past – and might as well be left there.'[92]

Critics were quicker off the mark than supporters of court dress. The
pattern of left-wing opening shots followed by right-wing response was
a standard *Herald* letter-page pattern, suggesting that the left still saw
it as their paper. For example, J.C. Dempsey of Rothwell, Northants,
asked: 'Did we pour our energy and strength at the last election so that
our leaders might go riding with Royal Princes and patter about in gold
braid and toy swords at King's parties. Oh, for a whiff of Keir Hardie.'[93]
The issue simmered on throughout the year. The *Herald* decision to
highlight its summary of the 1924 party conference resolutions with
the eight court dress motions, complete with quotes such as South
Kensington's 'Ridiculous and harmful', was calculated to strike
MacDonald as gratuitous.[94] The Premier's unhappiness was expressed
in an anguished correspondence with Fyfe which appears not to have
survived. If Fyfe's account is accurate, one has to wonder where he
found the time on top of running both the government and the
Foreign Office. Is it possible that expressing anger and frustration in
this way provided him with an emotional safety valve?

> He protested against our publishing anything that questioned his
> wisdom or acts of his Government. To my submissions that it was
> the duty of a newspaper that belonged to the Movement, to all the
> Trade Unionists and all Labour Party members throughout the
> country, to allow opinions to be expressed and the words and acts
> of leaders discussed, he fretfully objected.

Over and over again, in long letters written by his own hand, he complained not only of what had appeared in our columns, but of my letting correspondents have their way.[95]

Hostility rose still further in May when a leader criticising a Conservative committee chair led to Fyfe being summoned before the Commons committee of privileges. The committee was chaired by the Prime Minister, who considered the offence serious.[96] The *Herald's* persistent use of the term 'antiquated' made it clear it did not.[97] But the *Herald* had yet directly to attack government policy. That final, *in extremis*, sanction of the candid friend was invoked in the summer when the government continued the previous administration's policy of bombing fractious Iraqi tribesmen. The *Herald*, deluged by hostile letters and resolutions on the subject, offered junior air minister William Leech, a conscientious objector during the First World War, the chance to justify the policy.[98] He argued the 'realist' line – that Britain had promised to stay in Iraq, the alternative was greater British costs in money and lives and that the RAF were 'invariably a model of chivalry'.[99] Fyfe's comment a day later was distinctly double-edged, conceding that 'were I in his place, I might be behaving exactly as he behaves', but warning: 'We must always be careful to keep ahead of the people who govern. If they are wise they will see that this is useful and necessary.'[100]

Quite how far ahead became apparent in mid-August. 'Realism' over air credits could perhaps be rationalised with the thought that credits themselves did not kill anybody. The Iraq policy did, an actual wrong against the principled wrong. Fyfe's own, relatively recent, conversion to socialism was largely a consequence of revulsion against what he had seen in the First World War.[101] And if pressures of office were rendering MacDonald unusually tetchy, it is possible that the burdens of editorship plus the stream of complaint from Downing Street were having a comparable effect on Fyfe. Thus the tone of Fyfe's leader was one of pent-up frustration unleashed. It bitterly indicted Leech, Air Minister Lord Thomson, a close friend and associate of MacDonald's, and, by extension, the entire government:

What would be said if they enforced private claims by throwing explosives into their neighbours' homes. How could they defend themselves against national indignation by saying that their neighbours were imperfectly civilised and that it saved trouble to throw hand grenades among them? Yet that is exactly the attitude of Lord Thomson and Mr Leech, and with them the whole of the Cabinet, in a matter affecting not themselves personally, but the whole country ...

This will not do. The Labour Movement did not make General Thomson a peer and put him into an official position in order that he might officially repudiate one of the principles upon which the Movement is founded. As for Mr Leech, his conversion to the Creed of Militarism can only be explained by Shelley's lines:

> Power like a devastating pestilence
> Pollutes whate'er it touches.

Is he, or any of the Cabinet, going to speak at the No-More War meeting this month? If so, *what are they going to say?*[102]

It was typical of 1924 that this row triggered another. Letters column controversy reached a logical conclusion by debating the *Herald's* right to criticise the government. Reader opinion, measured in these terms, was overwhelmingly on its side, summed up by J.W. Roberts of Birmingham's opinion that 'criticism is helpful: it enables the government to see it as others see it' and that of L. Ingham of Brighouse who thought 'the day when the editorial columns of the *Daily Herald* become an official gramophone, it will cease to be a leader of public opinion.'[103]

MacDonald, whose anger at the *Herald* was noted by Beatrice Webb, could hardly wait to respond.[104] In September a four-page handwritten diatribe told Fyfe it would be better 'if the *Herald* came out honestly in the open as an organ hostile to the Government, or at any rate to me'.[105] Fyfe's reply restated his pluralist policy:

> The *Herald* is the organ, not of your Government, not of a Party, but of the Labour Movement. In that Movement there are many currents of opinion ... it would be foolish to aim at making the policy of the *Herald* fit in with all these currents of opinion, but it is very important that no section shall feel resentment at not being allowed to express its views in its own newspaper ...
>
> If I were to say to any section of them 'I will not publish your opinions because that would be unpleasant to the Prime Minister', there would be good reason to retort that I was setting the momentary interest of a Ministry above the permanent interest of the Movement, which is beyond question the greater of the two.
>
> I never publish complaints or criticism of the Government unless I know – from my study of correspondence which comes in every day – that it represents a fairly large body of opinion. You could not point to any letter, much less to any article – which did not voice the feelings of a great many people in the Movement ...
>
> You tell me I don't know my business as an editor. Assuredly I have much yet to learn, but I have been in training for thirty years. You have been Prime Minister for eight months without any

experience. Isn't it just possible that you have some things to learn as well?[106]

Fyfe's claim that his forthrightness restored relations and that MacDonald was 'soon writing as usual' has to be doubted.[107] On Fyfe's own account his 'usual' writings were deeply unfriendly, and an independent if slightly confused account of his views as relayed to the *Guardian*'s veteran editor C.P. Scott by Noel Brailsford of the *New Leader*, stated in November that 'he was furious with the *Herald* which was perhaps not wonderful as its editor was a Communist and perhaps hated MacDonald more than any other person in the world'.[108] Fyfe was no more a communist than he was, and it is possible that either Scott or Brailsford had misunderstood one of MacDonald's diatribes against Ewer. But he was still unhappy, and by his own lights he had reason to be. Even when the *Herald* was being supportive it had a knack of putting things unfortunately. It may have been true that 'severe pressure' from left-wingers like Lansbury, James Maxton and Scurr persuaded the government to drop hastily-brought mutiny charges against Communist editor J.R. Campbell, but the image of a government prone to surrender from the left was not one that MacDonald wished to project, above all on the issue which was to bring the government down.[109] If the *Herald* verdict on the government was broadly positive, it closed with unwelcome candour:

The chief fault of the Ministry was a tendency to be more official than the politicians of the Old Parties and an anxiety on the part of a good many to prove that a Labour Government was no different to any other. That was certainly a mistake. A Labour Government must be different, or there is no need for it to exist. More individuality in matters of minor importance would have fully made up for Ministerial impotence, imposed by the conditions under which they took office, to do more big things.[110]

Its leader on MacDonald's re-election to the leadership was headlined 'A wise and indeed necessary choice' and affirmed his huge popularity among labour supporters. Yet it contrived to suggest that his detractors were better informed: 'Whatever criticism there is of Mr MacDonald's leadership is confined to a small circle who follow events closely and know something of what goes on behind the scene.'[111] Repudiating his pursuit of respectability at all costs by means of the code of attribution to unidentified critics, it endorsed the right of criticism more emphatically than it did MacDonald: 'He will lead his party all the better now that he has been told openly of certain causes of discontent.'[112]

Rights of debate and criticism were fully used over the next 18 months. Debates were not always on party matters. Issues debated included the composition of a socialist Ten Commandments, the pros and cons of gambling and the requirements for happiness.[113] But politics predominated, and the *Herald*'s willingness to facilitate debates on issues such as the reaction of Labour governments to strikes in 'essential services' was bound to look unfriendly to MacDonald, giving the left an opportunity to attack his government's record.[114] Hardly more welcome was the extensive and favourable coverage given to Labour parliamentary rebellions. The leader column equivocated when Clydesider Davie Kirkwood defied party discipline to protest against a grant to the Prince of Wales, but two columns of front-page coverage plus an extensive letters page almost exclusively critical of the leadership left little doubt where the *Herald*'s heart lay.[115] MacDonald complained that 'if the Socialist and Labour press had given as much attention to the Geneva Protocol as to the Prince of Wales there would be no need for putting conscientious objectors to jail in 1950.'[116]

A further irritant was persistent *Herald* championing of the Independent Labour Party's *Socialism in Our Time* programme, including a living wage proposal based on the underconsumptionist theories of J.A. Hobson. An open challenge to the orthodoxy espoused by ex-chancellor Snowden, it was a symbolic issue used by the left to attack MacDonald. It was, said the *Herald*: 'A big programme, but one for which we believe the Labour Party is ready.'[117] It says something for the exigencies of politics that amid all this, MacDonald was willing to become a *Herald* columnist and that the paper should regard this as a coup worthy of a front-page banner headline accompanied by a picture of the party leader at his desk, glasses in hand and giving the distinct impression that he wished both interviewer and photographer would go away.[118]

The paper portrayed MacDonald's competent but predictable weekly commentaries, ghosted by Ernest Hunter, a former member of his Downing Street staff, as conferring special intimacy with the great:

> The purpose of these articles is to keep touch between the Labour Movement and its leader. Mr MacDonald will here reveal his ideas and purposes: he will express views that would otherwise be confined to the narrow circle which can meet him individually. He will chat to the wider movement as he does to his friends around the fireside, answer doubts and difficulties and, by frank, homely, methods seek to establish valuable contact between a great party and those whom it has placed at its head.[119]

The alleged frankness of the interviews did not extend to MacDonald confiding his view – expressed in the same month in his letter to Turner – of the *Herald* as a mischievous influence.

The limits to the *Herald's* appetite for free and frank exchange were reached in a vicious exchange between the right-wing railwaymen's leader J.H. Thomas and far-left miners' secretary A.J. Cook in early 1926. Having exercised its own freedom of inquiry and expression in printing Thomas's broadside, then sending a reporter to get Cook's reply, the paper refused to print readers' letters attacking its actions:

> The idea in the minds of most of our correspondents is that we should disregard our function as a newspaper and suppress anything with which we do not agree.
>
> Such intolerance, such intemperance of language, such incomplete conception of the duty of a newspaper, do great harm to the cause which they, and we, have at heart.[120]

It is doubtful that there was anything more vicious and harmful in the suppressed letters than the ugly public exchange between two major union leaders. These were fractious times on the industrial side of the movement, with the novelty of dealing with a Labour government, the arrival of the Minority Movement as a focus for Communist and far-left influence and the mounting coal crisis – ultimately to lead to the General Strike of 1926 – all potential flashpoints. For all its proclaimed appetite for intra-movement debate, the *Herald* was never happy when it turned into outright conflict. The first half of 1924, with Labour in power and a rash of disputes ensuring that Bevin was on the front page almost as often as MacDonald, was particularly uncomfortable.

When the National Union of Railwaymen fell out with ASLEF over the drivers' strike, Thomas proclaimed a 'fiasco' at the same time as Bromley of ASLEF was claiming an 'amazing response', its reports showed the same deliberate even-handedness as was seen during the 1923 Docks strike – both points of view were given exactly equal space, although news coverage left little doubt that the strike was seen as effective.[121] Even more discomforting was the government's decision to use Emergency Powers against the London bus and tram strike after the *Herald* had derided the idea as impossible.[122] Not for the first time, when confronted with tricky choices, the leader column response was a resounding silence. A settlement saved the *Herald* from making an unpleasant decision between government and the unions.[123] The government's main industrial tactic was the Court of Inquiry. The unions were wary of them – Bramley told *Herald* industrial editor George Thomas that inquiries might reduce their role – but the *Herald* took the government view, arguing that 'prevention is better than cure'.[124] The inquiries provided classic *Herald* copy, combining detailed examination of pay and conditions with partisan polemic. The Mines inquiry in May was said by the *Herald* to show 'a wonderful revelation of the capitalist mind and attitude towards the human needs of people', in the evidence of mineowners' representative Evan Williams.[125] It was even happier with the 1924 London Docks strike. The issues, low pay and casual employment, were little different to the 1923 dispute, but this time the strikers had official Transport and General Workers Union backing and this made all the difference: 'They will have, in this fight for the elementary decencies of life, the sympathy, and if need be, the active help of the whole working-class movement.' Subsequent headlines would include 'Dockers never so determined' and 'Organised labour supports the dockers'.[126] The dockers struck for an extra 2s per hour, and after rejecting a compromise offer of 1s derided in a *Herald* crosshead as a 'Useless trick' settled for 1s now and a further shilling later.[127] This was greeted with the headline 'IT IS A GREAT VICTORY – Ernest Bevin' and a leader which restated the *Herald* commitment to follow-your-leader trade unionism: 'By following solidly their leaders, who knew so well when to be prudent and when to be bold, they have established their claim to the rise in wages for which they put forward so irresistible a case.'[128]

This argument put the *Herald* firmly in the centrist, centralising mainstream. Yet at the same time the paper would come under constant, censorious union pressure for its attitude to the Communist-controlled Minority Movement (MM). It took Bramley's intervention to stop the tabling of a 1924 TUC resolution from the Workers Union condemning the extent of MM coverage in the paper, while a year later Brown of the Iron and Steel Trades Confederation asked, 'Is the *Daily Herald* to be the property of the Minority Movement?', implying strongly that it currently was.[129] Allen thought it was 'a semi-minority movement conspiracy'.[130] The *Herald* had thought the MM's founding conference as worthy of a full column report, just as it devoted two-thirds of a column to the communist platform at the 1923 election, emphasising its support for Labour,[131] but Brown and Allen appear to have been unfair. In 1925 the *Herald* gave full coverage to MM events and James Larkin's blistering invective:

The hope of the working-classes of the world lies in Russia. If the Clyneses, the Thomases and the MacDonalds had remained true to the revolutionary fervour they used in the old days, it would be a different story today. We might have had the working class in power.[132]

But it was equally prepared to give space to attacks on the MM by Thomas and Clynes, condemn the howling down of Thomas at a railwaymen's meeting as 'totally at variance with the spirit of the movement', and criticise advocates of revolutionary violence: 'A rising of the people, if it took place – we do not see signs of it at present – would make things worse instead of better.'[133] It was all a question of whether or not the communists were a legitimate part of the movement, entitled both to a voice and to reports of their events. The *Herald* view had always been that they were. This brought it into conflict with party loyalism as Labour progressively excluded communists. In 1924 membership of the two parties was declared incompatible by conference. The importance the *Herald* attached to this was shown by a four-column news report on the debate, its discomfort demonstrated by the absence of a leader.[134]

By the time Labour next met, leader column opinion had hardened, arguing that 'an energetic left wing of a constitutional organisation is a very different thing from a body of people who denounce peaceable action as a back number'.[135] Support for exclusion was still lukewarm, even if the juxtaposition of an advert headed 'That flatulence' with the headline 'Labour Conference: closing debates' was probably more subeditorial mishap than comment.[136] If the head backed exclusion, the heart was divided and the leader has the air of an internal dialogue between different opinions on the paper, again citing unnamed sceptics as a signal for disquiet short of outright dissent and turning on a bureaucratic appeal to rules and unity rather than vigorous advocacy of official policy:

> By many members of the Labour Party this decision, as was made obvious in the debate, will be regretted. They fear heresy hunts: they point to the incessant work of the Communists in the struggle against capitalism as a definite set-off to any differences of principle: they regard it as an obstacle to a united movement. To them we would say that the decision has been made by the governing authority of the Labour Party, that it carries the imprimatur of that authority, and that the primary requisite of the moment is that decisions by that body should be accepted by all who belong to it.[137]

MacDonald was as worried about foreign as home coverage, expressing concern about the possible communist allegiances, doubted by Fyfe, of Italian correspondent Giglio and expressing consistent doubts about Ewer which Fyfe rejected on the grounds that he was the best journalist on the paper, among the best in London and kept his views out of the paper.[138] Nevertheless Russia dominated foreign coverage. This did not itself prove communist sympathies. Andrew Williams, in his extensive study of the subject, points to a firm movement consensus behind the aborted Soviet trade treaty of 1924, extending to confirmed anti-communists like Snowden and MacDonald.[139] Nor was a pro-Moscow line in defiance of TUC views – the left traditionally dominated international debates, as the right dominated on pay and conditions, and a delegation returned from the Soviet Union with glowing reports in late 1924.[140] This was reinforced by a leftward lurch in 1925, culminating in a TUC vote for a single Socialist International including the Bolsheviks, a path firmly rejected by the social democratic parties of Europe.[141]

This enthusiasm was not particularly ideological. One reason why Bolshevism had become so acceptable to the TUC was the assumption, across the left–right spectrum, that increased trade with the largest country in Europe could ease the depression and reduce unemployment. The connection was made explicit in a news story headlined 'Ports that want Russian trade: unemployment in the Humber towns: position becoming worse' and developed in subsequent stories, including the discovery that British bankers were refusing the credit need for a £5m Russian machinery order, which underpinned its argument that capitalism was conspiring against Russia.[142] Even so there were times when the *Herald*'s backing for trade and contact with Russia looked remarkably like continuing enthusiasm for Bolshevism. The leader when the MacDonald government recognised the Soviet Union referred to 'the only system which could have held Russia together', while clear identification with the Russians as fellow standard-bearers of the working class was reinforced when Soviet delegates arrived for treaty negotiations to be greeted by a reference to 'the first negotiation between two working-class governments'.[143] The TUC delegation report was hailed as 'burying fantastic fictions of reigns of terror and starvation' while the International Federation of Trade Unions' disinclination to affiliate the Bolsheviks, citing among other things Labour's expulsion of communists, was ascribed to 'a strange confusion of mind'.[144]

Direct identification with Bolshevism was sharpest when Lenin died in January 1924, indicated by Ewer's statement that he was 'the greatest spokesman, the greatest leader that the working-class has yet known'. His two-column obituary 'Best-loved leader of Russia's people: his work for the Revolution' was summarised by the cross-heads 'Wonderful career: a terrible blow: his word was law: world for workers.'[145] The leader, though less effusive, still called him 'certainly the greatest Russian since Tsar Peter'.[146] This was followed by an unsourced funeral report that recalled *Herald* descriptions of the Poplar revolt. Headlined 'On his comrades shoulders: Lenin's return to Moscow: weeping crowds: workers march hand in hand', it started by telling of a four-mile journey to the station on friends' and workers' shoulders, followed by a procession including 'hundreds of peasants from the villages around who had walked, 20 miles or more through a Russian winter night, so that they might follow him one last time'. It went on to describe the arrival in Moscow:

> No pageantry, no pomp, but line after line of workers, in their working clothes, marching hand in hand, an endless column. Such a friend as no man has ever had ... By the coffin, night and day, passes the endless procession of his people, come to look once more upon his face before they lay him there under the Red Wall, among his fellows.[147]

Other foreign coverage remained preoccupied by the threat of renewed war in Europe. MacDonald was lionised with happy partisanship as the co-author with French premier Maurice Herriot, welcomed warmly as a replacement for the feared Poincaré in May 1924, of the settlement of the Ruhr crisis. It was, said the *Herald*, the 'First real peace treaty since the war.'[148] Its pages periodically resounded to the warnings of Labour experts like E.D. Morel of the Union of Democratic Control: 'Europe a vast arsenal' or Philip Noel-Baker who told an ILP summer school of 'incendiary bombs which can destroy an entire town in a day or two' and would make the 1914–18 war seem 'child's play in comparison'.[149]

Anti-imperialism remained deeply ingrained, with the old battle against the British variety given a neat twist when Indian journalist St Nihal Singh was commissioned to write a long series of articles on the Irish Free State. The conclusion to his first, 'Youth at the helm', could taken as relevant to India as much as Ireland: 'These young, inexperienced men are managing Irish affairs much better than they were conducted by the wiseacres in Whitehall.'[150]

The *Herald* of this period sometimes gives the impression of regarding non-political news as mere space filler. It is hard to know what else accounts for the extraordinary front page of 19 March 1926. Maidstone Grammar School's production of *Macbeth* and Swaffield Road LCC School, Wandsworth's *Twelfth Night* may well have merited front-page coverage in their local weeklies, but their appearance on the front of a national daily – however hard-pressed and however late an alternative story may have collapsed – is inexplicably bizarre even by *Herald* standards.[151]

Directors' memos written in the summer of 1925 show that they saw Labour news as the priority. Ethel Bentham commented that 'a small paper with limited resources has to fulfil two different functions – that of the ordinary daily newspaper and that of the organ of the movement'. With other news sources available, she suggested that it concentrate on the movement role.[152] Bevin was concerned that 'if one went away to a place where the DH was the only procurable paper and returned after a period, one would be out of touch'.[153] It is easy amid the splenetic rantings of Allen's paper to miss the significance of what he was saying about news coverage, his analysis of the paper's failings echoing Philip Snowden's 1919 critique of the left press. There was simply too much overt politics for the paper to have broad appeal:

> We advertise ourselves as a Labour Daily when all the time we want to be considered as an attractive newspaper ... there should actually be less inches of Labour matter and less Labour headlines in the DH than in other papers, simply because the public is especially sensitive in thinking of us as a propaganda paper. Labour propaganda and Labour's point of view should only be introduced into our columns when it is justified on its merits as news ... our eyes should always be set on the general reader, who does not want 'doing good' but wants a bright general newspaper.[154]

Fyfe was unimpressed, arguing that 'It is quite impossible that a paper [that] exists in order that the Labour point of view may be represented in the Press should serve up its news and comments exactly as the *Daily News* and *Daily Mail* do. If it did, what need would there be to keep going?'[155] The Allen critique, however, would exert increasing influence as the 1920s went on and the *Herald* continued to struggle. One observer credited Allen as the 'chief architect' of the new post-1930 *Herald*.[156] Putting these ideas into play, however well they were obscured by the tone of the remainder of his paper, was arguably his first significant contribution. Not that Fyfe was unmindful of popular taste. In early 1926 he told the Postmaster General's Committee on broadcasting:

> What the mass of newspaper readers required was amusement rather than information of a serious character. They wanted something to occupy their attention while they were travelling to and from work.
> What they liked best were the spicy little bits, attractively displayed, which they got on the principal news stories.[157]

The *Herald* still carried a mass of small items drawn from courts and other agency copy. A typical news page on 24 April 1926 carried 26 items including coverage of a slander action between an actress and producer, complaints about restrictions on women students at Oxford University, a honeymoon couple's double suicide, the imprisonment for fraud of a tax inspector and a bulletin on the baby princess.[158] But the clear view was that *Herald* readers were not 'the mass of newspaper readers'. The paper remained distinct, on occasion proudly and noisily different. Its view of the standard human interest story as an opiate, not only pointless but harmful, diverting readers from important matters, was crisply expressed in a leader 'Dope – and the reason why', which explained the sparse coverage of Lady Cathcart's exclusion from the USA for being the guilty party in a divorce:

> We do not of course, give prominence to the matter. The Capitalist newspapers treat it as the most important matter of the day. It is important to them. So long as the British nation can be doped in this way, so long the present system will last. They are getting all the advantages they can from the fact that the Englishman 'dearly loves a lord'.[159]

It is questionable sense ever to tell newspaper readers what they are not getting. The *Herald* patently did not 'love a lord'. It acidulously compared the tolerance extended to Lord Curzon after a succession of driving offences and to drunkenly riotous undergraduates on Boat Race night with the likely treatment of the less privileged under similar circumstances.[160] Yet news pages occasionally contained their own variation on 'society news', with the families of Labour leaders in place of jaded aristos. The wedding of Arthur Henderson's daughter in July 1924 prompted a short front-page story on the arrangements, followed by a front-page picture and a two-thirds of a column account indicating that most of the Cabinet had been among the guests.[161]

While rejecting the traditional human interest story, the paper was developing a variant of its own – aimed at evoking anger at injustice and pity for its victims. Politics were never very far away, with interest often following a Labour cue. Murders are always good copy and in 1924 the *Herald* found a campaign in the case of Jean Pierre Vaquier, a Frenchman tried for the murder of a Surrey publican named Jones.[162] Until the trial and death sentence it appeared little different from the other spectacular case of 1924, the Crumbles murder which provided several days of front-page agency-style copy and an execution which caused the *Herald* little apparent regret.[163] But once sentenced Vaquier became the focus for a fresh assault on capital punishment, his victim status based on condemnation via an unfamiliar language and legal system. Initiated by *Herald* director Ben Turner, a typical political cue, a 10-day assault was sustained by daily updates in the right-hand front-page column.[164] Readers were told that the paper was 'Snowed under by appeals', that 'All classes join in demand for reprieve' and 'Public feeling grows daily'.[165] There were reports of a 17,000-signature petition and a heavy anti-hanging postbag, although some wanted the law to take its course.[166] Unhappily for Vaquier, Home Secretary Arthur Henderson was with the minority, but the *Herald* never forgot where its loyalties lay. While Turner's Labour role was played up, the case was presented throughout as a Home Office matter rather than personal to Henderson, who was never criticised directly. The parallel case of William Smith shortly after the Conservatives regained power in late 1924 showed the advantages of opposition. Ninety thousand signatures were collected for his reprieve in Hull and this time the *Herald* had no compunction about getting personal: 'Home Secretary refuses a city' was the headline on the report of 'anger which rapidly gave way to bitter indignation' in Hull when his appeal was refused.[167]

An even more fruitful running story, which mixed rapacious capitalism with downtrodden employees, centred on the Empire Exhibition at Wembley, signalled on this occasion by a threat from Bramley of the TUC to withdraw union co-operation following complaints about poor pay and conditions.[168] This was too good to miss, there already having been letters-column criticism of high prices at Wembley and the main caterers were Lyons, lacerated the previous autumn in a 'Teashop slavery' series focusing on low pay and conditions.[169] A front-page full column investigation detailed low pay, long hours and reliance on tips, typified by a description of:

One white-faced girl ... on the verge of tears as she told me that up to three o'clock yesterday she had made 2d.

'I don't know what I am going to do', she added. 'I am in debt to my landlady for the first time in my life since I came to Wembley. Even if, as they tell us, we make plenty of money when the season really starts, it will take it all to clear our debts.'[170]

Similar stories ran throughout the summer, with unexpected Lyons pay rises in July attributed to the Ministry of Labour's collection of statistics.[171] When Lyons reportedly banned staff from speaking to the *Herald* and denied claims of staff discontent, the paper flourished a crop of letters from employees.[172] A front page cartoon captioned 'An exhibit we would rather not see at Wembley', showed a caged lion – the pun obvious – chewing on bones marked 'waitresses', 'sweated labour' and 'low wages' while the company's annual profits of £665,377 and a 25 per cent dividend were juxtaposed with a 15s a week waitress left with 3s after two customers left without paying.[173]

Scientific progress continued to enthuse. A series of 'Death Ray' reports in 1924 were something of a nine-day wonder, though reckoned worthy of front-page coverage and several cartoons.[174] There was genuine enthusiasm for long-distance flying with D'Oisy's flight from Paris to Calcutta in 1924 hailed as marking 'progress towards air journeys becoming as common as railway or steamship travel'.[175] Even after the Paris Mail aircrash in late 1924, with eight deaths, the *Herald* was convinced 'flight will become commonplace'.[176] Nineteen twenty-five was the year in which the *Herald* discovered the motor car, though not as something its readers were likely to own. The success of the Motor Show was quoted as proof that 'the comfortable classes of this country are doing very well indeed and are provided plentifully with money'.[177] With this in mind 'motor bandits' and road deaths – 'The Moloch of the road' according to one leader – were emphasised more than the potential freedoms created.[178]

Similarly reflective of the paper's outlook was the continuing seriousness of the reviews section. If the letters page was any guide, this is how readers wanted it. The bulk of those published argued, if anything, for greater austerity. For example, J. Lydon of Liverpool demanded 'definite working-class literature' in place of reviews of best-sellers while 'Student' of London N22 spoke for the most austere traditions of the self-educated and politically committed with his claim that 'the majority of *Daily Herald* readers find sufficient reading matter to occupy their spare time from the vast field of literature which is in some way connected with the Labour Movement'.[179]

Sport was, by contrast, oddly detached from the rest of the paper. In the summer of 1924 cricket columnist 'Titwillow' discussed the prospects for the England captaincy. Ramsay MacDonald's government was at that very moment demonstrating the working-man's ability to run the country. Yet Titwillow chose to discuss the professional cricketer's ability to lead England in conventional-wisdom terms that would have brought down leader-column derision if applied to any political, industrial or artistic issue and could with only minor adaptations have been deployed against the viability of Labour governments:

> In practice I doubt if it would succeed. First it is a well-known fact that a professional is not so apt to give of his best if he is under the control of a brother professional. There is bound to be an element of sub-conscious rivalry between them.
>
> And a captain's duties do not end on the field. He has a certain amount of social work to do. An England captain on tours abroad is in the position of being a kind of ambassador, and has to attend all kinds of functions and make speeches.
>
> I do not mean to suggest that a professional of today could not do this part of the work just as well. But I would wager anything that not a single professional cricketer would like to take the task on![180]

This was an isolated incident. In 1925 the *Herald* was the first paper to abolish the amateur–professional distinction in scorecards and gave three days of condemnatory front-page coverage to Yorkshire president Lord Hawke's infamous outburst against the possibility of a professional English captain.[181] That cricket was the one sport occasionally deemed worthy of moving from the back to the front page is not as odd as it might seem. Historian Tony Mason points out that soccer had yet to develop a national consciousness or figures comparable to Jack Hobbs, whose record-equalling 126th century was also front-page news for the *Herald* in 1925.[182] But given the context, Titwillow's musings are as jarringly incongruous as Fyfe's brief enthusiasm for Mussolini. Would a comparable piece have been allowed to slip through in any other part of the paper?

The *Herald* showed an equally unsure touch in dealing with the new craze of crossword puzzles, arguing that 'Cross words will pass. We shall be bored by them and seek out new inventions'.[183] But this was a matter of preference. The paper pragmatically provided a more or less regular puzzle from the start of 1925, beginning with 'The Swastika' – a symbol still to acquire sinister connotations – and with a typical *Herald* touch carrying an Esperanto puzzle in February.[184] It evidently did not love its new feature, and was convinced it had found a more palatable alternative in 'Labour limericks' with a political message in October, cheerfully claiming that 'only a few readers regret the passing of the cross-word'.[185] That entertaining puzzles were likely to outlast political messages in popular appeal was a message that the *Herald* remained reluctant to accept. It was, however, applied in one part of the paper. The one concrete consequence of the board inquiry of 1925 – one more than most *Herald* committees achieved – was a picture page, funded by £7,000 extracted from the General Council by Bevin.[186] Launched in February 1926, it reflected the Allen critique by being more newsy than political and closer to popular press style than the news pages. The first spread included two pictures of current floods, the Oxford boat loaded for race trials and a hat from the Paris fashion shows.[187] The mix of something newsy, something sporty and at least one pretty girl became the norm. Politics obtruded rarely, as when shots of an eroding wall near Lloyd George's Criccieth home provided an irresistible opportunity for pointed comparisons between the wall and Lloyd George's Liberal Party.[188]

So it was evidence of how serious the industrial situation had become in May 1926 that the picture page should have been devoted largely to pictures devoted to the coal crisis. Not every *Herald* reader would be enthused by the intensive coverage of the miners which provided the paper's central theme for much of 1925 and 1926. In August 1926 one would write to complain: 'I have been wondering these last few days if the *Daily Herald* is a paper for the whole of the workers or just for the miners.'[189] There were complaints that the paper gave too much space to miners' leader A.J. Cook, the Minority Movement's most prominent supporter.[190] Cook, however, was charismatic, quotable and an indefatigable speaker at a time when speech reports were the staple of political and industrial coverage. His union, by far the largest in the TUC, was to embroil the entire movement in Britain's only General Strike in May 1926. Historian

Keith Middlemass, no ultra-leftist, argues that: 'The history of trade unionism in the 1920s resolves around the perpetual crises of the coal miners.'[191]

Herald coverage of the lead up to the crisis points of 1925, when the government conceded a one-year subsidy to the industry as a delaying tactic, and of 1926, when the TUC slid reluctantly into calling the General Strike, was characterised by great restraint. There was no doubt which side the paper was on, stating the case for the miners in ethical, humanitarian terms: 'The men will stand firm. They are lights for life, a life that is worth living, not a mere existence of toil, existence and semi-starvation.'[192] It believed conflict could be averted either by reasonable behaviour by the owners or by nationalisation, an aspiration expressed in 1926 that mixed ethical argument with socialism as modernism, accompanied by a heavy dose of the paper's propensity to emphasise important concepts with capital letters:

A great Movement, inspired by Faith in the Future, by determination to move with the times, and by the spirit of Comradeship which aims at turning our resources to full account for the benefit of everybody, no longer for the advantage of a privileged few ...

There will be no Bureaucracy, no political conflicts over labour conditions, management will be by experts ...

A great occasion has called forth a great design. Nothing more encouraging to those who follow the Labour Movement, nothing more hopeful for the creation of the New Order, has ever seen the light.[193]

The *Herald* had no doubt that conflict was inevitable, in line with its conviction that the Baldwin government was no more than an instrument of the employers. Its coverage was comprehensive, progressively driving other stories from prominent places in the paper. But while expecting a fight, it was not spoiling for it. When the stakes were so high an official paper, reflecting the alarm of the General Council, who did not want a General Strike but saw themselves being dragged inexorably towards it, would not make rash statements that might make a bad situation worse. In both years there was a marked absence of polemic in news coverage. In 1925 headlines in the last ten days included: 'Mineowners pressed to withdraw demands', 'Coal crisis: Labour's General Staff in command', 'Government meet miners and mineowners', 'No coal imports if miners are locked out' and 'Premier conducts long-distance parley' with only the references to 'demands' and the General Council as 'General Staff' betraying sympathies.[194] In early April 1926 a lead story headlined 'Great coal crisis threatens' devoted two columns to a strictly factual report of the owners' position combined with comments from the miners.[195]

In 1926 the *Herald* was prepared explicitly to reject its syndicalist heritage: 'No responsible trade union leader has ever proposed a General Strike, which would hurt most of all the people it was intended to help' and to reflect its growing distance from the far left with an assault on inflammatory Minority Movement statements: 'A godsend to the Mineowners Press ... nothing but harm can be done by small and unimportant bodies butting in.'[196] Only when conflict appeared inevitable was cool objectivity abandoned and the *Herald* recast in partisan, election-campaign mode. On both occasions mobilising readers became a priority. The two oddly contrasting appeals run in 1925 did as much as the equivocal leader on Communist exclusion to reflect diverse elements within the paper. One offered hints of the old Lansbury direct appeal approach, identifying reader and paper as a single body: 'We all have a duty to the Miners. We can all state their case. We can all plead for sympathy for them.'[197] The other, noting a statement by movement leaders, was imperious, impersonal and treated readers as abstractions rather than individuals in an invocation of the traditional totems of union solidarity, discipline and trust for leaders:

> It is more than an appeal; it is a definite Trade Union instruction for, and on behalf of, powerful and well-established organisations, bearing the signatures of tried and trusted leaders and representatives ...
>
> Will our leaders therefore constitute themselves a voluntary army of canvassers in order to point out these really self-evident facts to those who have hitherto placed their individual whims and caprices before the duty they owe to themselves and their dependants.[198]

The following year found the TUC's decision to strike greeted with a voice-of-the-centre editorial titled 'Trust your leaders!'[199] Headlines in the the final pre-strike issue conveyed a mix of exhortation and information: 'Stand firm and we shall win', 'How to help', 'Stand fast! Be loyal to Labour and the miners' and one story 'Beware of wireless! The government controls it!', that prompted a police raid on the following day.[200] Fyfe's leader, as ever in moments of crisis, went back to the ultimate purposes of the movement, expressed in ethical supra-class terms. It concluded on perhaps the high-point of *Herald* millenarianism during the 1920s:

> If before victory comes we have to suffer, we must suffer gladly because of our Great Cause. If we must make sacrifices, we shall make them readily, looking to a rich reward. Not a reward in personal benefit, but in the knowledge that we have steadfastly borne our part in the eternal conflict between Progress and

Stagnation, between the forces which we symbolise as Christ and Satan, between Darkness and Light.[201]

In 1925 that conflict had been postponed, with the *Herald* hailing victory for 'the forces of organised Labour standing solid behind the miners'. Looking back to the disastrous defeat of 1921 it proclaimed that 'Black Friday can now be forgotten. Red Friday has washed it out.'[202] In 1926 there would be no such escape. Like every other national paper, the *Herald* was subject to the strike, but it continued, in the guise of the *British Worker*, the strike sheet issued by the TUC in response to Winston Churchill's *British Gazette*.[203] Its type and headline face were those of the *Herald* while regulars such as 'Gadfly' and 'Tomfool' provided a small leavening of humour alongside a mass of serious strike news and exhortation. Fyfe, Mellor, Williams and print manager Barrow continued to run the paper, although the editorial side was firmly subordinated to the TUC's Publicity Committee whose secretary Herbert Tracey firmly overruled Fyfe's desire to run other news alongside strike accounts.[204]

The tone and content of the *British Worker* were those of the *Herald* election issues, the voice of the centre addressing the activist on the periphery crystallised in 11 words in one issue: 'Stand firm. Be loyal to your instructions and trust your leaders.'[205] Unlike the *Herald* it was, with other papers closed or producing miniature editions, overwhelmed by demand. On 12 May it sold 713,000 copies – including just under 200,000 printed outside London.[206] The final issue's farewell message following the defeat of the strike was an exhortation to readers to transfer their support to the *Herald* – Fyfe suggested retaining the *British Worker* name to cash in on strike loyalties, but was again overruled.[207] He was not to go on being overruled for much longer. The *Herald* returned on 18 May 1926 believing that the twin objectives of a 500,000 sale, against 360,000 in late April, and profitability were within its grasp.[208] The print run was 554,000 on 18 May, and peaked at 562,213 two days later.[209] But returns rocketed with the print run. Within a month sales were below 450,000, with relatively poor performance in Wales and the North-East evidence of growing privation in the still-striking coalfields.[210] Advertising also showed the pattern familiar after political or industrial drama. Poyser returned to 'A fine basketful of cancellation orders' but reported a steady revival in June and July.[211]

Relative prosperity gave Fyfe his opportunity to resign. After promising to stay for three years, he was well into a fourth with no break longer than 10 days. He had no doubt he left the paper stronger than he found it: 'Its circulation had more than trebled. Its advertisements had largely increased. It was now a very fair newspaper, thanks to the efforts of its staff. It would have been a first-class newspaper if

Figure 5 'They always did what he told them to do'; Ernest Bevin, painting by Thomas Cantrell Dugdale, 1945 (National Portrait Gallery).

we had not had to cut and pinch and scrape in every direction.'[212] His resignation in July 1926 reflected continuing tensions with the directors. He blamed Williams and Bevin 'intriguing with more than their usual energy'.[213] No evidence is cited against Williams, but an anonymous memo in the TUC archives, bitterly critical of Fyfe's management, may provide the answer.[214] The author had a good day-to-day knowledge of the paper's workings and saw its movement role as paramount – both characteristics point to Williams. He commented:

> The editor has not the real co-operation and confidence of the staff and this is not due to any lack on the part of staff to co-operate, but purely a temperamental weakness of the Editor, it is made worse by the fact that his judgment is unstable and erratic, that he has not the knowledge of the different phases of the movement that several members of the staff possess and is too susceptible to personal influence.[215]

Fyfe recalled that Bevin attacked him at a meeting for having told a reader that *Herald* inadequacies were the board's fault for providing inadequate resources. He was certain he could have won the argument: 'I had only to appeal to results to defeat Bevin, and maybe drive him from the field.'[216] This is extremely doubtful. Bevin was not in the habit of losing battles and the memo suggests Fyfe's position was not as strong as he believed. But, remembering that the board had paid off Lansbury's deputy Gerald Gould, he saw an opportunity for making them do the same. He recalled telling them: 'I understood from Bevin that they would like a change of editorship. Some of them looked surprised, but they always did what Bevin told them to do, so they assented.'[217] Bevin's response is not recorded.

Fyfe left the *Herald* on 31 August 1926 with a £750 payoff.[218] His final months in charge were also dominated by the miners, continuing their dispute after the failure of the General Strike. The *Herald* maintained restraint, fast becoming second nature, accepting the TUC position that there should be no debate over the General Strike while the miners were still out. Its one lapse from this came in Fyfe's penultimate issue. Clearly feeling that he need no longer defer to his directors, he launched a ferocious broadside at the Minority Movement's bitter criticisms of the General Council, by implication critising the Miners' executive's decision to continue.[219] Communists were predictably furious, but so was the ever-loyal Turner, who expressed his regret when the issue was discussed shortly afterwards at the TUC.[220] It was a fitting conclusion to Fyfe's relationship with the *Herald* board.

Yet Fyfe's farewell was hardly out of line with the *Herald's* previous post-strike policy, and in lacerating the Minority Movement openly he was only a little ahead of his time. The General Council's cessation of the General Strike was a decisive, divisive moment in the movement's relationship with the communists and their organisations. To the Minority Movement it was a betrayal; they said so vigorously and often.[221] The General Council declared that there should be no debate while the miners were still out, while right-wingers attacked Cook's verbal and tactical recklessness.[222] There was no middle way amid such contention. The *Herald*, as it was bound to, chose the General Council. By refusing to debate the issue, and on one occasion refusing to publish a speech by Cook – 'We deliberately refrained from publishing the spicy bits of a speech that was intended to do as much harm as possible' – it had already aligned itself clearly against the Minority left.[223] But in so doing it was also elevating political priorities above journalistic ones.

The miners continued struggle provided the *Herald* with a story covering all three main home news categories – political, industrial and human interest. As such it completely dominated the paper from its return on 18 May – not until 19 June was the front-page banner headline unrelated to the strike – with devotedly detailed reporting chronicling every twist.[224] There were periodic loaded headlines such as 'Government playing the mineowners game', but the bulk of reporting at national level remained factual – on occasion lapsing into bureaucratic union circularese as when the TUC discussed plans for relieving conditions in the coalfields:

> Plans for a far-reaching movement to help the locked-out miners and their families, and to meet the developing attacks on the workers generally are rapidly approaching completion at the headquarters of the Trades Union Congress, and it is probable that the General Council will be in an position to make an important announcement of policy next week.[225]

The human interest element was drawn from the resistance of mining communities: one report on Lancashire was headlined 'No surrender!: Lancs miners stand firm: wonderful spirit of men and leaders: funds exhausted, money and food wanted – but no weakening'.[226] But enthusiasm cohabited with concern about the implications of fund exhaustion. Within days of reappearing the *Herald* was campaigning for relief funds – 'Miners bairns need help – you must give it' was not so much a suggestion as an order printed across six columns.[227]

The evacuation of children from coalfields provided the opportunity for emotion-inducing reports, larded with sentimental terms such as 'bairn' and 'mite', emphasising the helplessness and poverty of the evacuees and the uncaring attitude of owners and government. The story 'Bairns needing homes: flight from the wrath of the coalkings' included a typical description:

> Dr Marion Phillips, one of the secretaries of the Women's Committee, drew one girl to her, a frail mite of seemingly nine years, whose pallor was in marked contrast with the healthy colour of the women around.
> 'I think the seaside will do you good', she said.
> The child smiled wistfully. 'How old are you?'
> 'Fourteen next October', was the astonishing answer.[228]

In case anyone doubted the desperate seriousness of the situation, Bobby Bear was mobilised to appeal to children: 'Are you HELPING THE MINERS CHILDREN? ... Little children in the coalfields are suffering so much because their fathers and mothers cannot given them enough food ... Lots of children are helping already ... Will YOU do what you can to help?'[229] A consequence of such privations was that early faith in the miners' prospects receded fast. Having trumpeted on 29 May 'Why the miners are bound to win', the *Herald* was by August expressing 'a general feeling of relief' and commenting that 'fights to a finish are always conclusive' as the miners' delegates accepted the inevitability of negotiations.[230]

Given the *Herald*'s deep seriousness on the dispute, it is odd that it should have carried an agency space filler on the headmaster of Alleyn School's jarringly complacent levity on a thoroughly unfunny subject – that following his refusal to allow boys to drive buses during the General Strike, 'he believed there was a movement on foot to present him with the Royal Humane Society's medal for having saved life (more laughter)'.[231] But perhaps the *Herald* needed all the levity it could get. The sole light touch among lead stories came in August when the England cricket team recovered the Ashes. This relegated an attack on Cook at Chelmsford station, which ultimately contributed to his loss of a leg in 1931, to a single column second-lead.[232] There had earlier been proof that Titwillow's aberration of 1924 was well behind the *Herald* as columnist Robin Bailey lacerated the choice of amateur Percy Chapman over the supremely qualified, but professional, Jack Hobbs as England captain: 'This concession had to be made to snobbery, which has so often handicapped England in the sports arena'.[233] No such controversies were to beset the *Herald* board as they made an equally significant selection of their own, an editor to succeed Hamilton Fyfe.

5
The Second *Daily Herald*: 'A Decline Which Is Lamentable', 1926–28

> Every daily newspaper in London was competing madly against its rivals in the matter of insurance and offering princely bribes to the citizens to make a fortune by breaking their necks.
>
> P.G. Wodehouse, *Ukridge*.

William Mellor, deputy editor since 1922, was the obvious successor if, as *Newspaper World* said was likely, the search was confined to internal candidates.[1] There is no evidence that the board ever seriously considered anyone else and the 37-year-old Mellor was appointed on 26 August.[2] He was a formidable character – Margaret Cole described him as a powerful personality whose emotions were easily aroused, formidably effective in argument but prone to bullying.[3] Michael Foot, who worked with him on *Tribune* in the late 1930s, remembers him as a shouting editor and described him as an 'endearing ogre'.[4] Margaret Cole would describe him as 'stronger in the spoken than the written word'.[5] Unequivocally of the left, successively guild socialist, conscientious objector, proponent of direct action and founder member of the Communist Party of Great Britain, he was never to move far to the right, and later became the first editor of *Tribune* as well as being denied endorsement as a Labour candidate in the late 1930s because of his Socialist League activities.[6]

All this mattered less to the *Herald* board than the breadth of support and respect he enjoyed. Allen, proponent of conventional news values rather than socialist controversialism, nevertheless provided a reference.[7] Fyfe had praised him for his work on the *British Worker*.[8] MacDonald, so fearful of Ewer's influence, appeared to have no such worries about Mellor – although Fyfe suggests that in this MacDonald was misguided.[9] An anonymous memo writer was also an enthusiast:

> His wide, unbiased and very thorough knowledge of the movement enables him to correct errors of policy and fact ... his corrections are not always agreed to by the Editor ... it is because of the personal affection of the staff for him, his journalistic ability and his

knowledge of the movement that under such conditions of stress he is able to carry out this unequal task.

Wittingly or not, the memo writer made a strong case for promoting him: 'In the periods that he has acted as Editor he has created a different atmosphere in the office.'[10] Deputies, particularly those with Mellor's connection with a paper – his first contributions were before 1914 and he had been on the staff since the postwar relaunch – are frequently more popular than editors.[11] Allen, like Mellor, had been imprisoned three times as a conscientious objector and MacDonald had been a prominent, much-vilified critic of the war,[12] so this created a bond with others who had shared the same views and experience of persecution.

In backing so unregenerate a leftist, Allen knew what he was doing. Proof can be seen in Mellor's statement to the 1926 TUC when he defined himself: 'as a Labour journalist'.[13] Mellor was unequivocally of the labour movement. Where Fyfe, a late recruit, gave the impression that he was doing the movement a favour, Mellor had no qualms about regarding himself as its servant, prepared to tolerate its disciplines and idiosyncracies. Though well to the left of Fyfe he would be far more prepared to accept direction from the leadership. External circumstances would also aid this stronger sense of central direction. While Ben Turner would note wryly at the 1927 TUC that 'I think it would be the millennium coming if we got something to satisfy us all', the bitter political recriminations which followed the failure of the General Strike and the progressive falling out between the TUC and Russia meant that the two sides of the movement increasingly agreed that communists were to be regarded as a threat rather than allies.[14] Mellor, in spite of his own sympathies, would conform to this view.

Finances would also have their effect. Fyfe was reinforced in his independent line in 1924 by knowing that the paper was reasonably solvent. It is much harder to take a robust line against the influence of your paymasters, by now exclusively the General Council, when you have also to seek periodic subsidies in order to survive. While never remotely recalling the financial avalanche of the early 1920s, this would again be the lot of the *Herald* in the years following the General Strike. It would also be a period in which reasons for maintaining the *Herald*, always manifest at times of great political and industrial excitement, would be rather less obvious. While Fyfe's four years encompassed three general elections and the General Strike, Mellor's first couple of years found the Conservatives secure in mid-term with a comfortable majority and unprecedented industrial peace following the General Strike.[15]

If the anonymous memo, which provides the only picture we have of the editorial side of the *Herald* at this time, is to be trusted, Mellor's journalistic inheritance left something to be desired. He could count on the support of his deputy, the Welsh ex-miner W.H. Stevenson, 'a very nice-mannered person, methodical, but not an innovator'. Ewer, the memo-writer said, was as competent a journalist as any on the paper, but news editors lacked authority for historic reasons.[16] These were not explained in the memo, but the *Herald* was to run through 13 news editors between 1919 and 1932.[17]

The current chief subeditor (almost certainly Arnold Dawson) was literate and popular but lacking authority because of the 'sordidness of his private life and habits'. His staff were mediocre, clique-ridden and maltreated good stories in the desire to be 'safe'. Not that good stories were likely to be common with reporters who rarely left the office and spent most of their time reworking cuttings from other papers:

> The reporting staff of the paper, with one exception, is rather slothful and there is an unwholesome atmosphere in their habits, an interest in Labour or Trade Union affairs is absolutely lacking, selfishness and petty jealousies are often manifest and no journalistic rivalry is noticeable.

The industrial department had been in flux for 18 months, leading to inadequate and inconsistent coverage.[18]

Mellor might reasonably have hoped for increased editorial budgets. Instead he came under constant pressure for reductions, losing £40 a week in editorial costs by November.[19] He managed to extract the money for a branch office in Cardiff, whose coalfield hinterland was important both for looking at the longer-term consequences of the 1926–27 strike and as a heavily-canvassed circulation battleground, in early 1927, and was subsequently barraged with complaints from Williams about its cost. It was closed in March 1928.[20] In September 1927 the *Herald* had only four general reporters, less than half that of any other national daily, and in early 1928 its total editorial complement was 44, compared to 66 on the *News* and 68 on the *Chronicle*.[21] The problems this created would be summed up by Mellor, citing Monday 19 March 1928 to illustrate difficulties that had 'in not so extreme a form, to be faced daily'. He wrote:

> The sub-editorial staff consisted of 10. The chief sub-editor was taking his fortnightly day off; the industrial sub-editor had a day owing to him in consequence of the previous illness of the industrial editor; and one man was away sick. These 10 had to work a seven-hour day (with their time off) beginning at 12 o'clock and finishing

at 1 am (in actual fact they finished at 1.30). Two men finished their day when the First Edition went through, 1 man finished at 9, 4 men finished at 10, 1 make-up man finished when the Second Edition went through, leaving 3 men for the Third Edition and the Parliamentary Sub, who worked overtime. That night the whole paper had to be remade on the Second Edition, owing to the course which the Zinoviev debate took, and on the Third Edition extensive changes were necessary. The result was that on the Third Edition the paper was terribly understaffed, and it was necessary for myself and the Night Editor to take a very active, but not purely editorial part in the making of the Second and Third editions.[22]

As Fyfe had already found, the impact of a new editor on a national daily is likely to be gradual rather than immediate. Mellor was further constrained by the domination of the coal strike, which continued until December. Yet there were gradual indications of a new style. The editorial line was little different, but the terms in which it was expressed changed subtly. Fyfe's semi-mystical references to the 'City of God' and 'New Order' placed him firmly in labour's ethical tradition. Mellor, the ex-communist, demonstrated his Marxist grounding by using 'scientific' as a positive adjective. Pugh's 1926 TUC presidential address was commended as 'an important contribution towards scientific trade union policy', while another leader called for 'pulling this basic industry to its feet by the application of scientific methods of production and making it serve national ends'.[23] At the same time came mild reminders of the Lansbury style. The appeal to support the miners in Mellor's third issue was couched in terms of the readers' own experience as workers and the importance of their contribution: 'PAY DAY IS TO-DAY: or tomorrow for most workers'. Two per cent of miners were back at work: 'The other 98% DEPEND ON YOU'.[24] This technique and timing were used periodically for the rest of the dispute. The November Revolution anniversary leader, dropped under Fyfe, was reinstated: 'In an age of kaleidoscopic change, with crowned heads "ten for a penny" and Governments crashing in every other corner of the earth, the Soviet Union alone has remained stable.'[25] Gerald Gould, poet and Lansbury's long-time deputy, was recalled as the main Saturday columnist. He wrote in a philosophical, literary style, citing Shaw and William James in one early contribution, and dealing with subjects that were political by implication rather than current controversy.[26] But this was a rare example of overt politicisation in retreat. In early November 1926 Mrs Roscoe Brunner, wife of Sir Alfred Mond's business partner, was shot dead only hours after visiting the *Herald* offices and being interviewed by Stevenson. So strong a news story might have struck a less political editor as a natural lead story. The interview and her letter to Stevenson seeking a meeting were run on the front page, as was the following day's report that the interview had created a sensation, but both still took second place to the coal dispute.[27]

Mellor was also much more disposed to leaders on the same topic day after day as the story developed, and less inclined to leaven the mix with the softer, more whimsical leader on a general topic, which had been characteristic of Fyfe. The leaders on 25 November dealt with the death of Krassin, the Poor Law, by-elections and the state of the Liberal Party.[28] Fyfe, not a generous critic, said that the propoganda element in the *Herald* became more noticeable as soon as he left, with speeches by certain trade union leaders abounding.[29] This is not incompatible with the countervailing view of Beatrice Webb that Mellor had 'distinctly improved' the *Herald*, crediting it with 'more character and consistency, better news'.[30] Mrs Webb was nothing if not austere and serious-minded in her tastes. But neither was Fyfe necessarily being unfair.

Articles by MPs proliferated more noticeably than General Council speeches, and not only on political topics. One six-issue spate in the spring of 1927 saw five contributions ranging from Wheatley on 'The Tory attack on the Guardians' to Snowden on 'Why I like detective novels'.[31] Routine interviews with leaders were treated as front-page news events in themselves – not only MacDonald's equivocating views on the miners, 'I know that right will win in the end' but also 'The plight of Britain's chief export industry', based on an interview with the leader of the Cotton Operatives.[32] The tone of movement stories became more propagandist. Advertising and bureaucracy mix in a report that 'an inspiring tale of progress is contained in the report, published yesterday, which the National Executive of the Labour Party is to submit to its annual conference'.[33] The language used was often a reminder of official status – jarringly so when juxtaposed with the name of the iconoclastic former editor in May 1928: 'The DAILY HERALD is authorised by Mr George Lansbury MP, chairman of the Executive Committee, to make the following statement regarding the Labour Party's electoral programme'.[34] An occasional tendency to reproduce circulars verbatim crept in, while some stories just read like circulars:

> Strenuous efforts, which are certain to be sustained, are being made by the opponents of Labour to prevent any further encroachment by the working-class forces into the important sphere of local administration,

was the intro on a local elections story explaining that

Keen hopes are entertained at the Labour Party headquarters that November will witness great Labour victories in all the Boroughs. These hopes were voiced to me yesterday by Mr Egerton P Wake, the Labour Party's national agent.[35]

At the 1928 TUC Mellor would define the *Herald* as 'a centre paper trying to keep a level head in the midst of great difficulty'.[36] That alignment had been resoundingly confirmed with the issue of the *Labour and the Nation* programme in 1928, apotheosis of the ethical gradualism epitomised by MacDonald's resounding but imprecise belief that a Labour government 'could not accomplish impossibilities, but would steadily go forward to something nobler and better'.[37] On the left John Wheatley said that there was little in it that Liberals could not accept and that the programme might take 40 years and still fail to bring about socialism.[38] James Maxton saw it as imbued with ideas of 'long, slow gradualism'.[39] Mellor the man may have sympathised with them, Mellor the editor excused the programme's deep moderation by saying 'there was much to destroy before even the foundations can be laid'.[40] The paper's report called it 'the most important political document of modern times. A brilliantly written exposure of the failure of Capitalism and a convincing restatement of the case for Socialism, it will inevitably command the attention for many months to come of those concerned with the well-being of the nation.'[41]

'Centre' was more than a location on the movement spectrum, it also increasingly expressed the *Herald*'s position in relation to the grassroots, lecturing readers on their duties as followers. This tone was clear after a poor by-election result at Buxton:

There must be in every constituency a keen, zealous and well-informed body of voters, men and women, prepared to carry out the vital work of talking to electors on the doorsteps and winning them over. If the rank-and-file awaken to the realisation of their duty; if attention is paid to the voters list; if a strong and efficient electoral machine is built up in every constituency, Labour will beat the Tories and Liberals out of the field at the next national appeal to the electors.[42]

This did not necessarily rule out debate. Bevin, at the 1926 TUC, had given the *Herald* a licence for some dissent: 'Unless the editor and staff can express their thoughts, and are prepared at times to face even your hostility if they believe they are right, then the paper is not worth its salt in developing thought and in moulding public opinion.'[43] Mellor held that 'criticism of leaders is not only a right but a duty'.[44] But there were limits to this right. Left MP John Beckett's assault on Thomas and

Figure 6 'Keeping a level head in the midst of great difficulty'; William Mellor, *Herald* editor 1926–30 (photo: NMPFT/Science & Society Picture Library).

MacDonald at the 1926 Labour conference provoked a leader arguing that dissent through party structures was conditional on not giving enemies ammunition: 'There is criticism and criticism. Criticism that is necessary and helpful: criticism that is superfluous and unhelpful. It is not hard to place Mr Beckett's Margate speech in its proper place in that dichotomy.'[45] Mellor also made it clear to the 1928 TUC that he was determined to control the agenda and rules of any discussions:

> I have tried to run five controversies in two years on matters of urgent importance ... and I have had to stop every one of them because within three days the words 'Traitor', 'Communist', 'Anarchist', 'Bolshevik' cropped up, letters came and the whole thing had, as we journalists say, to be put on the spike ... We could have had discussions in the *Daily Herald* if only we could be sure that the dissenters are going to discuss what they are asked to discuss and not what they think they want to discuss.[46]

As well as controlling debate from the centre, the *Herald* was prepared to exercise self-restraint where it suited either the leadership or itself. The self-denying ordinance on the General Strike was maintained up to and including the special TUC held in January 1927. It was reported that Mellor had attended not as a reporter but as a matter of courtesy and that he would not give a full account.[47] This was not just acting as the leadership's paper rather than a normal newspaper, but making a point of broadcasting it. The communist *Sunday Worker*'s breach of the embargo on the reports from the General Council and the Miners' executive was greeted with a reproving leader: 'It is no use filling the air with shouts of "Traitor" on one side and "Bolshevik" on the other', while the *Herald* finally printed both reports in full plus a summary of the proceedings in which the General Council prevailed.[48] Laying blame on neither, a typically accentuate-the-positive leader implicitly backed the General Council, emphasising highly familiar themes of better organisation and co-ordination.[49]

Self-denial as a means of ducking the issue would be seen in 1928 when the National Union of Railwaymen conceded a two per cent pay cut. Such a settlement was totally opposed to the *Herald*'s declared principles on pay and conditions – Henry Ford's view that low wages were a significant cause of British unemployment had been seized upon gleefully – but it could hardly attack an agreement reached by a major union.[50] It squared the circle, when the deal went to the union's conference, by invoking the principle of non-intervention in internal union affairs: 'With all the facts before them it will be for the delegates to decide and outside advice would be sheer impertinence'.[51] The argument at least had the virtue of unexpectedness from a paper that existed for the purpose of propagating opinion.

There were never two opinions about the party political scene. Labour leaders delivered 'slashing attacks' while Liberals were derided for divisions, similarity to the Conservatives and the machinations of Lloyd George. Attacking Conservative Premier Stanley Baldwin was a little trickier, with the *Herald* never quite sure whether indolence or malevolence explained his failure to deal with social ills. A happy medium was eventually located on 29 August 1927 when a leader argued: 'Actively and inactively he has done more than any other man to sharpen the class struggle in this land and elsewhere.'[52]

There was little doubt about one of the sins of commission, the Trade Disputes and Trade Union Act of 1927, which restricted the rights of unions and enforced contracting-in for political contributions. The entire movement knew what it thought about this, making the choice of editorial line easy. The *Herald* went into campaign mode, first denouncing the bill then talking up resistance to the extent that it was prepared to see Clydesider James Maxton's call for '100,000 shock troops, all fighters and rebels' as a 'ringing call to the workers' rather than the veiled incitement to violence it might have diagnosed on other occasions.[53] The *Herald* ran 12-page editions throughout the bill's passage through Parliament, commending 'Labour's able and devastating attack'.[54]

Another consequence of the General Strike was the renewed interest displayed by some movement leaders in conciliation and arbitration. The *Herald* response was deeply sceptical, arguing against Snowden's protégé William Graham that 'strikes and lockouts are born of Capitalism and under Capitalism conciliation and arbitration only pay heed to economic power'.[55] Robert Williams placed the paper in a serious dilemma by endorsing conciliation in his chairman's address to the 1926 Labour conference, provoking uproar by comparing the miners to Samson in the temple: 'This despairing policy may be magnificent, but it is not war.'[56] The *Herald* leader in response was carefully balanced, implicitly rejecting the left by asserting Williams's right to say what he thought, but stopping short of endorsing what might be seen as class collaboration.[57] Even when the formidable trio of Pugh, Clynes and Henderson added their voices to the discussion in early 1927, the *Herald* continued to resist, albeit in terms some way from the 'Hurrah for the rebels' tradition, quoting approvingly Clynes's view that 'generally speaking the most effective agents for industrial peace are trade union officials'.[58]

Nor was it impressed when its old enemy Sir Alfred Mond offered the General Council talks on conciliation and joint consultation: 'Capitalism depends on there being "two nations". And in that is to be found the root of industrial and social unrest.'[59] When the General Council, in line with the view of recently-elevated general secretary Walter Citrine that consultation and conciliation offered a more fruitful way forward, accepted this 'without prejudice', the *Herald* had to tread warily.[60] It could not condemn the General Council, which was chaired by Ben Turner, but it continued to counsel both against capitalist assumptions that the talks signalled the end of conflict and against the left's shouts of betrayal.[61] The first meeting was reported straight and full endorsement came a week later with a leader saying that the General Council had been 'presented with an opportunity for raising and posing issues of vital concern to all workers'.[62] That would remain the line, with the *Herald* endorsing the General Council's motivation, but it never became wildly enthusiastic, went on reporting rows between critics and supporters through the summer and was always happy to expose an employer who lacked the conciliatory spirit. One attack on Lord Londonderry infuriated Citrine, who claimed Mellor was trying to sabotage the talks.[63] This was unfair. Had the *Herald* had these intentions it would undoubtedly have endorsed Mond–Turner's competing double act of 1928, Cook–Maxton. In June the duo issued a manifesto arguing that class war was being subsumed in collaboration, destroying the movement's fighting spirit and 'energy which should be expended on fighting capitalism is now expended on crushing everybody who dares to remain true to the ideal of the movement'.[64] The *Herald* of 1921 would have agreed; its successor of 1928 relegated the manifesto to page two and subjected it to withering, detailed criticism, accusing the duo of 'serious and unsubstantiated charges' and 'enfeebling solidarity'.[65] Four days later Mellor returned to the attack, accusing them of 'putting the Mond conference totally out of proportion' and employing the allegation, eternally levelled at the radical left by the centre, of a poor grasp of reality.[66] This went down badly with the *Herald*'s more left-wing readers and a heavy mailbag resulted, with equal numbers of pros and cons printed every day.[67] But Cook–Maxton had little impact except as an indicator of the movement's fault lines and the *Herald*'s changing relationship to them.

The attitude to Cook–Maxton was an extension of the *Herald*'s ever-hardening attitude to communists and the Minority Movement, who were invariably portrayed as subverters of that now most fundamental of *Herald* values, movement solidarity. The harder line anticipated by Fyfe in his farewell barrage became reality in late 1926, claiming a victim in the Herald League. This was by now something of a dwindling relic of the paper's days as an independent force, but still functioned as a propaganda and political education body through a rump of around twelve branches and 40 to 50 study groups.[68] Its fate was sealed when Citrine complained that the Birmingham branch was planning a joint meeting with the communist *Sunday Worker* and that the propaganda caravan was being used in tandem with MM publicity.[69] Williams, arguing that the League had no publicity use, recommended closure and it was wound up in December 1926.[70] It seems unlikely that a well-established, if declining, group had suddenly lurched to the left. What had changed was the *Herald*'s toleration of what might be associated with its name and, above all, its self-perception as an activists' paper.

Such thinking finally found full editorial expression just before the 1927 TUC with a leader arguing: that 'Trade Unions have no need to form a Society of Critics in order to make their voices heard. The place to do that is within the trade union' while a leader during the conference said MM policy was 'calculated and designed to create not unity and steady progress, but indiscipline, doubt and drift.'[71] Old friends were now enemies. The *Herald* unhesitatingly condemned Alderman Vaughan of Bethnal Green, once a key Poplar ally, when he attacked the anti-communism of the 1927 Labour conference.[72] Communist candidates fighting Labour were attacked with the vigour reserved for apostates. For example, the description of the communist candidate at Aberdeen North might have come from a Conservative paper:

> His round face and merry eyes take on the true aspect of the fanatic when he is in the thick of the fray ... His bitter denunciations of all of his opponents and particularly of the Labour Party, are harsh and violent, like the policy of armed rebellion and civil war for which he stands.[73]

Events previously reported straight came in for hostile treatment. There was more than a hint of irony in the report on the MM's annual conference: 'Complete harmony prevailed ... there were no amendments and no speeches in opposition to the resolutions ... there was hardly a speech which did not denounce either the General Council of the Trades Union Congress or individual members of it.'[74] The General Council had its revenge at the 1928 TUC, which set up an inquiry into 'disruptive elements'. The *Herald* welcomed this decision with a gesture in the direction of Tory and Liberal trade unionists before laying into the real enemy:

> The dictated activities of the Minority Movement ... reducing the power of the Unions to secure the rights and protect the interests of their members ... Disruption whether through the apathy and ignorance of the 'paying member' or through the ill-judged activities of the 'Left' means the postponement of the hopes of the intelligent worker for a civilised and human life.'[75]

The important words are 'dictated activities'. The *Herald* had spent years shouting 'hands off Russia'. In the aftermath of the General Strike defeat, with the Russians and the MM offering bitterly critical comments on the conduct of the TUC General Council, the *Herald* demanded that the Russians show similar restraint towards Britain. Relationships deteriorated fast once the Russian union chief Tomsky, banned by the government from attending the 1926 TUC, sent a deeply unfraternal telegram speaking of the 'unforgivable tactics of the General Council leaders' and calling Thomas the 'main instigator of defeat'.[76] Even the habitually sympathetic Lansbury was soon complaining that the Russians 'refuse to accept any person as honest, sincere or sensible who disagrees with their theory, tactics and policy'.[77] Krassin was greeted as an old friend when he returned to Britain in late 1926, and accorded both an immensely warm leader and a lyrical account, recalling the *Herald* coverage of Lenin, of his funeral when he died suddenly in November.[78] But this was the last blast of the old relationship. The continuing deterioration in 1927 was epitomised by the *Herald's* cautious response when the police raided the Soviet Arcos trade commission in May.[79] It condemned the government for basing policy on party political expediency when it used the incident as a pretext for breaking off the diplomatic relations established by MacDonald in 1924.[80] Much more striking though was the wary circumspection of the *Herald's* reaction to the raid, which would once have provoked instantaneous, furious denunciation.[81]

Citrine had responded to a fresh verbal assault by Lozovsky of the Russian-controlled Red International by saying that 'the limit of our tolerance has been reached', and the 1927 TUC broke off relations with the Russians, a decision backed by the *Herald* on the grounds that 'the methods of the Russian leaders are at the moment out of harmony with the methods and traditions of the British Trade Union Movement'.[82] The MM's angry reaction to the decision earned a *Herald* denunciation of the ferocity reserved for enemies: 'They do not argue, they do not reason. They throw mud at their fellow-delegates ... not only does the Minority Movement vilify British trade unionism, but it is doing a grave disservice to Russia, of whose interests it professes to be the custodian.'[83]

The movement leaders on the *Herald* board were equally concerned that communist influence on their own paper should be limited, taking the chance to cut it back when foreign subeditor Walter Holmes left early in 1928 to become editor of the *Sunday Worker*.[84] Mellor's permission to replace him was strictly subject to assurances 'that the man had no connection whatever with the Communist Party'.[85] This did not mean that there was any dramatic change in foreign coverage. The *Herald* retained its internationalist, anti-imperialist outlook. Although the British labour movement resented Russia's interventions in its own internal divisions, it continued to argue against isolating Russia within the international movement. This allowed the *Herald* to go on advocating Russian inclusion in the International

Federation of Trade Unions and to give massive coverage to the discovery that, back in 1925, an IFTU official had proposed action to exclude Russia without telling the British – demonstrating a belief that the affairs of international union bodies were as interesting to the average *Herald* reader as they were to union general secretaries.[86]

Russian coverage in the paper remained broadly sympathetic. The leader on the tenth anniversary of the November revolution celebrated the lone survival of 'this great working-class society', albeit with the normal reservations.[87] *New Leader* editor Noel Brailsford's accompanying feature expanded on the same theme, concluding:

> The great gain which overshadows every other, and dwarfs the sins and omissions of this new era, is the liberation of the working class ... Workers children grow up, for the first time in the world's history, without the deadening consciousness that they belong to an inferior caste. They know that they are members of a society organised for the purpose of aiding them to develop all the talents of human nature. That is the glory of Russia, and in the wide world she boasts it alone.[88]

The view that the world was dominated by imperial oppressors still influenced other foreign coverage. If a labour angle could be found, so much the better. Immediately after the settlement of the miners' strike, the paper was dominated by events in China, where the nationalist Kuomintang came to power and British troops intervened after a series of incidents in international concessions.[89] The war scare occupied the front-page lead for a fortnight, with heavy coverage of military and diplomatic manoeuvres supplemented by frequent stories on labour protests in Britain.[90] The *Herald* had no doubt that the irresponsible sabre-rattling of a British government, bent abroad as at home on maintaining privilege, in this case foreign concessions in China, was to blame. The war party, it said: 'Hate the very notion of a China that has no concessions and that wants organisations for the workers and non-interference by external powers.'[91] The Kuomintang were warmly endorsed as fellow-progressives: '[A] strong movement for national independence and real freedom ... wholeheartedly for the working-class.'[92]

The *Herald* was not always willing to endorse the tactics of national movements. As MacKibbin notes, British mainstream labourism has no rejectionist tradition, preferring to reach accommodation with existing systems.[93] So the *Herald,* in deploring the decision to boycott the Simon Commission on Indian government, was for once at odds with Indian nationalism: 'The negative spirit of boycott which seems to predominate at the moment is one that is least likely to help forward the immediate progress of India towards the desired goal of self-government'.[94] Heavy coverage of the Indian Assembly vote for boycott possibly owed something to straightforward relish of a good story. Amid the uproar following the vote, an excited journalist dislodged his typewriter, which crashed onto the head of the Finance Minister sitting immediately below, stunning him.[95] But half-a-loaf pragmatism was in evidence when it endorsed the Indian Home Rule Committee's call for Dominion status. Always a supporter of full independence, the *Herald* recognised the compromise involved, but argued that the idea was a 'tremendous step away from the present impossible impasse and would not debar India from further advance'.[96]

It also concluded a fortnight-long campaign to save leftists Sacco and Vanzetti from execution after seven years on death row in Massachusetts by rejecting the boycott of American goods proposed in a letter to the paper by 'Gadfly', writing under his real name of C. Langdon Everard.[97] It argued that a boycott would be hard to organise, would hit British workers and miss the point that capitalism generally, not only the American version, was to blame. The best response was to fight against 'Mammonlaw' in Britain.[98] This reasoning also underpinned continuing scepticism about attempts to legislate international peace. The *Herald* argued that the League of Nations, the Kellogg–Briand declaration on the renunciation of war and the Geneva disarmaments were only as good as the participating governments. The League's ineffectuality, it said, was down to 'the predominantly reactionary character of the principal governments'.[99] Peace would only be achieved if the League were dominated by socialist governments 'pursuing not imperialist objects, but those aims of international co-operation and concord which lie at the very basis of the Socialist creed'.[100]

Under Mellor's editorship, the *Herald*'s coverage of general news also continued along broadly similar lines, but with some concession to external pressures. The extent to which it defined not only itself but other newspapers in exclusively political terms was revealed in February 1928 when Lord Rothermere announced plans for new papers in 14 provincial cities. The treatment was totally political, with no sense of any possible commercial motivation, a serious blind-spot showing limited comprehension of its competitors. A six-column front-page headline 'New press offensive against labour' topped a report of 'a determined effort to extend *Daily Mail* ideas to the workers in the big cities' and a cartoon showing 'Printers Dope Ink' spreading across Britain.[101] General manager Williams's monthly reports showed that he saw the paper in movement propagandist terms, but he found the paper cheerless: 'It emphasises the adverse side of our national life more than the energetically hopeful. Socialism and Labour to me suggest a gospel of hope more than a policy of despair.'[102]

Allen argued again in mid 1927 that political fixation was the paper's main problem. The *Herald* was speaking only to a committed minority. Where lively and varied presentation of news in other papers reached the non-political mass, influencing their view of political and industrial events, the *Herald* was addressing only a committed minority. Most readers, he argued, lacked 'the psychology of the political enthusiast, seeking an informative tendentious pamphlet. The average reader is out for distraction and not for a daily diet of self-improvement'. The definition of news should be broader 'even if it seems trivial to our enlightened minds, should be more fully treated ... the love romance of Pola Negri may seem stupid to the more quietly wedded editor and directors of the *Daily Herald*, but it is not for that reason foul, and it figured prominently in all other dailies, and not at all on the most important day in the *Daily Herald*'. It should reduce its mass of 'labour' headlines unless justified by news value and avoid the belief that it should automatically be different to other papers. If this attracted a wider audience, it would ultimately be more politically effective, instilling 'our subtle medicine all the time into a vast clientele'.[103]

Automatically or not, it clearly was different. London circulation traveller Howard looked at the main popular dailies on 28 November 1927. He found that the 1,080 column inches of the *Herald* made it little more than half the size of the *News* and *Chronicle* and around a third that of the *Express* and *Mail*, yet within that cramped space it contrived to run 197 inches of parliamentary, political and industrial news against 56 in the *News*, 105 in the *Mail* and 36 in the *Express*. Against this all the other papers were running two to two-and-a-half times as much general news and features.[104] Howard admitted that his categorisation might be arbitrary. Mellor performed his own study, comparing the *Herald* with the *News* over a week in December. His findings were a little different, but emphasised the difficulties of the *Herald*'s size. The *News* could carry as much political news while taking up much less of its available space. By dividing categories he demonstrated the intensiveness of *Herald* industrial coverage, running 415 column inches against only 87 in the *News*.[105]

So the *Herald*'s test continued to be, not commercial news value, but was arrived at by asking: 'Is it important?' Mellor did give some ground, however, giving prominence to stories he felt were trivial, but which had clear interest to readers. A Marx-influenced rationalist, he could hardly contain his impatience at rows over the rejection of the new Anglican prayer book or the Bishop of Birmingham's views on evolution: 'It would react disastrously if the quarrels of the Anglican church were to be superimposed on much more vital social issues.'[106] But he knew that church controversies interested his readers and the stories duly ran.[107] Similar treatment was given to the 1920s phenomenon of female channel swimmers: 'One of these days a long-suffering public may intimate that it is growing tired of these overdone long swims.'[108] Yet one swimmer, London typist Mercedes Gleitze, was consistently reported, her news value greatly enhanced by recognition that London office workers were a potential *Herald* audience.[109]

Even more of a natural *Herald* human interest story was provided by unemployed Mountain Ash miner John Penar Williams, labelled 'the Welsh Chaliapin' after winning the solo voice prize at the 1928 National Eisteddfod.[110] Miners were typical *Herald* readers, the paper was fighting insurance competition in Wales, it could be shown as a benefactor, meet Robert Williams's demands for happier stories and yet tie John Williams's experiences to the political angle of human waste in the coalfields. When he was offered a BBC audition, the *Herald* brought him to London, pictured and reported him over the next few days – climaxing in his radio debut which was headlined 'Enter Mr Williams: *Daily Herald* singer's spectacular debut: BBC SURPRISE: millions of excited listeners'.[111]

Yet perhaps even more archetypally *Herald* was its twist on a hugely successful popular press stunt, the *Westminster Gazette*'s 'mystery man' Lobby Lud, who created great excitement in the slow news days of summer 1927 by travelling around seaside resorts handing out money to those who identified him.[112] Where Lobby Lud gave out money, the *Herald*'s incognito 'Traveller' collected opinions: 'His aim is to draw from all sorts and conditions of men their inner thoughts on the things that matter today.'[113] The 'things that matter' were overwhelmingly political in nature or implication. Even when wanting to avoid people normally quoted in the *Herald*, his definitions were couched in political terms: 'Decide to steer clear of Labour Party and trade union officials. Must try to meet rank-and-filers and get them to talk. Hope to meet a member of Spencer Union.'[114] The member of the Spencer Union, a post-General Strike breakaway from the Miners, turned out to be a *Herald* reader while his Miners Federation counterpart took the *Express*. Both held 'very low views of the intelligence of a section of their fellow workers ... Yes, our chaps have a Triple Alliance of their own – Football, Racing and Beer'.[115] They were followed by, among others, a Canadian businessman with a low opinion of British capitalists, a socially-aspirant teacher who had forsaken his nonconformist Labour background for Anglican Toryism and East Anglian farm workers distrustful of Liberal agricultural policy.[116] As the 'Traveller's' travels ended, his conclusions were similarly political: 'There are more Henry Dubbs in this world than you and I wot of, but the youngsters who are coming on have a wider vision ... I am confident that the Labour Movement is making sure, steady and permanent progress.'[117]

Faith that scientific and social progress could go together was maintained – 1926 was hailed as 'A Year of Achievements' with Baird's television experiments given front-page prominence and seen as having similar potential to cinema and wireless which were 'broadening the minds alike of town dweller and village'.[118] When long-distance fliers suffered a string of fatalities in the summer of 1927, the *Herald* rejected a call by one of its favourite Labour MPs, Harry Day, for restrictions on flights: 'The aeroplane and the airship are destined to bring about a tremendous change in the habits and outlook of mankind, and few people would wish to see them impeded so long as they are not used for the purpose of war.'[119] The social progress basis of this viewpoint was underlined by a very different attitude to speed records. Britain's victory in Schneider Trophy races was rated a front-page lead, but a leader headlined 'Cui bono?' assumed readers' knowledge of basic Latin as well as rejecting speed for its own sake.[120]

As ever it was happiest if two interests could be combined. The rescue of a stranded Italian arctic expedition by a Russian ice-breaker, after they had been located by wireless, could be hailed as a triumph for modern science and international co-operation.[121] Amelia Earhart, in 1928 the first woman to fly the Atlantic, combined glamour with interests so calculated to appeal to the *Herald* that its reporter evidently fell in love on the spot:

'I wanna see your Toynbee Hall; your welfare centres interest me immensely; my social work in America is to me my life's ambition', she said.

Who is this heroine of the Transatlantic? Well, when I saw her she was all smiles and charm. Tall, I should think about 5ft 8in, slim, the '1928 woman' type in fact with a mop of curly, bobbed hair shielding a laughing face.

Miss Earhart is a true woman. 'I dunno' she told me, 'what I'm going to do. Cause you realise that I'm tired' – this while she pulled her finger wearily through her hair.

Can you imagine a tall, lissom girl with that delightful hair, and the happy laughing face, in a khaki shirt, red tie, brown jumper, black riding trousers, stockings to match ...[122]

Mellor's own enthusiasm for sport was reflected in a redesigned Monday results page, the occasional sports leader – in February 1927 he analysed the social roots of the decline of Welsh rugby – and an extra Monday page for football coverage from the start of the 1928–29 season.[123] Cricket was still the one sport which could command front-page space – notably a delighted response to Yorkshire's offer (later declined) of its captaincy to professional Herbert Sutcliffe in October 1927.[124]

The arrival of greyhound racing in Britain, the distinctive sporting event of the period, found the *Herald* in one of its less perceptive moods. Its initial welcome was based on support for better working-class entertainment and a loathing of hunting, often expressed in leaders attacking stag hunting.[125] It had 'little doubt that this new pastime will achieve a great domestic success' and quoted approvingly the slogan 'thrill of the race without the cruelty of the chase'.[126] The first day at White City was given a full-column front page story headlined 'Dog racing has a great start', a picture and full results.[127] A colour feature in August 1927 found 80,000 at White City: 'Only a minority made bets. The vast majority sat or stood on the upper tier around the stadium with scarcely a thought beyond seven half-minute thrills. There were 120 minutes of waiting.'[128] Reality dawned a month later, bringing a very different attitude. A fresh White City feature showed a very different world to August's benign scene. On the journey there: 'Only one subject was discussed – the chances of certain dogs and the prices to be offered by the bookmakers. Not a word was heard about sport.' At White City there was 'a wildly gesticulating mob', promoters who 'gazed with approval on the great oval wall of men and women who represented the half-sovereigns and shillings that matter so much to the track-owner' and 'a mad rush for money for nothing'.[129] Unhappy that current legislation did not cover dog racing, the *Herald* called for local licensing.[130] But the old loathing for gambling was on the wane. A leader on the 1928 Derby had commented that 'moralists may condemn, economists talk of waste, enthusiasts for world reformation groan – but among the flutterers are moralists, economists and enthusiasts! Derby day is a holiday in more ways than one!'[131]

By then it was evident that few working-class speculations could be riskier or costlier than their own of running a daily newspaper. By the autumn of 1928 the *Herald* was at its lowest point since the near-closure of five years earlier. Speaking at the 1928 TUC, editor Mellor pointed to six reasons why the paper was struggling: 'Insurance, size, quality of the paper, editions, staffing and policy.'[132] It appeared to be in inexorable decline.

Ironically, the habitually problematic area of advertising was the least of their worries. Advertising income was up ten per cent to £72,450 in 1927, and continued to rise in 1928, allowing the paper to contemplate turning down adverts placed by birth control clinics.[133] Since 1919 the *Herald* had been the only London daily to carry them, but circulation manager Le Good argued that the income of £35 to £37 per week was outweighed by damage to the paper's standing. Poyser was less convinced, and with Mellor persuaded the board to accept the view that proven reputable clinics and publications should still be accepted.[134]

The shift away from subjective analysis to market research was working in the *Herald*'s favour. From 1927 the London Press Exchange, among the largest of the agencies, included the paper in its mass-market campaigns.[135] This factor should not be overplayed, however. The *Herald* continued to draw only 20 per cent of its income from advertising, against the 60 per cent quoted by Lord Beaverbrook for his *Evening Standard*.[136] Howard's content survey showed how little space it was selling compared to its rivals – only 128 column inches in the sampled issue against 899 in the *News*, 855 in the *Chronicle*, 1654 in the *Express* and 1680 in the *Mail*.[137] Marginal advertising progress was being made in the face of the *Herald*'s overwhelming worry – constantly declining sales. The directors would note in early 1928: 'Whilst the *Herald* is only using its net sales certificate when it must, its principal rivals are broadcasting theirs showing substantial increases. Advertisers do not need telling to make their deductions.'[138]

The *Herald*'s certificate for January to December 1927 showed a decline of 45,000 compared to its predecessor.[139] That was putting the best possible face on it, as sales went on plunging between May 1927 and August 1928, it lost around one fifth of its circulation – falling from around 380,000 to 310,504. With returns at 16 per cent, the net sale was around 260,000: 'Perilously close to the 250,000 we are wont to regard as the nucleus of those who buy the *Herald* at all costs', said Williams, who nevertheless saw no possibility of stabilisation.[140] Losses were heaviest in the impoverished coalfields, down nearly a third in the North East and a quarter in Wales, and gathered pace at holiday times as readers cancelled their papers before going away, then chose not to reorder.[141] The paper was, said Williams in September 1927, contemplating a loss of 6,260 copies in 20 days, which was drastic even by *Herald* standards, in 'a decline which is lamentable'.[142]

There was little doubt about the reasons why. Bevin told the 1928 TUC: 'No one, I think ... could foresee the tremendous development of the publicity side of the Press of this country that has taken place in the last eight years.'[143] Circulation manager Le Good described the *Herald* as 'assailed on all sides by the extraordinary efforts on the part of the capitalist press in the eagerness to demonstrate, regardless of cost, their enormous sales increases'. The squeeze was well co-ordinated: 'Increase in sales of the capitalist dailies synchronises with the increased size of the issues, the printing of editions in the north, and the increased benefits offered.'[144] While the *Herald* was losing 15 per cent of its readership, the *Mail*'s daily sale rose 140,000 to 1.96 million and the *Express*, aided by starting to print in Manchester in 1927 and Glasgow in 1928, rocketed 400,000 to 1.5 million.[145] The two 'pictorial' dailies, the *Sketch* and the *Mirror,* started insurance schemes, the *Chronicle* was sold for £1.45m while holding steady at 950,000 and the *News,* aided by swallowing the *Westminster Gazette* in February 1928, rose from 650,000 to a million.[146] The *Herald* pitched for *Gazette* readers with bills saying 'Now buy the *Daily Herald',* but to little effect. Le Good reported that 'the insurance bait ... proved too strong for us'.[147]

The *Herald* line, expounded in leaders and by Turner at the 1927 TUC and in his 1930 memoirs, remained anti-insurance,[148] but from worrying about any scheme's cost, its managers had come round to the view that not having one was even more expensive in lost sales. In January 1927 the board reported that 'our circulation travellers constantly report that we are under an enormous disadvantage compared with our competitors because we have no insurance scheme'.[149] A month later they ingeniously appealed to the class and political outlook of the General Council, noting that 'working class organisations like the Trade Unions, the Friendly Societies and the Co-operative movement have taught thrift, and the necessity for various forms of insurance'.[150] The key conversion appears to have been that of Williams. The February 1927 board meeting set up a finance sub-committee to look into insurance and costs.[151] When they met in March, his evidence was their main item.[152] He reported that the case for a scheme was so overwhelming that he had the support of the editor, circulation manager, advertising manager and accountant in pressing for the 'More or Less Immediate' establishment of a scheme. He argued that the financial benefits in sales and advertising would more than outweight the cost, projected at £20,000 for a sample scheme, and that the alternative was continued inexorable decline. Williams supported his case by pointing to the success of the Liberal *Chronicle, News* and *Gazette* which had all but doubled their sales during five years of chronic electoral decline: 'In my judgment the principal and overwhelming reason is the pull of the insurance scheme.' His arguments were backed by reports from circulation travellers who said that sales in the East Midlands might have been doubled if the *Herald* had had an insurance scheme in the last few years, while in the Eastern Counties, it was 'a well-known fact in workshops, railroads and factories, [that] workers take other papers in preference to the *Daily Herald* believing they are covered against every known risk, and in groups of six, are buying it each morning and are sharing it, taking turns to pay, as they cannot afford two morning papers each'.[153]

From then on, Williams campaigned incessantly in his monthly reports for an insurance scheme. When the *Mail* and *Express* made capital out of payments – including £20,000 to one family – after the Sevenoaks and Darlington railway disasters, he noted that it was 'the kind of argument the average newspaper reader prefers to political propaganda'.[154] The best characterisation of the appeal of insurance for the *Herald*'s target readership, and the handicap imposed by not having it, would come from Le Good, following the 1928 Carmarthen by-election: 'I encountered five railwaymen at Llandeilo, one of whom takes the *Herald*. The other four had a spokesman who said, "We vote Labour all right, but we are railwaymen. I am married with children. The *Daily Express* covers me with the insurance, so you cannot blame me for taking it".'[155]

The *Herald* directorship went on looking for means of making the paper competitive. A development plan informed by Williams's thoughts on insurance and Allen's on content, arguing that an unchanged paper was doomed to go on losing sales and money, was put forward in February 1927. Rejecting the option of a Sunday paper, the directors called for a three-year insurance and promotion drive to take the paper to a self-supporting sale of 550,000. If the paper could reach this target and pull in projected advertising income it would cost £88,400, or only £10,000 more than maintaining a small declining paper which would still be a loss-maker after three years.[156] Neither Allen's nor Williams's reasoning impressed *Herald* chairman Ben Turner. He was happy with the paper as it was: 'We don't want the same kind of news as other papers. We are a specialist paper and that is what it was started for.' He doubted that the money was available for insurance or increased staffing and called instead for 'a steady six months – until the end of the year – going on as we are and seeing what effect the attack has upon the circulation'.[157] Allen won the battle when the *Herald* finance committee endorsed his proposals, but lost the war on 14 June 1927 when the *Herald* board deferred changes other than make-up alterations until the TUC and Labour Party had been consulted about money.[158] Nor was a 1927 TUC resolution from the engineers, calling for a shilling levy to fund a Northern edition, any more fruitful. It was dropped after Herbert Smith of the miners and J.H. Thomas for the railwaymen, both unions with unimpeachable records of support for the *Herald*, warned that they could not afford it. Bevin said that a vote against could be used against the paper.[159]

Desperate as the *Herald* was, it was a bad time to be asking for more money. Falling membership was hitting unions, while the 1927 Trades Disputes Act cut Labour's income. Herbert Smith had told the TUC that there was a time when the miners might well have found the £40,000 required by the proposed levy: 'But if I were to say I could do it now I would simply be betraying you.'[160] Labour had contributed only £1,000 to the *Herald* since 1924 and nothing since the end of 1926.[161] It bowed to the inevitable at the end of 1927, telling the TUC that further payments were impossible.[162] By the end of 1928 it had agreed to transfer its shares to the TUC, although the process would drag on for another year.[163]

The *Herald* finance committee continued its search for solutions, rejecting the traditional short-term remedy of production economies in November 1927.[164] They pressed the General Council for a response throughout the winter of 1927–28, warning that 'a situation of some gravity is likely to occur in the near future, but the Directors believe that on this occasion it is possible to foresee and so prevent this by at once taking stock of the present situation and probable future of the paper'.[165] Sales had fallen by 35,000 in five months since the Allen–Williams plan was submitted in June, but the case for investing in a stronger paper rather than continuing to subsidise a chronic loss-maker was as strong as ever.[166] The General Council remained unmoved, even when a joint *Herald*–TUC sub-committee meeting in February concluded that 'the present method of the *Daily Herald* had run its course'.[167] Any doubts about this were ended over the next few months. Asked for a decision on the alternatives of sustaining current losses or guaranteeing a capital development scheme, the General Council did nothing until May, when it cut its annual *Herald* subsidy from 2d to 1d per affiliated member.[168] This was, ironically, a consequence of a *Herald* success – its campaign for a stronger, better-resourced General Council. A doubling of staff from 1923 and the creation of new departments increased the administration's share of budgets, putting pressure on the 3d affiliation fee created in 1922. Reducing the *Herald* share to 2d in early 1926 had been uncontroversial in view of its stability at the time, but this was different.[169] *Herald* losses between 1924 and 1927 were small by previous standards, but a handwritten note in the TUC archives pointed out that the penny subsidy would raise around £15,000 a year, compared to the £19,000 it had already drawn out in the first nine months of the current year.[170]

The General Council had undergone a process of serial disillusionment with the role of press proprietor. Straightforward movement loyalty, whether induced by simple exhortation or the pledge scheme, had been insufficient to hold readers. The attempt in 1923 to create a paper which could compete on its merits was equally unsuccessful. The political excitements of the 1924 Labour government and the 1926 General Strike had provided a respite, but no more, in the downward pressure on the paper's sales. The paper was caught in a vicious spiral of underfunding, inadequate size and declining sales, exacerbated by ferocious competition. After six years of struggling with a paper lacking either the broad editorial coverage or the other inducements offered by rival papers, the board had been convinced that the *Herald* had no alternative to matching them, but there was no chance that the movement could fund this from its own resources.

The TUC was not preparing to abandon the *Herald*. Bevin later explained that the Allen–Williams scheme was seen as insufficiently ambitious to guarantee success.[171] His estimate, revealed to the 1928 TUC, was that a minimum of £1m would be needed.[172] Rejection of methods tried so far was implicit in Bevin's comment:

> It is no good appealing for shillings, or appealing for pence, appealing for more affiliation fees, in order to go on from hand to mouth ... It may mean going to the market for money: it may mean using affiliation fees in the future to guarantee the interest on that money, but we must get sufficient at least to launch out on a wide footing.[173]

It would be, as J.H. Thomas promised, 'A big scheme, a scheme that you have never before considered, a scheme which I repeat is going to be a capitalist scheme, because you cannot run the "Herald" on sentiment.'[174] The 1928 TUC's acceptance of the General Council's proposals was a collective admission that the means adopted of running the *Herald* since the movement takeover had failed. The movement's resources were exhausted, and the involvement of external funders was now inevitable.

6
The Second Transition, 1928–30

Wealth is not without its advantages and the case to the contrary, although it has often been made, has never proved widely persuasive.
John Kenneth Galbraith

However hard it was for organised Labour to accept the inevitability of a capitalist scheme, finding a partner for it was to prove even trickier. Meanwhile the *Herald* continued to decline. Bevin would write to Allen in November 1928: 'I know that you sometimes feel almost driven to despair about the *Herald*, but I think I have already got there.'[1] Circulation fell below 300,000 on 27 October, with rising returns taking sales below 250,000.[2] Two per cent of northern sales were lost in a month.[3] Advertising was holding up, but Poyser warned that a slump was inevitable when it became clear that the *Herald* dare not issue a 1928 sales certificate. The first warnings came in December when three major agencies 'very much embarrassed me with a direct question regarding our net sale ... it is a portent of what we must expect next year ... Any hesitation on the part of a newspaper in supplying a net sales certificate is soon recorded ... and a silent, though deadly, pressure in the shape of diminution of business results.'[4]

A fresh development plan was commissioned from Allen, then dropped.[5] The General Council offered five options – complete with costings – for improving the paper, but acted on none.[6] Instead yet another sub-committee was set up to explore the possibilities of raising capital and setting up an insurance scheme.[7] Turned down by the National Provincial Bank, they were advised that an insurance company might prove more receptive.[8] The sub-committee – Allen, Thomas and Citrine – opened negotiations with Prudential Assurance, whose company secretary Sir George May was destined in 1931 to enter labour demonology as chairman of the committee whose call for spending cuts would precipitate the fall of the MacDonald government.[9] This time he was more accommodating of labour desires. Negotiations, in such secrecy that many General Council members did not know until early March which company was involved – minutes referred simply to 'the Lending Body' – started on 5 February and ran to the end of March.[10] The Pru offered a loan of £300,000 at an annual interest rate of five or six per cent, with a repayment period of around

20 years. Guarantees requested included acceptance of responsibility for debt by union chief officers, an increase in TUC affiliation fees, the full participation of *Herald* directors as a guarantee that the paper 'is not likely to be run by extremists' and the right to recall the loan at three months notice – with assurances that this was highly unlikely.[11]

Advised by A. Geilinger, who had run the *Express* insurance scheme for Eagle Star, that any insurance scheme must match that offered by its rivals to be an attraction, the *Herald* secured a £50,000 per year quote for a scheme matching the *Chronicle*'s, plus some special features.[12] Meanwhile Allen considered possible uses for a loan. His argument that 'every other alternative is a greater gamble' was reinforced by Williams's February report showing 'the most disquieting period since I became the General Manager' with sales down to 288,324.[13] Renewing his vision of expansion he said that £300,000 would be exhausted in two years with insurance and a reshaped staff and called instead for an initial £400,000, to be followed by an issue of £1.2m, backed by levies of first 1d then 3d. It was, he said, the minimum needed – in line with sums being spent by better-heeled rivals.[14] At the same time Allen called for an extensive staff reconstruction combining a raid on Fleet Street's left-leaning talent with a purge of the main survivors of the Lansbury era. Ewer, Brodzky, Dawson and Slocombe should be sacked 'irrespective of whether we know who shall be appointed in their places', Mellor demoted and 'Gadfly' put to work outside the office and used less frequently.[15] Allen told Citrine that the staffing sub-committee accepted most of this settling of old scores, but Turner – also a member – remembered differently.[16] Allen then refused to put his proposals to the board.[17] A further intervention from Turner then also helped derail the Prudential deal. Thinking only to head off complaints that it had not sought a labour partner, the TUC went through the motions of seeking a loan from the Co-operative Insurance Company, which as expected declined.[18] But Turner concluded that if the CIS had refused much the same deal as the Pru had been offered, he was none too happy about it himself.[19]

It would be easy to dismiss Turner as bemused and uncomprehending of the paper whose board he chaired. His statement to the 1927 TUC that not having a report of Ramsay MacDonald's speech in today's paper did not matter because 'it would read just as well tomorrow' is the classic illustration of Fyfe's contention that *Herald* directors did not understand newspapers.[20] Yet he was a substantial figure, immediate past president of the TUC and soon to be Minister of Mines.[21] His scepticism about expensive development plans was probably more representative of the union officials who had to determine the *Herald*'s future and take financial responsibility than Allen's expansionary vision. As the habitual voice of immobilism when action meant spending movement money, he tended to get his way.

He did again this time. On 18 March the TUC's lawyers warned that only the Transport and General Workers had rules wide enough to indemnify leaders for their personal responsibility for the loan guarantee.[22] The idea that a rule change, often a long and complicated process, would be needed to avert personal liability for around £30,000 was calculated to chill any union official's blood. On 27 March the General Council rejected Allen's development plans and Thomas's presentation of the loan proposal by 15 votes to four.[23] The minutes are minimalist, but Citrine's letter to May tells the essential story: 'The General Council decided that they were unable to incur the responsibility of undertaking the loan, particularly having regard to the difficulties which were anticipated in respect of securing the necessary individual guarantees.'[24] A conference called to sanction the increased levy was cancelled, and the *Herald* informed that future support would be confined to the present 1d per member from the annual levy.[25] The TUC was not left totally empty-handed – they had finally persuaded the Labour Party to give up its shareholding in March.[26] As the loan was the TUC's last ploy in seeking to maintain movement ownership, which was doomed by the failure, the *Herald* was back to square one, and all indications were that this was a thoroughly unhealthy location.

In the circumstances the long-awaited 1929 General Election, finally called for 30 May, could hardly have been better timed.[27] Not only would it boost sagging sales, although Williams had already warned, on the basis of by-elections, that these were unlikely to match the benefits of previous polls, but it also gave the *Herald* an unparalleled opportunity to remind its sceptical owners of its usefulness.[28] Even so the start of the campaign had less obvious effect on the paper than usual. This was because, unlike previous elections in the 1920s, it was possible to see the 1929 poll coming from a long way off. The certainty of a poll in the next few months dominated the paper from autumn 1928 on, accentuating the already strong trend towards the loyal follower style.

All the symptoms of election coverage were present in this pre-election period. Routine political stories like MacDonald's everyday feat of seeing off a communist heckler at Seaham were given front-page lead treatment.[29] A by-election victory at Midlothian in late January was hailed as a 'Portent of Victory'.[30] Politics pervaded areas of the paper like Gerald Gould's column, normally only implicitly political. In April 1929 he proclaimed: 'There is a plain truth between truth and falsehood, between right and wrong. There is a Crusade – and it is Labour's.'[31] Claims of unity were made even when they flew in the face of the paper's own reports. When the 1928 party conference debated *Labour and the Nation*, the *Herald* commented that 'no fundamental

Figure 7 'Election fever'; *Daily Herald* front page, 11 May 1929.

differences of opinion' were revealed even as its news team were reporting Maxton and Wheatley's trenchant criticisms.[32] Critics accepted as legitimate, like Maxton and Wheatley, were subjected to mildly antagonistic reporting. The conference reports said Clynes 'scored a palpable hit when he asked Mr Wheatley if Liberals would support the Programme proposals for the nationalisation of land, mines, power and transport'.[33] Communists, outside the pale, were now overtly equated with fascists.[34] And election-time double standards applied to the reporting of enthusiastic meetings. MacDonald was reported as inducing 'memorable scenes and magnificent expressions of loyalty' in Seaham in the same week as Lloyd George was greeted with an 'outburst of wonderfully contrived applause' at an Albert Hall rally.[35]

The paper's role in the election remained the same as in earlier polls – to act as a central rallying force, enthusing and informing the party worker and monitoring the activities of opponents. Informing came in the form of three series: specially commissioned features from labour leaders, starting with MacDonald on 22 April and ending with Lansbury on polling day: front-page 'Little letters' to different sections of the population explaining why they should vote Labour and a bold-print box in each issue from as early as 4 March outlining the records of the three main parties on different issues. This series was reprinted in booklet form during the campaign.[36] Ability to expose other parties' lies was always cited as a prime *Herald* role. It had a genuine success in exposing a Scottish Conservative leaflet misquoting Cardinal Bourne as saying Catholics should not vote Labour.[37] When Conservative chairman J.C.C. Davidson called the story a 'complete fabrication', the *Herald* joyfully reproduced the letter which accompanied the leaflet, crowing that 'every statement ... was vindicated yesterday by no less a person than Sir Lewis Shedden, the Tory chair in the West of Scotland'.[38]

MacDonald's national tour was again lovingly described. Although the breathless novelty of 1923 and 1924 had gone, reports still recorded 'triumphal meetings ... unforgettable scenes of enthusiasm ... smashing attack ... reception at Carlisle was notable chiefly for its spontaneity'.[39] This matched the tone of all election coverage, with headlines proclaiming 'Labour sweeping forward to victory' and 'Labour's whirlwind campaign for power'.[40] Heavily regionalised constituency accounts were similarly bullish, with Labour making 'great progress in Tory strongholds' and former *Herald* editor Hamilton Fyfe's candidature supposedly 'winning converts every day' in Sevenoaks.[41] Polling day headlines were a reminder that this was the paper of the centre, issuing orders to the periphery: 'Give Labour a clear majority today': 'Our readers must work today. majority will be won on the doorstep' and 'Why you must cast your vote for Labour.'[42]

After the fierce optimism of the campaign, *Herald* readers, fed on demands for a majority, may have been a little disappointed that Labour, which won 287 seats to 260 for the Conservatives, was merely the largest party. This was hardly evident in the giant headlines that gave so comprehensive an account of the outcome that reports were almost superfluous 'Labour on top! The strongest party!: Electors give Baldwin's government emphatic notice to quit: Tory strongholds stormed by advancing might of workers' and '"Red letter" majority shattered: Fiasco of "Great Liberal Revival".'[43] Just in case anyone missed the implications for the press, the issue of 31 May carried a front-page story 'Our good record: how we have roused public interest: signal service: Beaverbrook papers on the Tory trap exposure' and a leader calling for readers to go on supporting the *Herald* as they had supported Labour.[44] The *Herald* had no doubt of its relationship with the new government, formed when Baldwin resigned the week after the election.[45] As soon as MacDonald took office, the board mandated Williams to write to him asking that 'the Prime Minister and Government will regard the *Daily Herald* as being in effect the official organ not only of the Trade Union and Labour Movement, but of the Labour Government'.[46] MacDonald's precise response is not recorded, but the request was in itself an indication of how completely the *Herald*, candid friend in 1924, had become a loyal follower in 1929.

There is no doubt that it received privileged treatment. In early July Mellor reported: 'We have been able since the Government came to office, to secure a number of exclusives and to lead the Press generally.'[47] MacDonald did not consult widely on Cabinet appointments, but the *Herald* was clearly well briefed in advance. It accurately predicted that J.H. Thomas would be put in charge of unemployment and went on offering justifiably 'confident predictions' and well-founded 'reasons to believe' to its readership as the government took shape.[48] Where necessary, the relationship included the *Herald* facilitating as well as reporting government policy. It not only treated Chancellor Snowden's robustly nationalistic tactics at the Hague conference on reparations much more indulgently than it would a Conservative government acting in the same way, but also intervened directly when reporter George Slocombe helped arrange a meeting between Snowden and French Premier Aristide Briand.[49] When the conference ended the British delegation – Snowden, Willie Graham and Arthur Henderson – wrote thanking Slocombe for giving 'great assistance on the political and financial sides'. This was reproduced as a front-page splash complete with a full facsimile of the letter and Ewer's profile of Slocombe.[50] The reporter was also singled out for praise by Bevin, conveniently forgetting that he had at least acquiesced in Allen's attempt to sack him only six months earlier, at the 1929 TUC.[51]

While cheerleading – Bracher was as ever particularly willing – the *Herald* also aimed to dampen down expectations of the minority administration. When it welcomed the new government, its voice was that of the centre, warning followers of the difficulties to be faced: 'It will not be all done at once. There must be patience, faith and loyalty – and these will be repaid in full ... Labour will not disappoint them.'[52] This mix of considerations was seen in its welcome for the decision to raise the school leaving age: 'Another triumph for the Labour Government. After years of neglect there are a mass of items banging at the legislative door. The task of picking and choosing as to which should come first is bound to create differences of opinion.'[53] Where such differences occurred the *Herald*, in marked contrast to its role as forum for debate in 1924, downplayed them. In July Home Secretary Clynes excluded Trotsky from Britain on the grounds that 'persons of mischievous intent' would exploit his presence for their own ends and to embarrass the government.[54] Three years earlier the *Herald* had deplored the exclusion of Tomsky, even as it condemned the message he intended to bring.[55] Now, confronted with a similarly political exclusion, its leader columns said nothing – even when Trotsky, possibly out of date on the *Herald's* standpoint, wrote to it blaming secret police activity for his exclusion, and Bernard Shaw mischievously suggested that it live up to its traditions by inviting Trotsky to Britain.[56]

The criterion for dealing with critics was not 'Is it right?', but 'Does it help our government?'. Twice in 1929, Glasgow left-wingers found themselves at odds with Minister of Labour Margaret Bondfield. In August George Buchanan complained at the way his constituents were being treated by Labour Exchanges, and in December John Wheatley was angered at her refusal of a concession which would have cost only £50,000.[57] Bondfield's reply to Buchanan had been that administrative changes were under way, but that her powers over the exchanges were limited.[58] In both cases the demands of the poor were pitted against administrative and financial restraints. The *Herald* would not have accepted inaction from a Conservative government, or in 1924 a Labour one, but in 1929 it came down both times against the protestors, accusing Buchanan of allowing 'his heart to run away with this head' and attacking Wheatley via a leader on a speech by MacDonald.[59] Its rebuke to the rebels, couched in terms extraordinarily reminiscent of those used by moderates against Poplarism, showed how far the *Herald* had moved since the early 1920s:

Mr MacDonald did well to bring his listeners back to fundamentals. If it is true, and it surely is, that the mere distribution of money is not Socialism, then it is entirely wrong to turn it into a test of Socialist faith. No greater disservice could be done than to create in the public mind a picture of Socialism as one huge national workhouse and the reckless pouring in of public or private charity. That is only a caricature of the real thing, with which the enemy can do untold harm to the Socialist cause.[60]

Mellor did accommodate a debate between left-winger W.J. Brown and loyalist John Clarke about their respective points of view within the parliamentary party.[61] The *Herald* argued consistently for more robust treatment of the government's Liberal allies where disputes arose.[62] But the government was openly criticised only when it disagreed with the TUC, first when Bondfield declined to accept a more liberal view of the 'Not genuinely seeking work' clause under which thousands were refused employment benefit, and then over its moderate Coal Mines Bill.[63] On both occasions, the *Herald* reverted to 'candid friend' mode, offering support, sympathising with the government's difficulties and suggesting improvements.[64] But this was hardly editorial independence. In offering mild criticism of the government, the *Herald* was simply reflecting the views of its proprietor.

Loyalty occasionally went as far as misrepresentation of the news. Robert Skidelsky has argued that, though its privileged position gave it access to the truth, the *Herald* consistently downplayed and misreported the financial crisis of 1931 which would bring down the MacDonald government and lead to its replacement by a 'National' administration.[65] If so, this was not the first time. In February 1930 the *Herald* complained of 'venomous press attacks' on Thomas and reports that Oswald Mosley, Lansbury and Tom Johnson – the rest of the employment team – had resigned. It argued: 'Political journalism in this country is certain to discredit itself if every time a controversial memorandum is before a Cabinet the occasion is represented as a crisis of the first magnitude.'[66] *Herald* reporters must have known the extent of the division within the government over the 'Mosley memorandum'. It would precipitate an offer of resignation from Thomas and lead ultimately to the departure of Mosley, briefly Labour's rising star, from both Cabinet and party. If this was not 'a crisis of the first magnitude', it is hard to know what was.[67]

Industrial coverage had also moved a long way from the abrasive style of the days of Larkin, Direct Action or even the General Strike. As the TUC was increasingly dominated by its conciliatory, pragmatic General Secretary Walter Citrine, so was the *Herald* much more inclined to call for an inquiry rather than a strike. Industrial correspondent Vivian Brodzky, always an assiduous follower of leadership fashion, displayed the extent of the conversion with an exposition of the new style following the 1929 TUC. He argued that Congress was no longer moved by the inspired orator, but those like Citrine who provided 'facts, figures and constructive speeches and criticism'. The style was to:

> Ferret facts, let us say, of amalgamation and industrial unionism, it sorts and analyses them and thus prepares the raw material for impartial and constructive memorandum upon which well-informed decisions can be taken ... with this new type taking the place of the wordy sentimentalist or the acrimonious debater, the future of Trade Unionism is bright with promise.[68]

Being 'impartial' and 'constructive' fitted well with the Mond–Turner talks, which the *Herald* continued to support even when employers rejected proposals for a bipartite National Industrial Council.[69] Even so Sir Alfred Mond, chief anti-socialist protagonist when the Commons debated socialism in 1923, must have been amazed when the mildly ameliorative measures proposed in the March 1929 report on unemployment were hailed as 'a vindication of the Socialist diagnosis of the ills of capitalism and in part of the Socialist treatment of these ills'.[70]

Discussions and inquiries were in much better supply than serious strikes in the late 1920s. The *Herald* of old would have echoed Maxton's view that the 800 workers from the Rego tailoring factory in Edmonton, north London, who struck in the last three months of 1928 'deserved the thanks of the working classes of Britain for having broken up the deadly industrial peace which had hung over the country since the National Strike'.[71] After the strike, organiser Sam Elsbury thanked the *Herald*: 'Without your publicity we could never have gained the sympathy and financial support that had been achieved.'[72] Yet *Herald* coverage – in spite of the London location, absence of other disputes, the convenience of 'Rego' as a headline word and the novelty of female strikers – was less than might have been expected. Coverage was never less than sympathetic, with the normal sketches of happy and determined workers: 'Mostly girls between 16 and 21 years of age and the determined spirit they are displaying is a pleasing feature of the dispute' and 'they were in a cheery mood, singing and dancing as they waited for their money ... so catchy was their song that at least two of the policemen caught themselves humming the tune'.[73] But the dispute failed to win official support and was strongly suspected of communist inspiration – Elsbury was a party member and the strike provoked a communist-led split in the Garment Workers Union.[74] It did not therefore attract the same coverage as an official dispute would merit, and made the front page only once, as a picture and caption when strikers took collections in Fleet Street and visited the *Herald* office.[75] Most coverage was consigned to page six with the rest of the movement news, and declined significantly once the Rego company had alleged communist influence, although the strikers' denials were reported.[76] There was no leader on the dispute.

Fear of communists was seen again in late 1929 when drivers at Barking Bus Garage struck, 'causing much inconvenience to the working-class districts of Dagenham, Becontree and Barking'. This censorious note was not normally associated with *Herald* strike reports, but this dispute, it reported, was 'proved by literature that has been issued to be a Minority Movement stunt'.[77] It was rapidly settled, leaving an embarrassed Bevin to admit that he had been wrong when he claimed that 'literature now issued proves that the stoppage is a Minority Movement stunt'.[78] The similarity in the wording shows that the paper had reprinted Bevin's views, without attribution, as uncontested fact but it did not feel obliged to replicate Bevin's apology.

The centre may have established firm control over home political and industrial coverage, but it was less sure of its hold over the foreign pages. Citrine had contracted MacDonald's aversion to Ewer and bombarded Mellor with complaints about him, arguing that he was giving foreign news a heavy pro-Soviet slant.[79] Mellor's responses are not recorded, but Ewer survived. Andrew Williams, looking at Labour–Soviet relations in this period, argues that the *Herald* acted throughout as 'the voice of patience', with relatively positive portrayals of Stalin, but with little to justify Citrine's anger. Its emphasis on the loss of Russian trade during the 1924–29 Baldwin government reflected labour's priorities.[80] While the *Herald* still preferred Russian communists to the British variant, sticky negotiations over resumed diplomatic relations and continuing Soviet dictation of British Communist Party policies ensured that, if anything, attitudes hardened once Labour took office. It was delighted when a delegation of Kent miners returned from Russia with unfavourable impressions: 'The natural reaction of men fed on silly Communist propaganda designed to prove that the Soviet Union has established a new heaven on earth.'[81]

Support for Snowden's antics at The Hague breached traditions of internationalism, but elsewhere in foreign coverage there was continuity. With a Labour government in London, the *Herald* grew yet more indignant about Indian boycott tactics, describing them as 'surely the last word in futility'.[82] When Congress voted for a boycott in pursuit of complete independence, the paper argued: 'Mr Gandhi and his colleagues have made, not indeed so far a Himalayan blunder, but a singularly foolish one. Their policy to which they have succeeded in definitely committing Congress is ... a futile one of mere negation.' The self-designated official paper of the Labour government predictably felt that Gandhi might have done better to co-operate 'with a government the sincerity of which he has frankly acknowledged'.[83]

The Wall Street crash in October 1929 was accorded a single front-page lead and a leader showing some grasp of potential international implications: 'It would all be as unimportant as the Monte Carlo gambling tables were it not that, on this gigantic scale, it affects credit the world over ... So inter-connected is the world economy today that a miner in Durham or a cotton operative in Saxony may go hungry because of the follies of gamblers in New York.'[84] The full consequences of bankers' priorities and international financial collapse would not be fully visited on British labour until 1931.

In a period dominated by serious political news, general coverage was squeezed. Recognition that an unleavened diet was far from ideal was signalled by deputy editor Will Stevenson in a feature on 'Letters to the Editor' which said:

Do not complain that your letter on Marx and the Great Contradiction was overlooked in favour of one describing a queerly-shaped potato dug out of an Ilford allotment. Too many of us Socialists try to make man in our own image. We forget that the average worker, good Labour man and trade unionist though he may be, demands diversity in his daily news diet. Man does not live by politics alone.[85]

The *Herald* continued to inch in this direction. The King's serious illness in 1928 was deemed worthy of lead coverage on a day when Parliament was debating controversial rates reform proposals and run as a major story, though with no leader, for several days.[86] A further step in the direction of what was once regarded as frivolity was provided by the occasional apparently syndicated Hollywood feature ostensibly written by stars such as actress Marion Davies.[87] Court stories, previously dotted around the paper, were consolidated as 'Cameos of the Courts' in 1929.[88] Just occasionally even the *Herald* could be tempted by an irresistible headline. On 20 December 1929, it might have been expected to lead on rural council attacks on Neville Chamberlain's poor law policy. Instead the main headline was 'Hunchback shot dead in billiard saloon'; undoubtedly the closest the *Herald* ever came to the *New York Post*'s immortal 'Headless man in topless bar'.[89] But it was still far from accepting mainstream commercial news values. In March 1929 it reported the exploits of the female 'Colonel Barker', who had successfully masqueraded as a man for years, and had been 'the talk of the country this week' – a near-definitive definition of the commercial lead story. It appeared regularly on the front, but was kept out of the lead by political stories, only winning six-column headline treatment when she was charged with perjury.[90]

The *Herald* still had its own variants on standard commercial stories. In place of society gossip came lighter items from the lives of Labour leaders and their families. A half-column news report plus picture on the Oxford v Cambridge women's hockey match owed everything to the presence of Sheila MacDonald, daughter of Ramsay, at inside-right for Oxford.[91] Police scandals offered the chance to draw social and political morals from the news. When officers were jailed for conspiring in a false charge against a woman, the *Herald* showed itself thoroughly representative of late 1920s Labour by calling for a Royal Commission.[92] As Egon Wertheimer, the acute London correspondent of the German labour paper *Vorwarts* had noted in analysing the responses of British Labour to complex issues, it was 'amazing how many times it falls back on the expedient of a Royal Commission'.[93]

The conviction of Sergeant Goddard for taking bribes from night-club keepers induced a classic *Herald* response, seeking explanations in the corruption inherent in capitalism and blending plain-man distrust of opulence with rejection of puritanism:

The average night-club is not half as cheerful as the tap-room of a village inn; nor as merry as a suburban dance-hall ... How many have censured the society which makes the Meyricks and tempts the Goddards to their destruction. How many have expressed disapproval of the crowd of rich idlers who, in a country stricken by the plague of poverty, turn its capital into a city of dreadful night clubs? Yet they are the real criminals, for it is they who paid Mrs Meyrick to bribe Goddard to let them break the law.

Or rather not even they are the criminals; they, wretched, bored creatures are themselves the victim of a social order which has given them a surfeit of 'filthy lucre' and the spending of it is their only job. Goddard, the dreary extravagances which corrupted him, and the stricken villages through which the Prince of Wales is touring are all symptoms of that same disease which is capitalism.[94]

Faith in scientific progress was undimmed. The link with social progress was made explicit in September 1928 when an autogiro flew the Channel: 'A new era of scientific revolution is developing. By co-operative endeavour it can be made an era of prosperity and progress for all.'[95] Nor was all progress airborne. Six-column prominence was given to the first wireless transmission of photographs to the *Herald*, which in its enthusiasm hailed a grim, grainy picture of the King as 'clear as any newspaper picture'.[96] Support for innovation applied just as much in the arts pages. *World's Press News* might convict it of 'highbrowism', but the *Herald* stuck to its role as junction-box between the intelligentsia and the self-improving worker.[97] Literary editor Arnold Dawson gave vigorous support to Radclyffe Hall's pioneer lesbian novel *The Well of Loneliness*, reviewing it as 'a profound and moving study of a profound and moving problem' and treating its banning by Home Secretary Joynson-Hicks as an assault on serious literature as whole.[98] Dawson asked provocatively 'Should the Bible be banned?' and won the support of 45 literary figures when he called for the reform of laws which made a single magistrate the arbiter of taste and generated idiocies such as a policeman's opinion being elevated over that of writers and other eminent people.[99] The *Herald* was similarly supportive of Robert Graves and Erich-Maria Remarque's demythologising of war in *Goodbye to All That* and *All Quiet on the Western Front*, which it serialised during the 1929 election campaign, defending them against critics and noting that the vast majority of a heavy postbag supported Egon Wertheimer's view that 'Never has the war myth been more fearlessly exploded' in spite of the disconcerting choice of verb.[100]

Possibly the paper's finest hour as a cultural junction-box came in early 1930 when an exhibition of Italian masterpieces was staged at the Royal Academy. It gave the exhibition heavy coverage and offered a series of reproductions described as mixing two favourite themes 'Modern science and the art of the world's greatest painters', receiving 70,000 orders.[101] Delighted to see readers responsive to its high-culture values, the *Herald* noted the large number of orders from industrial workers as evidence that 'the workers of today are determined that they should not live by bread alone'.[102] It campaigned for the exhibition to be extended with a statement of its creed that high culture should be made available to all:

> For too long the great masterpieces of the past, and even of the present, have been enjoyed only by a very few people. Now at last the masses are being awakened to a new beauty by the joy and colour of the artist. Ugly as life may be, the painters, the poets and the musicians can bring light and happiness to many minds that have only lived in dark places. That this is being so widely understood is a great achievement and one for which the Italian exhibition is largely responsible.[103]

When its demands were partially met, the *Herald* for once confessed itself 'not satisfied with the half-loaf', but made sure of taking credit for what had been achieved.[104]

The *Herald* had every reason for regarding 1929–30 with great satisfaction. The election had been won, the paper's role as loyal and vigorous supporter of the new Labour government freely acknowledged, and it had fulfilled its role as purveyor of high culture to the workers. Most importantly of all from its own point of view, it found a partner for the 'capitalist scheme'. The link with Odhams Press came after a long, dispiriting period in which it seemed, as Bevin told the 1929 TUC, that no partner would be secured.[105] As Williams had predicted, the 1929 General Election was not as beneficial to the paper as those of the early 1920s. Sales rose 78,000 between dissolution and the day after the results were declared, enabling the issue of a new sales certificate.[106] The appointment of Ben Turner as Minister of Mines, entailing his resignation as chair of the *Herald* and replacement by the forcefully competent Bevin, might also be regarded as a collateral benefit from the poll.[107] But underlying worries remained. In 1924 the sales increase, starting in any case from a higher base, had been one-third greater,[108] and attrition began as soon as the election was over.[109]

The search for a partner was ended by an unsolicited offer. Odhams Press was looking for another contract to occupy presses recently expanded to accommodate the success of their Sunday paper, the *People*.[110] They were at first sight unlikely partners for the *Herald*. Starting as printers, they had become publishers almost by accident, taking over both their main products, the weekly magazine *John Bull* and the *People*, when previous owners were unable to pay printing bills.[111] Odhams's managing director, Julius Salter Elias, was as far from the traditional image of the press baron as it is possible to get. Journalist and press historian Charles Wintour describes him as 'about the most ordinary fellow ever to run a large newspaper empire', living 'an intensely respectable, impeccably tedious life'.[112] Odhams's pre-1929 record was of unbroken success. Promotional techniques developed for *John Bull* – prize competitions, insurance and circulation canvassing – had been applied with spectacular success to the *People*.[113] Together with lurid 'confessional stories' and 'news stories of romance, passion, violence and changing fortune for which the *People's* editor Mr Harry Ainsworth scoured Britain and Europe', this formula had taken sales from 250,000 to two million in four years after Odhams took the paper over in 1925.[114] Elias was apolitical: 'Printing was a job of work: machines were machines – and 40 of them, great majestic presses, lay idle for six days of each week for 52 weeks of the year', recorded his biographer R.J. Minney. Having costed a new daily at around £2m, he concluded that it made better business sense to accommodate an existing one.[115] His search for another outlet took him first to the *Radio Times*, where he ran into BBC director-general John Reith's presbyterian integrity. Reith had married an Odhams and was determined there should be no hint of nepotism.[116] He looked then at the virulently High Tory *Morning Post* and the Liberal *Daily Chronicle*, to which he was beaten by the Inveresk Paper Company, also seeking an outlet for its main trade.[117]

Odhams and the *Herald* were not complete strangers. Odhams's print manager F.J. Cook advised the *Herald* during the 1923 crisis.[118] Minney and Francis Williams, City editor (1930–36) then editor (1937–40) of the *Herald* both stress the role of Odhams's editor-in-chief John Dunbar, a former left-winger, in initiating the link, with Williams saying that C.P. Robertson, a former Labour correspondent and mutual acquaintance of Bevin and Dunbar, acted as intermediary.[119] It is clear that the first approach came from Odhams, but it is more likely that it was made to editor Mellor and deputy Stevenson than to Bevin, who told the General Council 'subsequent to the Board meeting of the *Daily Herald* ... Mr Stevenson and Mr Mellor spoke to him with regard to a proposal which emanated from Odhams Ltd with regard to the *Daily Herald*'. The General Council minute continued: 'After Mr Mellor's discussion with them, he discussed the matter with Mr Bevin.'[120] Mellor was to explain: 'He first had the intimation from Odhams two days before he spoke to Mr Bevin about it.'[121] All three quotes point strongly to the conclusion that the journalists were approached before the directors in the first half of July 1929. Happily this does not rule out Minney's image of Bevin coming to see Elias in a 'dark wide-brimmed hat'.[122] Whoever started the process, Bevin was firmly in charge of the *Herald* side within a few days and pressing forward.[123] The Prudential experience had ruled out any chance of a loan saving the *Herald* in its present form. Odhams had the means and could see the potential implicit in Labour's 8.5 million votes.[124] Far from worrying Bevin, Elias's lack of interest in politics probably attracted him. Bevin liked getting his own way. Elias had already given the charismatic charlatan Horatio Bottomley a free hand as editor of *John Bull* and, although a Jew, had been prepared to consider dealing with the intermittently anti-semitic *Morning Post* before switching attention to the unswervingly Liberal *Daily Chronicle*.[125] With such a record, he was likely to be similarly tolerant of Labour views.

The main details of the partnership were worked out by the time the *Herald* board met on 19 July. Odhams would either purchase the paper or set up a new company jointly with the TUC to provide a 16-page *Herald* complete with a Manchester-produced Northern edition and an insurance scheme linked to the *People*. Shares would be divided 51 per cent for Odhams, and 49 per cent for the TUC with a means devised of ensuring that the paper was firmly tied to Labour political and TUC industrial policy. Any lingering hopes of a partnership with the Co-operative Press were ended by Mellor's report that they had no expansion plans.[126] The directors backed the scheme, as did the General Council, convinced by Bevin's argument that 'he could see no alternative way of getting the money, and he believed that the policy of the paper could be safeguarded even more effectively than it was at present'. The only dissent came from railway drivers' leader John Bromley – a persistent critic of the *Herald*. He said the paper had been bleeding the movement dry and should have been wound up ages ago, avoiding the current crisis in which it was being given away. He doubted union directors could control policy, and said that if Odhams saw the *Herald* as a commercial proposition the movement should be asking how much they would pay.[127]

With General Council approval secured, only the details of policy safeguards and protecting existing staff remained. Odhams rejected Bevin's bid for a TUC majority on the board, and legal advisers disliked plans for a Trust Deed running along the lines of Lord Northcliffe's *Times* Trust.[128] In its place came an ingenious division of the board and shares into two categories. Odhams's 51,000 'B' shares would give them control of commercial policy. The General Council would hold 49,000 'A' shares and only their 'A' directors were allowed to vote on matters of political and industrial policy, which should conform to those laid down by the Labour Party and TUC at their annual conferences. The Lord Chancellor, Lord Sankey, would arbitrate on disagreements.[129] Bevin and Mellor had already endorsed Odhams's record as employers, and an agreement to use only union labour was written into the printing contract.[130] Existing staff were promised jobs, and no reduction in salaries, but not that they would stay in the same posts: 'The people on that new staff would have to retain their jobs on their ability to do their jobs', warned Bevin.[131]

Agreements, subject to ratification by that year's TUC, were concluded on 30 August.[132] The deal had gone through the complex *Herald* and General Council machinery in six weeks, a smooth passage reflecting the fact that no alternative existed. Or did it? True to form, the *Herald* attracted an oddball last-minute suitor, one H.D. McIntosh. This was almost certainly Australian entrepreneur Hugh McIntosh, popularly known as 'Huge Deal' for enterprises such as the Burns–Johnson heavyweight title fight in 1908. A former president of the Weekly Newspapers Association of New South Wales with high-ranking Australian labour contacts, he was active in Britain from the early 1920s and a Labour candidate at the 1929 General Election.[133] With consummate timing, on 26 August, he offered a £200,000 investment and division of shares and board similar to the Odhams deal.[134] It is hard to imagine the TUC would ever have accepted an individual proprietor, although an offer in the desperate hiatus between the Prudential and Odhams offer might have provoked a revealing debate. With the Odhams deal settled, however, a polite letter from Citrine explained that the TUC were in no position to take up his offer.[135] It was just as well – McIntosh went bankrupt in 1932.[136]

The 1929 TUC, meeting in Belfast, went into private session on 4 September at 2.15 pm. Before it were four resolutions embodying the Odhams deal, and a report from the General Council.[137] Bevin, opening for the General Council, promised a paper matching the size, insurance and publicity of its competitors which would 'fill a gap in the Labour Movement and embrace an opportunity which has not been presented this way before'. The alternative was to continue attempting the impossible on inadequate resources. TUC directors would safeguard policy. Mellor hailed 'an agreement unique in the history of journalism' and promised a paper with a million sale which would not sacrifice quality to quantity or sensation. He appealed for a decision now. A.J. Cook, saviour of the *Herald* in 1923, intervened briefly and apparently decisively. Miners president Herbert Smith, who said it was 'the fifth burial sermon on the *Daily Herald* at which I have been present', asked for the chance to go back and consult his membership, but was persuaded to accept a resolution, seconded by Cook, that Congress adjourn for no more than 15 minutes to allow consultation with delegates. When they returned a card vote endorsed Bevin's report by 3,404,000 to 47,000. The four resolutions were carried by acclaim, and the *Herald*'s fate sealed.[138]

The Odhams deal still had to be sold to a wider movement whose only pre-Congress warning had been a *Mail* leak in early August.[139] The privatisation of the *Herald* must have been a bombshell, yet the TUC and Labour Party archives show little evidence of protest. Not that the authorities were prepared to accommodate protestors. A Building Trade Workers' resolution of protest was suppressed by the Birmingham City Trades Council executive while Labour deputy secretary Jim Middleton attempted to choke off an animated correspondence with the South Marylebone ILP by arguing that as Labour had no say in the *Herald* the matter was outside ILP competence.[140] Citrine can hardly have reassured Derby Trades Council by responding to their complaint about the secrecy of the deal by saying he could not discuss private session deliberations.[141] Claiming a 'thrill of joyous expectation' from the bulk of readers when it announced its relaunch on 12 November, the *Herald* told the critical minority that they had lost sight of the policy guarantees outlined by Mellor in his article explaining the scheme.[142]

The officials might have quoted the paper's continuing travails. Under the old set-up it would have been close to disaster in October. Forced to request £8,000 from the TUC, they were greeted by Citrine's comment that of the £8,000 left in their fund, £7,000 was earmarked to guarantee paper supplies. With the Odhams Seventh Cavalry just round the corner, the TUC released the cash.[143] Without them the paper would have exhausted its auxiliary resources barely a month into the TUC year. Sales had gone on crashing, steadily wiping out the election gains. More than 15,000 sales were lost over the seven-week holiday period and by 17 October circulation was 332,554, only 17,000 more than when the 1929 election was called.[144] 'We are doing all possible to feed the old *Herald* while doing our share to help the new paper', reported advertising manager Poyser in November.[145] A new company, the Daily Herald (1929) Limited, was registered on 11 November with a nine-man board chaired by Elias, with Bevin as vice-chairman and Tillett, Citrine and Pugh as the other TUC directors.[146] Mellor, in a foretaste of the eventual change of editorship, was released from day-to-day duties to help with planning, leaving Will Stevenson in charge.[147]

Staff recruitment pulled in major recruits from other papers – L.M. MacBride from the *Express* as news editor, Austin of the *Sunday Dispatch* as features editor and Arthur Webb of the *Sporting Life* as night editor.[148] But the chief subeditor was an old *Herald* hand, Leslie Sheridan, returning after five years at the *Chronicle*.[149] Mellor and Stevenson apart, the conspicuous survivor among current senior staff was Ewer, retained as foreign editor.[150] This, as much as captures from other papers, showed an emphasis on journalistic skill over political conformism, although Ewer was to leave the Communist Party in 1930.[151] Poyser survived as advertising manager, although subordinated to advertising director Philip Emanuel.[152] By November it was reported that all but two refuseniks, whose identities are unclear, had transferred, most to better-paid jobs.[153] Williams was found a role as liasion officer between the *Herald* and the TUC after Bevin interceded with Elias on his behalf.[154]

The importance accorded the circulation campaign was shown by the quality of those in charge. The TUC seconded Vincent Tewson, who would succeed Citrine as General Secretary and a *Herald* director, to work with William Surrey Dane, a key Odhams figure over the next 30 years.[155] The aim was to mobilise Labour activists. Inadequate as a circulation figure, they were a different matter as a canvassing force. The top-down recruitment process began on 7 December in Cardiff with the first of 14 regional meetings involving 10,000 union and party officers and officials.[156] Centre-piece of each meeting was a statement from Bevin – who reckoned his endeavours for the paper took 35 consecutive weekends in 1929–30 – or in his absence, Citrine.[157] Organisation was not the only purpose, Middleton admitted that the aim was also to allow Bevin to explain the *Herald* deal fully to remaining doubters and answer any questions and worries.[158] Citrine's notes for a speech probably delivered in Sheffield on 4 January indicate a basically political appeal for a political audience – emphasising policy guarantees and the importance of a paper to defend the Labour government – at the same time as promising 20 pages, insurance and, from June or July, a Northern edition.[159] Suitably inspired, delegates passed a resolution promising to administer the circulation scheme and enrol as many canvassers as possible in the region covered by the conference.[160] Central organisers at the Odhams offices at 68 Long Acre, near Covent Garden market, operated a system of local co-ordinating bodies – Trades Councils and Labour Parties in boroughs, divisional parties in the country. Union branches were to canvass workplaces and local parties their districts. At the bottom of the pyramid came the infantry, the individual Helper operating under local direction.[161] A target of 100,000 Helpers was set.[162]

This was not the first attempt to mobilise the rank and file for the *Herald*. The pledge fiasco remained an unhappy memory. Requests for *Herald* canvassers had been made throughout the 1920s, but previous attempts had relied on political enthusiasm. Birt, the circulation traveller for the West Midlands, put the problem bluntly: 'Voluntary canvassing is no good – you must offer some payment', he had said, suggesting 1s per copy.[163] Odhams agreed, and the *Herald* campaign offered 1s 3d per copy – 3d each to the co-ordinating body and the party or union branch and 9d to the Helper – in return for which they had to return a plethora of coupons.[164] Formidable as this combination of financial muscle and movement numbers promised to be, the response to the enrolment campaign running through December was slow enough to worry Middleton – although Dane confidently predicted a January rush.[165] Although the numbers fell well short of the 100,000 target, 32,803 were enrolled as the campaign, intended to run until two weeks before the new paper was launched on 17 March, started on 9 January.[166]

The circulation drive showed the hallmarks of Odhams's previous campaigns. Each new reader was offered the choice of a camera or fountain pen plus membership of '£10,000 Free Family Insurance' advertised in a leaflet tastefully illustrated with train crashes, injured footballers, crashing motorbikes and other mishaps. Vast numbers of leaflets were issued – 450,000 with messages from MacDonald and Snowden plus a further 200,000 with details of the incentives offered to Helpers and messages from other leading movement figures.[167] Helper efforts were encouraged and directed by *The Helper*, an eight-page weekly intended to inform and inspire them with a feeling of crusading excitement as members of a great army fighting for the future of paper and movement. Leadership appeals were the staple, with parliamentary figures more prominent than TUC, Bevin apart. MacDonald, inevitably, was first.[168] He and Bevin were pictured in every issue while Snowden, Henderson and Clynes followed their leader on to the cover.[169] Lansbury, incongrously clutching a cricket bat, appeared in issue three while other appeals included one from the movement's 13 leading women and what was termed 'An inspiring message to *Daily Herald* Helpers' from Citrine.[170]

Rhetoric was supplemented by practical instruction. Every issue pictured the free gifts. Early issues featured hints on canvassing, succeeded in later issues by suggestions and anecdotes from Helpers – which as well as providing practical assistance aimed to create a sense of belonging. The language was conversational, recognising canvassers as movement insiders. A message in the fourth issue caught the flavour, as well as betraying an unconscious belief that all Helpers were male:

'You are now an experienced Helper. A valuable man in the service of the cause.'[171] Later issues set targets for emulation, quoting examples such as a Norwich man named Goldsmith who said he had recruited 400 new readers and was aiming for 1,000.[172] Both the *Herald* and *The Helper* were consistently bullish about the campaign, but it had to be extended twice, first to the 17 March launch and then to 21 March.[173] The extensions were accompanied by a 3d bonus for Helpers, taking their reward to 1s.[174] *The Helper* implied that this was to satisfy demand. It is equally likely that the campaign was undershooting, an impression reinforced by *The Helper*'s call for a 'great last two weeks rally', implying the need for recovery.[175]

On 3 March the total number of pledges was 400,566, which was not enough.[176] But an extra 219,188 enrolled over the next two weeks, plus 210,000 brought in by a press campaign and just under 100,000 old readers gave the *Herald* a registered readership of 922,000 by the night of 17 March.[177] The drive even aided the old *Herald*, with sales rising from the moment when Odhams took over printing on 17 February.[178] The last Victoria House issue, 15 February, had a circulation of 323,900 and by the time the last old-style *Herald* appeared on 15 March the figure was 348,030, recovering the previous seven months' losses.[179] Bowing out with the headline 'Success assured on Monday' the last old *Herald* reported a valedictory visit to the paper from Lansbury. While the new proprietors were effectively repudiating most of his traditions, they recognised the immense importance of his endorsement, linking the new paper to the *Herald*'s distinctive heritage.

A leader headlined 'Invincible' similarly linked old and new. Implicit in it was the promise that in future the *Herald* would depend on the financial and professional resources of a commercial publisher rather than movement goodwill.

> The paper began in a fighting spirit; in a fighting spirit it has lived. And from Monday it will carry on the fight with a power never before possible ...
>
> Behind it was the Socialist spirit, the Socialist ideal and these are invincible ... No paper has ever had such splendid supporters. They gave themselves unstintingly to the *Daily Herald*. Never will it fully be known what sacrifices they made in time and money.
>
> That is why the paper lived. That is why, despite its meagre equipment, it grew in power and influence.[180]

The leader was right insofar as survival was in itself an achievement. The *Herald*'s years under direct movement ownership were characterised by two broad trends – one political and the other commercial. Politically it faithfully reflected the movement it represented during a decade in which centralising, gradualist leaders strengthened control over both party and unions. As the 1920s went on the *Herald* became progressively more like the paper it had seen off in 1915, the official *Daily Citizen*. It shifted by stages from diversity to uniformity, from dissent to conformism and from left to right. This progress paralleled that of former reporter John Scurr. In 1921 he was an imprisoned Poplar councillor, in 1924 an MP so disillusioned by the first Labour government that he questioned the value of the exercise, and by 1929 a backbencher so conformist that he was described as one of the most loyal of 'loyalist' MPs.[181] The *Herald*'s existence guaranteed Labour a voice in the national press during the contentious decade in which it established itself as a serious competitor for political power, a countervailing force in an otherwise overwhelmingly anti-labour field. But struggles for circulation and commercial viability eliminated the options open to its management until sale to an external financier was the only option open to it. These struggles were rooted in the paper's poverty, vividly evoked by Hamilton Fyfe's 1924 Labour Party conference comparison of it with a ragged street beggar. But they were also to some extent self-inflicted. The *Herald*'s serious, informative approach served the movement's activists and loyalists, those whose interests and self-definitions were essentially political, very well. Like clubland papers such as the *Pall Mall* and *Westminster* Gazettes it was catering to a political elite, but with the difference that where their elites had been a socio-economic elite confined to a small area, the *Herald*'s readers had little money to spend while demanding the trouble and expense of national distribution. Other potential readers, whose interest in politics waned between elections and major industrial disputes, were less well served. The *Herald* was constrained in meeting their demands by poverty, lack of editorial space and a movement culture that made adoption of its competitors' style and attractions unlikely. But there was a choice that its owners might have made before it was effectively forced upon them in 1929.

They might have chosen to tailor the *Herald*'s serious-minded, improving outlook to serve the movement's activist elite, accepting in the process that a mass circulation was unobtainable. Alternatively they could have accepted that in the absence of a mass anti-capitalist counterculture they would have to compromise with dominant commercial values and make the financial commitment necessary from their own resources to secure a large popular circulation. They refused to make the choice and persisted in pursuing popular targets with elite values. In consequence the *Herald* contrived the worst possible outcome, that of being neither one thing nor the other.

7
The Third *Daily Herald*, 1930–64

'Why don't you print news, stuff that really matters?'
'You are twenty years too young, Mr Evans. The stuff that really
matters is not news. Anyone can find that. What matters is profit.'
Gwyn Thomas, *Sorrow for Thy Sons*

It is as well that the first issue of the new *Herald* covered a relatively
uneventful weekend, as there was only ever going to be one lead story
– itself and premier MacDonald's visit to Long Acre to start the presses.
It reported that 'the Prime Minister's visit was the outcome of a keen
willingness to identify himself with the new enterprise'.[1] This is
doubtful. As publishers of *John Bull*, Odhams had reproduced his birth
certificate, displaying his illegitimacy to the world, during the First
World War.[2] Furthermore, he turned down Bevin's suggestion that
Elias be awarded a peerage in 1931, and went on blocking him while
he remained premier.[3] Years later, Elias would still quote bitterly his
greeting on arrival at Long Acre: 'You're a very courageous man. You're
taking a great risk you know.'[4] But MacDonald and the *Herald* needed
each other's endorsement. After a dutiful hour-long visit, during
which, it was proudly reported: 'Never before had a British Premier
mingled so freely with the staff of a great journal', he sat at Mellor's
desk to be photographed by one of the *Herald*'s star recruits, James
Jarche, while penning a message:

> I hope that all supporters of Labour, and all those, whatever their
> views, who wish to have the Labour case put fairly before them, will
> buy it and read it. There never was a time when it was more
> necessary for the Labour Party to have a national newspaper devoted
> to its support; or for the public to have the Labour point of view
> continuously put before it.

The front page also carried a picture of Elias, although a passport-
sized portrait at the bottom of the second column could hardly be
described as Maxwellian.[5]

The new paper was dramatically different to look at, not only to its
low cost predecessor, but to anything seen previously in Britain. After
years of striving for political innovation, the *Herald* found itself a

design innovator – according to Le Mahieu the first British popular paper to use layout to create a distinct visual identity.[6] Design expert Allen Hutt recorded the benefits of Odhams's expertise as printers: 'Fleet Street's backwardness in make-up, text and machinery was put to shame by a "popular paper" ... with a consistently planned typography in the bold variants of one type family only ... with a strong-contoured text ... and with rotary presswork of a quality comparable only with that of *The Times*.'[7]

Content was also different. Mellor, in *Labour Magazine*, had explained the change: 'Political news ... must take its place as news and not sprawl over the paper covering every page and obtruding into every nook and cranny.'[8] Politics and industry each had their dedicated page, but these were two pages out of 20 rather than the ten or twelve of the old *Herald*. The promised full range of popular features included a leader page feature on peace by H.G. Wells and a specially-written serial by Edgar Wallace, the top-selling thriller writer of the day. A front-page plug for insurance was supplemented by a three-column inside page description of the scheme while full pages covered music, arts and radio and business and finance – the last signalling a changed view of readers with the headline 'Your investments' and a general diary column edited by 'Chanticleer'. 'Tomfool' and 'Gadfly' survived, but 'Way of the World' was relegated in truncated form to the arts page. A feature 'The truth behind the dope peril' referred to drugs and not the capitalist press.[9] Advertisements were complemented by an explanation assuming an ignorance of their purpose surprising even in purchasers of the anti-capitalist press: 'These advertisements are invitations specifically directed to you. They ask you to buy the goods of the firm who insert them in our pages' and betrayed an over-anxiety to please advertisers: 'You can have as much faith in the advertisements carried in this paper as you have in the integrity of the paper and the principles for which it stands. Remember: Good advertisements in the *Daily Herald* mean good goods.'[10]

This over-compensating embrace of the commercial ideal took even more startling form three weeks later: 'Readers in their turn have not been slow to appreciate that the firms which advertise most freely are those whose products are the best.'[11] The new outlook was epitomised by two 17 March insertions. Wincarnis, the one company to have complained consistently about birth-control adverts, took front-page space. H. and J. Searle, whose adverts while in dispute with the Upholsterers Union had caused such controversy in the first half of the 1920s, also advertised heavily, whether fortuitously or pointedly, on the industrial page.[12]

If any readers still doubted that politics was being kept within limits, proof came on 1 April, after a government defeat in the House of Lords. The paper's view that defeat made little difference to the

Figure 8 'A keen willingness to identify himself'; Prime Minister Ramsay MacDonald starts rotary machines in the new *Daily Herald* building, March 1930.

government echoed its attitude to a similar setback three weeks earlier, but where defeat in early March received a six-column banner treatment from the old *Herald*, its successor kept the reverse off the front, rating Kaye Don's world land speed-record bid the most significant story of the day.[13] Not everyone approved. Wilfred Fienburgh, a Labour MP and author of a book on the *Herald* in the 1950s, recalled: 'My own family almost wept at the death of the old, genuine, workers' *Herald* and sternly refused to buy the new capitalist paper.'[14] The Communist Party had attempted to cash in on such discontent by relaunching its *Sunday Worker* as a daily on 1 January 1930.[15] But official confirmation that this was a minority view came within three weeks, with the first net sales certificate. Again the *Herald* made itself the main story of the day with banner headlines hailing a figure of 1,058,588: 'Amazing feat in 14 Days: third biggest daily before Northern office opens'.[16] The Manchester rally held in late June to celebrate the Northern edition attracted such crowds that Manchester Tramways' takings record was broken.[17] Perhaps the most spectacular evidence of this early success was the demise of the *Daily Chronicle*, which had relaunched shortly before the *Herald* but was destroyed by its competition – 'torpedoed flat' in the argot of Fleet Street. [18] Within weeks it had been forced into merger with the *Daily News* to form the *News Chronicle*.[19]

This had the paradoxical outcome of strengthening the competition, relegating the *Herald* back to fourth place as it pursued the aim proclaimed at the Northern rally: 'Now for the Second Million'.[20] The *News Chronicle* was finally overtaken as the *Herald* topped 1.5 million in February 1932 and the long-time market leader, the *Mail*, later in the same year.[21] A furious race for two million followed, with the *Herald* beating the *Express* by a few days in June 1933.[22] For the next three years the *Herald* could proclaim 'The world's largest daily net sale'.[23] Historians Tom Jeffrey and Keith McLelland argue that the *Herald*'s success was to some extent understated: 'The narrowness of the new *Daily Herald*'s victory in the circulation wars of the early 1930s was as nothing compared to its clear victory in terms of readership.' They point to a 1934 survey showing it as the most-read paper in the West Riding, the South East, Greater London, the West Midlands and the North-West.[24]

If the labour movement hoped that a mass-circulation daily would guarantee electoral success they were to be horribly shocked in 1931. Finally granted this apparently crucial weapon, Labour went down to the most shattering defeat in its history, reduced to a rump of 52 seats and with Lansbury the only surviving Cabinet minister.[25] Yet it was in the crisis before the election, with the Labour government splitting over proposed unemployment benefit cuts, with idolised leader Ramsay MacDonald forming a National Government and the

Figure 9 Never knowingly understated; the new *Daily Herald* hails its first official one million-plus sales certificate, 8 April 1930.

distinct risk that his authority would persuade many party members and followers to support him against the bulk of Labour, which went into opposition, that the *Herald* proved its usefulness to many.

Editor Will Stevenson was among those inclined to give MacDonald, and Labour ministers who followed, him the benefit of the doubt. Hugh Dalton recalled the meeting with, among others, Lansbury, Bevin, Citrine and Henderson, at which he was persuaded into line:

> They send for X [Stevenson] of the *Herald* to settle the line of tomorrow's leader. Stevenson, still under the influence of JRM [MacDonald] and PS [Snowden] who had been working on him very hard – had proposed to begin by paying tribute to the courage of those who were staying in. 'And what about the courage of those who are coming out?', asks Uncle [Henderson]. So the whole emphasis is changed. The *Herald*, in the days that followed, under Bevin's influence, gave a fine lead.[26]

Hannen Swaffer, a long-time *Herald* journalist but with few illusions about his employer, told the 1947 Royal Commission on the Press: 'The *Daily Herald* was the only reason the Labour Party kept together in 1931.'[27] Yet by the late 1930s, the atmosphere surrounding this big-selling, politically loyal paper was one of rumbling discontent. In 1936 Labour's National Executive complained of a tendency 'to take the existence and services of the *Daily Herald* too much for granted'.[28] When *Herald* political reporter Maurice Webb, later a Labour MP and minister, polled 350 leading Labour figures in 1937 he found very few entirely satisfied and a minority extremely critical, arguing that 'people no longer talk about what the *Daily Herald* is saying or what it is going to say' and that it had 'lost its individuality'.[29]

The sacking of two editors – Mellor in 1931 and Stevenson in 1936 – may look routine to modern eyes, but was hardly characteristic of successful papers in this period.[30] The National Union of Journalists chapel, which boasted the only closed-shop agreement in Fleet Street, spent much of 1938 first conducting its own inquiry into the running of the paper, then being bitterly angry over the sacking of popular news editor Jim Barnes.[31]

There was disquiet over the means by which the massive sales figure had been obtained. It is possible to overstate the circulation wars of the 1930s – as Jeremy Tunstall has pointed out 'they ran for only a few months at a time in 1930, 1931 and finally from March to June 1933'.[32] Those brief eruptions have given the period its legends – the *Herald* circumventing a rule against free gifts by using its publishing capacity to generate thousands of cut-price editions of Dickens, Beaverbrook miming drawing a sword and running Elias through with the words 'This is war!' and the alleged ability of free gifts from one or other paper to clothe an entire family within ten weeks.[33] Anyone old enough to have been an adult in the 1930s has anecdotes about circulation canvassers, figures as evocative of the interwar years as crossing sweepers were of the horse-drawn age. My grandparents told with particular relish of an extremely persistent *Daily Sketch* canvasser who, challenged finally for his own opinion of the paper, admitted, 'I wouldn't take the *Sketch* if you paid me. I think it is a dreadful paper.'[34] The *Express* spent £270,000 before dropping out of the 12-week battle of 1933, when *The Economist* reckoned the combined costs of the four main competitors were £50,000–60,000 per week.[35] Odhams's tactics were simple from the start, to apply the methods that had been so successful with the *People* and outbid their competitors. While 1933 was a peak, the *Herald* was spending heavily throughout the 1930s. Its accounts point to expenditure of more than £2.1m including losses, around £1.20 for every extra reader secured, during the decade.[36] The insurance scheme cost around £2.5m during this period, peaking in 1938 at £474,000.[37] This compares to £310,000 editorial costs in the same year, and was approaching 30 per cent of the paper's sales revenue from a circulation of just over two million.[38] This need not have mattered if the *Herald* had pulled in the hoped-for advertising. As ex-editor Fyfe put it in the mid 1930s: 'When the *Herald* was in the hundred thousands, Mr Selfridge was asked if he would not take space in it. He replied courteously that he found it sufficient for his business to use certain other papers. The *Herald* with two million purchasers he cannot thus neglect.'[39]

The *Herald* certainly progressed immensely. The London Press Exchange told one advertiser: 'Though primarily it caters for an artisan and lower middle class market, it also reaches a considerable percentage of the population of slightly higher earning capacity.'[40] A 1934 survey showed that it had 50 per cent more middle-class readers than *The Times*.[41] Its 32 per cent increase in display advertising revenue between 1932 and 1936 was more, relative to sales, than any paper except the *News Chronicle*.[42] Yet the quantitative surveys that improved the *Herald*'s advertising competitiveness also showed up its continuing weaknesses. A national survey in 1936 showed that nearly 96 per cent of its readers had an annual income of less than £250 – against 75 per cent of *Express* readers, 57 per cent for the *Mail* and 87 per cent for the *News Chronicle*. Where it had 103,000 readers with incomes over £250, the *Express* had 510,000 and the *Mail* 720,000. Even the *News Chronicle*, with a substantially smaller readership, had more than twice as many.[43] In consequence, the *Herald* always ran fourth for advertising. In two weeks in April and June 1938 it ran 11,000 column inches of adverts. The *Express* had 43 per cent more, the *Mail* 32 per cent and the *News Chronicle* 20 per cent.[44]

In 1937 total advertising income was around £1.3m – 18 times what it had been a decade earlier, and accounted for 45 per cent of total revenue, up from 20 per cent.[45] But it still ran well behind the national press average of 53 per cent.[46] Combined with the massive promotion and insurance costs, this made nonsense of original calculations that the *Herald* should be profitable at a circulation of two million. In the two years to the end of March 1937, sales were steady between 2 and 2.05 million.[47] Over that period, the *Herald* lost £343,000.[48] Even massive promotional spending failed to keep the *Herald* top of the sales list. It plateaued firmly at just over two million for the rest of the 1930s.[49] The *Express*, which had pulled out of the frenzy of 1933, immediately shedding around 150,000 sales, then grew steadily through the rest of the decade, passing the *Herald* in 1936 (forcing it to shift to 'A world record: over two million for more than three years' in promotional material) and reaching 2.585 million by 1938.[50]

Odhams was driven by promotions and their printing capacity. Tom Hopkinson, later editor of *Picture Post,* joined their publicity department in 1932. He recalled: 'Everything was geared to keeping their machines going.'[51] They could match any company in these respects, but they had also to put out a good paper, which is a costly business. Other papers rapidly incorporated the new *Herald*'s design innovations, and proved rather readier to spend money on journalism.[52] Francis Williams believed that Elias begrudged all editorial expenditure except on big name writers who could be used for promotional purposes.[53] Here Odhams would spend, giving salaries of £5,000 to both the feature writer H.V. Morton and the cantankerously brilliant Hannen Swaffer, the 'Pope of Fleet Street', an all-rounder who 'would have written the whole paper given a chance' and whose publicity posters showing him from the back led him to grouse that 'I'm the only bugger in Fleet Street who sells papers with his behind'.[54] Elias offered even more to cartoonist Strube of the *Express*, creator of the archetypally English 'Little Man', only to be out-bid by Beaverbrook.[55] The *Herald* instead went back to Will Dyson, who arrived back in Britain in 1931, but with mixed success.[56] When he died in 1938, a series of triallists were given one week's chance, including Vicky, the Hungarian exile who would become one of the great postwar political cartoonists.[57] But, Vicky's biographers record, his skills were still developing and 'he muffed it'. The job went to the competent but rather uninspired George Whitelaw.[58]

Elsewhere there was deep reluctance to spend. Arthur Webb, a senior executive throughout the 1930s, recalled: 'When Beaverbrook brought in Christiansen [editor of the *Express* 1932–57] he poured out money on the editorial side of the *Express.* At the same time Odhams, hard pressed to find more money for canvassers, began to economise in the editorial department.'[59] Tom Driberg, on the *Express* in the 1930s, recalled that the *Herald* was 'notorious for parsimony over expenses'.[60] The *Herald* NUJ chapel was complaining about 'dismissals and salary cutting' by July 1931, and a list of staff changes sent by Dunbar to Citrine in June 1932 showed that there had been 16 sackings among the 58 editorial staff who had been on the paper in March 1930.[61] Dunbar argued that 'anyone who has worked in other offices in Fleet Street will tell you that comparatively the *Daily Herald* is heaven. This particularly applies to the *Daily Mail* men.' He conceded that some bad appointments had been made, but ten of the sackings were for economy reasons. Survivors of the old *Herald* seem to have been particularly vulnerable to economy cuts. Lance Mattinson, Slocombe, 'Gadfly' and Monica Ewer all went this way, plus Brodzky (indiscipline), Dawson (dereliction of duty) and the reporter Fox, whose shortcomings had so angered Fyfe, finally deemed 'unsuitable' in January 1931.[62] Dunbar, rather than the editor, had the final say on decisions which involved spending money. Francis Williams told the Royal Commission on the Press:

> He had to give his agreements to any arrangements with writers in the way of ordering a series of articles, or anything of that kind, unless the amount involved was very small. He had an overriding authority on financial expenditure; so that he could, if he so wished, curtail or prevent the sending of foreign correspondents to various parts of the world, not on the grounds of policy, but on financial grounds.[63]

One consequence of these priorities was that while the *Herald* had more than three times as many canvassers – 1,056 to 339 – as the *Express* in the late 1930s, it was considerably less well-off for foreign coverage.[64] Derek Jameson argues that 'like the public they serve, popular newspapers care little for what goes on out there in the wide world, unless it concerns Britain'.[65] But the years running up to the Second World War were a time when it was clear that what was happening in the outside world concerned Britain deeply. Arthur Webb remembered: 'We were without staff correspondents in Germany, Italy and the United States all through the crisis years.'[66]

This inhibition appears to have extended to news coverage in general. Swaffer warned in 1936: 'I think the *Express* will go ahead, more and more, and in the end, reach 3,000,000. It is doing this largely because it does, quite frankly, all those things which somebody or other would stop if they were suggested in our office.'[67] The 1938 NUJ inquiry complained of 'multiple control' leading to 'lack of consistency and coherence in direction ... while authority is dispersed, it is not delegated ... the effect of the inhibitions, prohibitions, taboos, conflicting instructions and "steam-rollering" has been to destroy initiative and to reduce the staff to mass-production units'.[68]

Swaffer fell victim to one prohibition in 1935 when he implied that some gifts to Lord Derby on the occasion of his being granted the Freedom of the City of Leeds had been given under duress. Dunbar cut his copy, and when Swaffer complained to Elias he was told that 'Lord Derby is a friend of mine and I know him to be ... the essence of honour'. Which while possibly true, was, as Swaffer's biographer Tom Driberg notes, hardly relevant. Swaffer, noting more relevantly that Derby was a prominent Conservative, had argued that: 'If I cannot refer to things like that, I might as well leave off writing for the *Daily Herald*.'[69]

In spite of such incidents, the *Herald* remained politically distinctive, as much in the extent as in the biases of its coverage. James Curran's analysis shows that in 1936 it had a higher proportion – 33 per cent – of public affairs news and features (political, social, economic, industrial,scientific and medical affairs) than not only any of its popular rivals, but also the heavy *Daily Telegraph* (22 per cent). The *Express* scored 18 per cent and the *Mail* 19 per cent.[70] There were occasional complaints – Maurice Webb's 1937 respondents wanted 'more movement inside news' – about the extent of union and Labour news.[71] But analysis of coverage in July 1938 testifies to the paper's commitment, with 1091.5 column inches against 301.5 in the *News Chronicle,* 171.5 in the *Telegraph* and 120 in the *Express*.[72]

It was unfailingly supportive of the Labour Party or TUC line of the moment. Former *Herald* journalist Douglas Jay records that labour correspondent George Thomas 'looked exactly like Walter Citrine and Citrine was in all things his hero and the fount of all wisdom and truth'.[73] Its loyalism in 1931 incorporated not only reasonable criticism – Stevenson's leader, after a suggestion by Henderson was headlined 'Not a National Government', while the paper put the phrase 'banker's ramp' into circulation – but apparent self-deception.[74] Swaffer said both MacDonald and Thomas were sure to be defeated at the 1931 election, and the leader comment following the disaster of polling day was that 'never was it so manifest that the Labour Party and the Labour Movement are deep rooted in the hearts of the masses of the people themselves'.[75] Only a day later did it admit that Labour had suffered 'a damn good hiding ... beaten at every point of the field'.[76] When the pacifist Lansbury clashed memorably with Bevin over defence policy at the 1935 Labour conference, the *Herald* was firmly in favour of Bevin and collective security: 'Sanctions, certain and overwhelming sanctions mean peace' it argued.[77]

It was similarly happy to follow the party line when Bevin and Attlee lined up against Edward VIII during the abdication crisis. Its front-page article when the story broke had the tone of an official circular:

> A constitutional crisis of a grave character has developed as a consequence of serious differences between the King and the Cabinet ... affairs which would be a private citizen's private affair are matters upon which a monarch should, and must seek the advice of his elected ministers ... Upon the King, in a crisis of personal wishes and public responsibilities, which comes so early in his reign, there rests a grave duty.[78]

All of which was in essence a long-winded, officialese rendition of Bevin's crisp statement that 'our people won't 'ave it' and helped earn Elias a peerage – as Lord Southwood – from grateful premier Baldwin, who admired 'the great dignity' of the *Herald* during the crisis.[79]

There were costs to being official. Stevenson's restraint on learning of Herbert Morrison's plans for transport in London in 1931 cost him an exclusive. When Morrison asked him to delay publication for a day so he could consult his superiors, he agreed – and saw a House of Commons statement issued on the advice of MacDonald and Snowden.[80] The left were unimpressed – Aneurin Bevan characterised the *Herald* as having 'the intellectual stringency of a parish magazine and the scepticism of a Holy Roller. It snatches at every incident of the royal panoply and serves it up with the sycophancy of an eighteenth century placeman ... childish rubbish.'[81] George Orwell, though similarly sceptical of the political line, saw other virtues: 'The one Socialist paper in England which could last a week on its merits *as a paper* is the *Daily Herald*, and how much Socialism is there in the *Daily Herald*?'[82] Fyfe noted the view of some readers that it was to be found in Swaffer's column, and nowhere else.[83]

But merits there undoubtedly were. Ritchie Calder gave readers a vivid picture of the Jarrow march and proved an adept interpreter of science.[84] Swaffer ranged widely and eloquently, even if he occasionally descended into cheerleading, describing the sanctions debate at the 1935 Labour conference as 'the finest debate on any vital subject that any political party has ever staged'.[85] Amid the bought-in stars, a new one developed in City editor Francis Williams, whose column 'aimed to link finance with political and economic policy in a way ... little done on City pages then' and developed into 'virtually a commentary upon world affairs'.[86] His story proving, by analysing figures for 25 key raw materials, that Germany definitely was rearming was a scoop to rank with any in the *Herald*'s history.[87]

A path-breaking *News Chronicle* readership survey in 1934 gave quantifiable substance to already-established journalistic instinct that the human interest story invariably captured wider interest among wider audiences than any other.[88] Swaffer argued that the *Herald* too frequently neglected personality and human interest in its serious political coverage: 'We must dig down and extract the fundamental issue in each story ... There is a basis of drama, colour and movement in each wage-fight, in every political issue ... the invention is always much easier to describe than the inventor. But the world wants the invention told and explained in terms of the inventor; the war in terms of the soldier.'[89] Political content and entertainment occasionally came together. Stephen Wynne, *Herald* journalist and Bevin's son-in-law, meshed the two in his 1938 serial story 'Murder at Transport House', including scenes in the *Herald* office.[90] More often they cohabited, generating some memorably incongruous juxtapositions. Readers startled in 1931 to find ultra-respectable Arthur Henderson sharing front-page billing with Hollywood siren Carole Lombard possibly recovered from the shock in time to enjoy the issue of 14 September 1935 in which Mussolini's antics prior to invading Abyssinia competed for attention with 'Freed dancer tells of her nights in cell: arrest of the wrong platinum blonde'.[91] But, true to its essentially serious nature, the *Herald* always preferred a news hook of a sort to the unvarnished pin-up, and was grateful for the high divorce rate among attractive actresses.[92]

The 1930s *Herald* also rapidly acquired some of the popular press habits its predecessor had derided. These included a keen interest in the aristocracy – the issue on May Day 1930 devoted two-thirds of a front-page column to the flying feats of the Duchess of Bedford, while debutantes started to appear with striking regularity on the picture page and 'Peer's nephew in an escapade' was deemed worthy of coverage.[93] It also happily capitalised on the misfortunes of insured readers, in July 1931 listing 17 who had died, complete with cause of death and amount of payment. This included one 'who was speeding along on his bicycle when the tyre burst. He was shot over a bridge and killed. *Exactly one month prior to the accident he had registered for the* **Daily Herald** *free insurance*. His foresight resulted in a substantial cheque for his dependants.'[94]

While the two could cohabit, all was reasonably well. But this ceased to apply by the late 1930s. Southwood was worried by the paper's failure to compete with the *Express* and believed that fears of war would hit business confidence and thus advertising. On both counts he was unhappy with the paper produced by Francis Williams, who had succeeded Stevenson as editor at the start of 1937.[95] Williams recorded: 'Each morning he spread all the morning papers on the floor of his office – it was rarely his habit actually to read them – and walked among them brooding.'[96] Williams, who admits, '[I] came to hate him more than any man I have ever known' is undoubtedly a jaundiced witness.[97] But not for that reason unreliable. R.J. Minney, author of a reverential, somewhat Pooterish, official memoir of Southwood, records him telling Williams: 'Look at the front page. Just compare one with the other. Do you think ours is the best?' and corroborates what Williams called an 'editorial compulsion to be bright': 'Make them smile – cheer them up. The news is grim enough. We ought to have something on every page to lighten their hearts.'[98] Hugh Cudlipp, a detached witness for the 1930s, if not the later *Herald*, recounts similar pressures on the editor.[99] Hugh Dalton records a meeting with Douglas Jay, Williams's successor as City editor, during a period when Odhams was operating a 'No gloom' rule and there had been an attempt to insert recent high company profits figures into Jay's column, in his absence, as evidence of continued prosperity. The business manager of the *Herald* was quoted as saying: 'Nothing should be printed in the paper unless it either helps advertising or interests the reader.' Stories noting that high average building society deposits concealed a large number of people with very little money apparently did neither.[100]

There is no doubt that Southwood was a supporter of appeasing Hitler during the late 1930s. Historian Richard Cockett notes that he was a frequent visitor to the Foreign Office and highly amenable to pressure from Lord Halifax, then Foreign Secretary.[101] Within the *Herald* he found some sympathy from Ewer, by now an unrelenting anti-communist in reaction to his earlier views, but none at all from Williams, whose support for a firm line against Hitler was buttressed by Bevin.[102] As Williams puts it, the *Express* was saying 'In the *Daily Express* every day is a sunny day' while his line was 'In the *Daily Herald*, the news must be given straight and the dangers into which appeasement is leading us made plain'.[103] There was little doubt which his proprietor preferred on either count. His views were made clear via Dunbar, remembered by Jay as 'offering advice in long telephone soliloquies to all and sundry on the staff from the Editor downwards. Being rather deaf, he did not listen to any reply', although Charles Leatherland, Father of the NUJ chapel at the time, recalled being able to win concessions from him by initially engaging him on a mutual interest in horses.[104] Less publicly, Southwood's outlook was being buttressed by a daily memo on the *Herald* from *People* editor Harry Ainsworth, a highly proficient practitioner of Sunday populism at its most basic.[105]

Pursued by these pressures, confusion and division within the Labour Party and an entirely reasonable desire to avoid another war, the *Herald* pursued a slightly lurching course through the dismemberment of Czechoslovakia in the autumn of 1938. First it headlined 'Good luck, Mr Chamberlain!' as the Premier went to meet Hitler in

Munich.[106] Within days it condemned the agreement he and Daladier reached, without consulting the Czechs, with Hitler: 'Never in recent history [has there been] so disgraceful a case of intolerable pressure brought to bear on a small power by two Great Powers' and giving heavy publicity to Labour protest meetings.[107] With the Czechs mobilising, the *Herald* felt that Hitler had exhausted the options open to the other powers: 'If war there must be since Herr Hitler is set on war, then it is better that it should be now when Britain has its allies behind her.'[108] The sense of relief when talks opened again – 'How London laughed again' was the headline on a Swaffer column which talked of 'the lifting of a cloud' – was perhaps natural.[109] Less logical, in view of the paper's stance only a few days earlier, was resigned acceptance of the deal under which the Czechs agreed not to resist: 'It is open to grave criticism on a number of points. Nevertheless Herr Hitler has had to abandon the most brutal of his ... terms.'[110]

Hitler's open betrayal of the agreement, swallowing the rest of Czechoslovakia in the spring of 1939, allowed Williams to be more direct, calling for Chamberlain's resignation – although the *Express* went on until August 1939 cheerfully proclaiming that 'Britain will not be involved in a European war' – narrowly defeating Tomfool's *Herald* reaction to Mosley's resignation in 1930: 'I prophesy with confidence that he will yet do big things for the democracy of this country' as possibly the worst prediction of the whole decade. [111]

The declaration of war in September 1939 appeared to solve some pressing problems. Williams might reasonably hope, although he was soon disillusioned, that Southwood would desist from pressuring him over his robust anti-Hitler stance.[112] Circulation canvassing and insurance schemes were cancelled, never to return, as soon as the war started, cutting around £500,000 from annual costs.[113] Newsprint rationing cut papers back to four pages by 1941, slashing costs again – having spent £853,000 on paper in 1938, the *Herald* spent more than £500,000 less in 1942 and 1943.[114]

There were inevitable casualties in shrunken papers. Sport virtually disappeared while the Germans accomplished what the 1923 TUC had balked at, and ended for good the long career of Bobby Bear.[115] Advertising, however, became a seller's market as advertisers competed for limited space.[116] Papers still sold at 1d and the public seized every copy they would print – *Herald* returns in August 1940 and 1941 were 0.006 and 0.009 per cent, equivalent to 100 to 150 copies on print runs of 1.6 million.[117] Paper and print restrictions meant that sales, which had dropped slightly to under two million just before the war started, continued to fall, dropping to around 1.6 million between 1941 and 1943, before climbing back to two million in June 1945.[118] But with all the other restrictions on costs, profits between 1941 and 1945 totalled £718,000, easily the most, indeed the only, prosperous period in the paper's history.[119]

War also created a demand for serious news. The miniature wartime editions were dominated by crisp, concise war and diplomatic coverage, so the *Herald*'s abiding seriousness was less conspicuous in the popular market. In 1946 it was still running more public affairs news and features than its popular rivals, but the gap – 45 per cent to the *Express* and *Mail*'s 39 per cent – was proportionately much less.[120] In a conventional sense, the *Herald* had a good war. Sports writers like Clifford Webb (football) and Charles Bray (cricket) redirected their efforts to war reporting – Webb accompanying the Eighth Army in North Africa while Bray was air correspondent.[121] Naval correspondent A.J. McWhinnie was one of 21 British war correspondents to receive the OBE in 1945.[122] Three *Herald* reporters – Bray, R.W. Pearce and A.B. Austin – were among the 22 mentioned in dispatches for 'distinguished services in the field', more than from any other news organisation.[123]

Two were killed. Stanley Willis, who in 1943 fulfilled his desire to become a war reporter after nine years as a *Herald* subeditor and was the only journalist present when the siege of the Seventh Indian Division on the Burma front was lifted in February 1944, died a month later in the crash which also killed General Orde Wingate.[124] Austin, killed in Italy in September 1943, had once been assistant features editor and parliamentary sketch writer on the ultra-reactionary *Morning Post*.[125] Contacts made while an RAF press officer early in the war gave him 'access to several well-placed sources' while writing daily war commentaries, but his most effective work was done in the field, where he was the only reporter to accompany the abortive Dieppe raid in 1943. Suzanne Bardgett sees him as coming close to Swaffer's ideal of 'war in terms of the soldier': 'Above all Austin wanted to involve his readers in his experience, as closely as if they were with him in the field.'[126]

The wartime *Herald* also regained a political edge. This was in spite of the departure of Williams after a row over the suppression of an article on Finnish resistance to the Russians at the end of January 1940.[127] Williams recalled: 'The phoney war had restored his [Southwood's] faith in the commercial ethos ... what lay between us now was he thought I was determined to stir up the war.'[128] The TUC directors, led by Citrine in Bevin's absence abroad, were prepared to support him but lawyers ruled that the position of the editor was a matter for the board as a whole, not just the policy directors.[129] After discussion, the General Council let the matter rest, as did the staff after Williams advised them against a strike.[130]

His successor was Percy Cudlipp, editorial manager since 1938 and eldest of a Cardiff-born trio who all became Fleet Street editors.[131]

Previously editor of Beaverbrook's London *Evening Standard*, he was regarded as a gifted writer and newspaper technician – the cartoonist David Low called him 'that rare phenomenon, an editor who knew what a political cartoon was, and how to present it' – yet his appointment was widely expected to depoliticise the paper.[132] He had famously described himself as 'an advocate, like a lawyer in court, rewarded for my skills in putting my client's case'.[133] Peter Howard, a Beaverbrook colleague, credited him with 'toughness, resilience and a sense of humour'.[134] All three would be useful while editing the *Herald*. Many critics of his appointment, like Jay, a close ally of Williams, were rapidly won over: 'He became less and not more cynical as his fourteen years of editorship wore on. He ... developed sincere principles.'[135] The barrage against the 'dead wood' of Chamberlain's government continued, the final reshuffle in April 1940 labelled 'futile' and a 'Mad-Hatters Tea Party'.[136] While inclined to back Lord Halifax ahead of Churchill for the premiership when Chamberlain fell, this was at least as much a reflection of the labour movement's memories of Churchill as a class warrior – particularly in 1926 – as of any influence Southwood could exert for his friend the appeaser.[137]

While *Herald* attacks on the Conservatives receded a little after Labour joined Churchill's coalition government in May 1940, it continued to push for an agenda emphasising fair shares for everyone – it had been a vigorous supporter of food rationing from late 1939 until its introduction in early 1940 – vigorous prosecution of the war, and the postwar reconstruction of a fairer society.[138] In this it was aided by the presence of a minority of non-ministerial Labour backbenchers, led by Arthur Greenwood, as the official opposition. Thus, while backing the coalition in a vote of confidence after the fall of Tobruk in mid-1942, it could do so with a substantial dose of scepticism, calling for 'sufficient adjustment of organisation and outlook [which] must at last and at once be made'.[139] Swaffer asked MPs 'but exactly how much confidence have you? Have you complete confidence? Have you a fair amount of confidence? Or have you only a little confidence? And how much do you really think your constituents have?'[140] Aneurin Bevan's assault on the government during the debate was hailed 'the most considerable performance of any backbencher since the war began, if not in the entire Parliament'.[141]

When the Beveridge report, outlining the bases of the postwar welfare state, was issued in December 1942, the *Herald* devoted two pages to a comprehensive summary, saying it 'would capture the imagination of the public', and being careful to claim political credit ('Trade Unionism and the Labour Party will feel a special satisfaction') while warily not committing its political masters by noting that 'obviously there must be an interval of weeks before the Labour Party and the TUC can issue detailed declarations'.[142] In an ingenious and revealing flight of fancy, reporter Hugh Pilcher described the imaginary 'Life under Beveridge', taking a young couple from the 1940s through all the stages and potential crises of life to come. At each stage 'they still found that they could manage nicely', a modest aspiration speaking volumes for the impact of poverty on the outlook of British Labour for much of this century. Their son suffered 'the usual childhood illnesses, but there was no worry about doctor's bills or hospital fees' and their grandchildren were 'big fine kids, much taller than the average in the 1930s'. The grandchildren 'used to marvel when Grandma talked about the days "when there wasn't any Social Security plan my dears. When I was a girl, if people hadn't the basic necessities of life and if you had a baby you never knew whether you would be able to feed it properly." It didn't seem credible.'[143]

When the government chose to defer Beveridge until after the war, the *Herald* loaded the blame on Conservative ministers, labelling Home Secretary John Anderson the 'Wet Blanket' and giving vigorous backing to the Labour opposition amendment demanding early implementation: 'Should the Beveridge plan be pigeon-holed, or should it be made a reality, an inspiration to our people at war, an example to the world?'[144] Only Conservative ministers were criticised by name. Labour Home Secretary Herbert Morrison was credited with a 'masterly winding-up speech' as he closed for the Cabinet.[145] It urged the opposition to keep up pressure on ministers.[146] Labour members of the government were not amused by these vigorous displays of independence. *Mirror* director Cecil King told Lady Cripps, wife of Sir Stafford, that Cudlipp's editorials – he wrote them himself after his leader writers went into the armed forces – 'caused the Government more annoyance than anything else in the entire press'.[147] Cudlipp was to tell the Royal Commission on the Press that he was only contacted three times by members of the wartime government about the paper's policy and that he had more editorial freedom at the *Herald* than he had enjoyed at the *Evening Standard*.[148] But Christiansen, who knew something about dominant proprietors, refers to Cudlipp's battles with Bevin as 'an act of personal courage'.[149]

Cudlipp was equally disinclined to take lectures from Citrine. He rejected a complaint about liberal coverage of a speech by Aneurin Bevan, accompanied by the warning shot that the General Council felt 'growing concern' about the *Herald,* with the reply that if it had not given full coverage it would have 'laid itself open to the accusation that it deprives its readers of news which they are entitled to have'.[150] It may not be a coincidence that the complaint came only days after Michael Foot, a close ally of Bevan's since the early days of *Tribune* in the late 1930s, had begun a 20-year association with the *Herald*, initially as a columnist.[151]

Yet, for all these positive financial and editorial indications, the war years were when the *Herald* began its long terminal decline. The signs were there in a 1942 report from Mass Observation. Amid a general shift from the broadsheet popular papers to the pictorials – in particular the *Daily Mirror* – the *Herald* had picked up 'conspicuously fewer new readers' than other papers since 1939. It was making almost no impact among the young and while its readers were more interested in news and more politically educated than those of other papers, a much higher proportion – 13 per cent – expressed serious discontent. Just as alarming was that when readers were asked to say what features of their paper they particularly liked, 22 per cent of *Herald* readers replied 'Nothing in particular' against an average of six per cent for all papers and nine per cent for the *Express*.[152] More anecdotal evidence comes from Sir Tom Hopkinson, who remembered: 'If you were late buying your morning paper, you would find that most of them had sold out. The last two were always the *Herald* and the *Sketch*.'[153]

Another reason for decline was that for the first time since 1915 Labour-voting working-class readers had a Labour-supporting alternative to the *Herald*, and a far more formidable one than the hapless *Citizen*. The *Daily Mirror* had made impressive circulation gains almost as soon as it began its transformation from genteel picture sheet to aggressively populist tabloid in the mid 1930s. But it had been held back by the advertising industry's aversion to pictures, believed to attract less notice than text, and a fear that going too strongly for a mass working-class readership would risk losing its existing middle and upper-class base. Newsprint rationing removed this fear entirely.[154] The contrast between *Herald* and *Mirror* is drawn out by A.C.H. Smith's analysis of coverage of the military debacle in Crete. Both were critical of the British leadership, but 'what is missing from the *Herald*'s editorial is the aggressive Us and Them tone of the *Mirror*'. While the *Herald*'s air was that of 'the armchair statesman' and mildly reminiscent of *The Times*, the *Mirror* 'situates itself among the people, a tribune loyal to its readers and owing no obligation of respectfulness to the government it criticises'.[155] John Beaven, who would later edit the *Herald*, would say in the 1950s: 'The *Daily Mirror* accepts people as they are, crude, sentimental, self-sacrificing, selfish – all the contradictions of human nature.'[156]

Tabloidese, owing much to the advice of American advertising techniques, may have declined into parody in the 1990s, but in the 1940s it was fresh, different and considerably better adapted than the more leisurely journalese of the broadsheet populars to the space restrictions of the time. Historian Adrian Smith argues that the secret of the *Mirror*'s initial prewar success was 'an embryonic working-class consumerism in those areas and occupations beginning to benefit from modest economic recovery'.[157] This appeal worked even better with the armed forces, munition workers and the young of all occupations during the war. The more conservative labourist reaction to its vigour, vulgarity, huge headlines, pin-ups and cartoon heroine Jane – forever on the point of losing all her clothes – was summed up by Tennant of the Navigation Officers Union at a conference called to allow union newspaper editors to discuss the *Herald* in 1946. Pointing to the large numbers of members who chose other papers, he recalled with some disdain: 'Two members came into my office and asked if Jane had stripped yet.'[158]

The *Herald* had answers to competitors in the 1930s – free gifts, insurance and intensive canvassing. Their abolition revolutionised the papers's finances, but removed its defence mechanism. Between 1943 and 1946 the *Mirror*'s audited circulation surged from two million – ahead, but not uncatchably so, of the *Mail, Herald* and *News Chronicle* – to three million, in an entirely different class occupied only by the *Express*.[159] The *Mirror*'s ability to capture the *Zeitgeist* was seen again at the 1945 General Election. Maurice Edelman, a successful Labour candidate in 1945, recalled: 'The mood of the electorate ... was admitted by all who took part in the campaign to be one of sober and thoughtful consideration ... As Election Day approached, the *Mirror* ... became more and more sober in its appraisal of the issues.'[160] Not so the *Herald*, noted by the first Nuffield Election Study for the 'abuse' and 'violence' of its tone. It 'depicted the Tory party as a collection of rogues, monopolists and profiteers, who lived to exploit the people; who had no policy, who meant to get through the election by means of a series of stunts and scares, but whose manoeuvrings were so pathetically incompetent that their intention was obvious to the simplest elector – when enlightened by the left-wing press.'[161]

This role reversal again found the *Herald* at the wrong end of the equation. It was true, as Wilfred Fienburgh wrote, that the *Herald* made its contribution to Labour's massive win in 1945: 'Not ... that it supported Labour during general election campaigns, but that it had, since 1930, given consistent support to a comprehensive philosophy of change.'[162] But when the moment of change came, it was the *Mirror* which the academic observers credited as running the most effective campaign, and their 'Vote for Them' slogan appealing for support for the returning servicemen, that provided the election's enduring media image.[163]

Southwood died in 1946, the year in which *Herald* sales reached their all-time peak 12-month average of 2.146 million.[164] Sales stayed over two million until 1950.[165] But by then the *Express* and *Mirror* had topped four million, with the *Mirror* over four and a half, and the success of the *Mail* had relegated the *Herald* to fourth place.[166]

Coverage of Clement Attlee's Labour government was proudly pro-prietorial. As it launched the National Health Service, National Insurance, the National Assistance Board and Industrial Injuries Insurance in July 1948 the *Herald* headlined 'All these great benefits are yours from this morning' and perhaps the most noticeable feature of the coverage is a distinctly weak cartoon – more party-line propaganda than humour – showing ministers Bevan and Griffiths as proud parents clutching 'Britain's Quads', four babies marked with the names of the new benefits.[167]

The paper also cheerfully adopted the nascent Cold War attitudes of the time, seizing on votes against Marshall Aid by communists, their allies and a group of Conservative members associated with Lord Beaverbrook to lambast them as 'fellow travellers'.[168] A TUC circular against communism showed that the muscle-bound prose adopted by the *Herald* for industrial matters, a literary version of Socialist Realist art, was alive and well: 'The central authority of the British Trade Union Movement, the Trades Union Congress, issued yesterday a call to action by all loyal trade unionists to combat the Communist menace.'[169] The *Herald* reprinted the 800-word circular almost verbatim, ran a leader which included the statement 'No sterner statement has ever been issued' and followed up, it being late October, with a cartoon showing a Beefeater locating 'communism', a shrinking, obviously foreign caricature indistinguishable from those used over the years by right-wing cartoonists, hiding Guy Fawkes-like behind a barrel in a cellar. In case anyone missed the message, it was captioned 'Out with him – the TUC calls on all loyal trade unionists to combat the Communist campaign of sabotage and dangerous subversive activities'.[170] New recruit Marjorie Proops, who would in time leaven the mix with her advice column, started like many great journalistic successes by accident – her predecessor died and her curiosity was attracted by the letters piling up unanswered on her desk.[171] But for the moment she was confined to fashion stories and denied a first name, billed curtly as 'Proops – *Herald* Fashion Expert'.[172]

If the first warnings of decline were apparent in the wartime *Herald*, its reality would be visited on the postwar paper, which finally closed less than 20 years after the resounding victory of 1945. The received version of the paper's demise points to two key dates in the process – March 1949, when circulation controls were lifted, and 1956, when newsprint rationing was abolished. The first at least does not hold water. Koss talks of the *Herald* dropping 100,000 copies immediately as the *Mirror* put on half a million.[173] But *Herald* sales actually went up by 13,000 in March and April 1949.[174] No more than 65,000 daily sales were lost between the 1946 peak and the end of 1950.[175] The decisive year appears to have been 1951, with a massive loss of 121,000 taking the paper decisively below the psychologically important two million mark and initiating the steady decline, averaging more than 50,000 annually, which would afflict the rest of its existence.[176]

Why 1951? Labour lost power that year, a rare example of the *Herald*'s fortunes running in parallel with rather than against electoral fortunes, but it also polled a record vote. It was in better shape for cartoonists, always regarded as a strong circulation puller, than at any time since the days of Dyson. David Low had joined in 1950, and Margaret Belsky, whose front-page pocket cartoons would be among the paper's trademarks for the rest of its career, had begun a career that would generate 6,000 drily humorous drawings over the next 19 years.[177] But 1950 also saw some important departures. The post of foreign editor was abolished, the Paris and Berlin offices closed down and weighty Central European correspondent G.E.R. Gedye was dropped. The *Herald* was the only national newspaper without a correspondent at the Korean War, a classic event abroad which mattered to Britain. For the rest of the 1950s, as *Daily Mirror* witnesses told the 1961–62 Royal Commission on the Press: 'There was no security leak about the *Herald*'s foreign news service: it scarcely existed.'[178] The one significant survivor was the sempiternal Ewer, who while reaching retirement age in 1950 continued as diplomatic correspondent, holding court almost nightly in the Radio Arms across the road from the *Herald* office, and receiving the CBE in 1959.[179]

In 1951 there was a major redesign, described by Allen Hutt as 'the first and only time that a broadsheet has been given the full tabloid treatment. This at least provided an object lesson in the error of such an approach.'[180] Successive reworkings of the front page – the *Herald* ran through 12 mastheads between 1919 and 1957 including a bizarre three-column box for a few months in 1957 – were symptomatic of deep uncertainty.[181]

Percy Cudlipp's long editorship ended in October 1953 under circumstances described by Douglas Jay: 'The Odhams management had been constantly pressing him to produce plans for "raising the circulation to four million" and he finally had the bravery to write a memorandum saying bluntly that this could not be done unless very large sums of money were spent.'[182] His departure came only three days after brother Reg's appointment at the *News of the World* had made all three Cudlipp brothers simultaneously Fleet Street editors.[183] Swaffer reported that 'Percy had his afternoon conference as usual ... without telling anybody he was leaving' and he had subsequently pinned the announcement of his resignation on the newsroom noticeboard.[184] His successor was Sydney Elliott, another former *Evening Standard* editor who had also run the Co-operative Sunday *Reynolds News* from 1930 to 1942.[185] Beaverbrook once flattered him that 'the *Reynolds* leader page is the best in Fleet Street', but the appointment was unexpected, even the habitually discreet Lord Leatherland remembered it as 'quite a surprise', and unsuccessful.[186]

Douglas Jay recalled: 'What organisation had previously existed at the *Herald* slid into chaos. Editorial conferences were often incoherent. Responsibilities were blurred. Hugh Pilcher, a professional journalist and political writer, whose sanity throughout all this was a breath of fresh air, once remarked to me that the situation was so bad that soon someone would be stabbed in the front.'[187] Jay's accounts may have informed the views of Hugh Gaitskell, Labour Party leader from 1955, who considered Elliott's appointment 'disastrous' and heard of 'nothing but trouble and friction with staff'.[188] For Gaitskell the *Herald* was, in the view of his biographer Philip Williams, 'a constant worry ... and a source of controversy in which he was rarely at his best'.[189] With *Tribune*, *New Statesman* and Richard Crossman's influential column in the *Mirror* ranged against him in the struggle with the Bevanites which dominated the party in the 1950s, he was constantly fearful of losing control of the *Herald* as well.[190]

Yet in the 1950s the paper epitomised loyal followership as never before. H.G. Nicholas, analysing its coverage of the 1950 General Election for the second Nuffield Election Study, noted that it 'judged its news by the test of whether or not it could help the party' and that 'all its themes and leader subjects seemed to be raised first in speeches and party documents', making loyal followership almost a literal state.[191] On the board the dominant TUC voice was that of Arthur Deakin, successor to Bevin as boss of the Transport and General Workers Union, whom Geoffrey Goodman, a distinguished industrial reporter for the *News Chronicle*, *Herald* and *Mirror*, recalls as having 'All Bevin's instincts for control, but none of his imagination'.[192] Leslie Hunter, *Herald* parliamentary correspondent in the 1950s, remembered: 'Few industrial correspondents in Fleet Street have not at some time or other heard Deakin's voice bellowing down the telephone about some paragraph or reference he considered "mischievous". The greatest crime in his eyes was "disloyalty" and since he had an abiding faith in the infallibility of his own judgment, the ranks of the mischievous tended to be swelled by all those who differed from Deakin.'[193]

The instinct to party loyalty above all else cost Hunter one of the best stories of his career in late 1954 when, in a totally uncharacteristic burst of loquacity, veteran party leader Attlee confided both his intention of retiring and his belief that Gaitskell should succeed him. Editor Sydney Elliott decided that it would be 'premature' and 'unwise' to run the story. As Hunter points out, 'Labour's official newspaper had felt inhibited from discussing Attlee's position all along and had merely reported briefly, and without comment, such public statements as were made from time to time'.[194]

This was reflected in coverage of the battle between the leadership and the Bevanites, in which the paper was consistently hostile to the left-wing rebels and their motives. Gaitskell's recent biographer Brian Brivati notes, 'The *Daily Herald* presented the Bevanites as a faction whose objective was to capture the leadership'.[195] It had backed Gaitskell firmly over the introduction of charges for Health Service optical and dental work in the 1951 Budget, flashpoint for the Bevanite split. The budget was presented as 'a masterly review of the people's social and economic problems', a headline proclaimed 'still free fillings' with the new charges buried at the bottom of the front page summary and described as 'regrettable; but we think most people will accept them as reasonable in the nation's financial circumstances'.[196] The 'circumstances' were Cold War rearmament, and the *Herald* lambasted Bevan for refusing to accept them: 'Mr Bevan wants peace, but he flinches from the responsibility of financing an adequate arms programme', it argued following his resignation.[197] It took another bite, labelling Bevan 'Idol of the Wishful Thinkers', when Harold Wilson followed him:

Though he is all for liberty, he leaves to others the unpopular task of telling the nation that liberty means sacrifices.

It was Aneurin Bevan who coined the phrase 'The language of priorities is the religion of socialism'.

If ever there were a number one priority, it is rearmament, because rearmament is the surest shield against aggression in this disturbed world.[198]

Low, who even before the resignation had depicted Bevan buying 'half price teeth for gnashing', followed up with a cartoon captioned 'Gone with the wind' showing Bevan, clutching a paper marked 'Escape into idealism' borne aloft on the winds of 'Unavoidable demands of rearmament' while Gaitskell, Morrison, Shinwell, still firmly on the ground, looked on.[199] By early 1953 the paper's assaults on the Bevanites had reached such a pitch that even the Labour Party executive, firmly in the hands of Gaitskellite trade unionists, felt compelled to rebuke it.[200] Gaitskell, once leader, could count on still more enthusiastic support, winning front-page headlines four times in the first week of 1956 for his attack on the government for selling tanks, concealed under the headings of 'scrap' and 'agricultural implements' to the Middle East.[201] When Parliament met, Pilcher reported: 'The first clash between Mr Hugh Gaitskell, new leader of the Labour Party and premier Sir Anthony Eden, has resulted in a clear victory for the opposition chief.'[202] The paper would be similarly supportive during the Suez crisis, giving Gaitskell's reactions liberal front-page coverage.[203]

Gaitskell was consistently worried about *Herald* journalist Basil Davidson, 'whom most people believe to be a Communist, and who ought not, in my view, to be employed on the paper. This is not the first time I have complained about him. I have written several letters ... about other articles of his', he said after a lunch with Elliott in early 1956.[204] Even the highly sympathetic Philip Williams considered this a 'rather unattractive habit', and it echoes Ramsay MacDonald's complaints about Ewer 30 years earlier, although with greater success as Davidson would fall victim to an economy drive in early 1957.[205] By this time echoes of the 1920s were becoming unpleasantly loud. While Davidson played the part of Ewer, trade union leaders were echoing age-old grouches about the 'disloyalty' of the rank and file to the paper. Vincent Tewson, vice-chairman of the *Herald* and Citrine's TUC successor told Dunbar in September 1952: 'We are asking for a stable $2\frac{1}{4}$ million when we should be able to get at least 3 million. If we were to accord the *Herald* the loyalty we expect the *Herald* to give to the Movement, the circulation figure should be the highest of any daily newspaper.'[206] In 1957 *Herald* director Tom O'Brien would complain of the 'appalling apathy' of people who 'enjoyed all the benefits of the welfare state'. Labour, he said was 'surely entitled ... to have a national newspaper with a three to four million circulation'.[207]

It showed no sign of getting it, inducing further 1920s echoes as continuing circulation decline and advertising worries led to the *Herald* producing much smaller editions than its rivals once newsprint rationing was finally abolished – eight pages to the *Express*'s 14 by late 1956.[208] Perhaps this was not surprising. Self-serving and self-satisfied as the *Mirror*'s evidence to the 1961 Royal Commission on the Press was, there was justice in its view that the *Herald* was not only politically predictable, but 'unrelieved by clever writing and sufficient entertainment. There is nothing more unpalatable than a politician's bread and butter speech on an inauspicious occasion on a wet afternoon ... The pudding appeared in the (Labour) *Daily Herald* and the sauce in the (Labour) *Daily Mirror*.'[209]

Not that the political bosses were invariably happy. The Labour National Executive complained of inadequate coverage after the 1955 General Election, backing their irritation with research suggesting that the space devoted was only half of that given in 1951.[210] Accusing fingers were pointed at the downmarket tastes of the veteran *People* editor Ainsworth, who had surfaced as editorial director of the *Herald* in succession to Dunbar, who retired in 1953 and died early in 1955.[211] A year earlier the national Trades Council conference criticised *Herald* coverage, and found sympathy from Tewson, who compared it unfavourably with the *News Chronicle* and grumbled: 'The *Herald* must be bright (whatever that means) but in striving after this it should remain informative and authoritative.'[212]

Goodman, then on the *News Chronicle*, recalls the amusement of journalists from other papers at the 'knee-jerk way it would react to complaints from the unions or the Labour Party'.[213] It was certainly informative on Labour Party politics. Adrian Smith summarises its approach in a decade when Labour was dispiritingly contentious: 'A world of composite motions and complex agendas which the *Mirror* rarely got bogged down in, but was food and drink for ... lobby correspondents only a taxi ride from Smith Square or Hampstead, whose idea of getting away from it all was a September break in Blackpool.'[214] Goodman recalls:

> As a reporter on another paper you didn't feel you had to read the *Herald* as you certainly had to read the *Mail*, *Express* or *Mirror*. As an industrial reporter you knew what it was going to do – it would quote trade union officials unquestioningly. When it reported conferences it would quote what the president of the union had said, with no attempt to get a sense of colour or animation. There was no attempt to find out what employers or the rank and file were up to.[215]

Socialist Realist prose continued, with the 1957 Transport and General Workers conference decision to reject a pay freeze reported: 'Strong words that will be of no comfort to the employers or the Government were spoken yesterday.'[216]

Attempts to be 'bright', a journalistic catch-word of the period, had mixed results. Appointing historian A.J.P. Taylor, later a great success with the Beaverbrook press, might have been a good idea, but, billed at different times as 'the man with the independent mind' and 'I say what I please', he himself conceded that during this period 'I had a great gift of expression and nothing to say'.[217] It was 'by no means to my regret' when the *Herald* dropped him at 24-hours notice in July 1956.[218] There was awareness of greater working-class spending power, reflected in the appearance – in what turned out to be Cudlipp's last issue – of the 'Herald holiday man' Arthur March, who introduced himself in rather patronising, indirect address, spell-it-all-out-simply terms: 'I am an expert on holidays – especially holidays abroad. And it is my purpose to be of use to *Daily Herald* readers in the coming weeks by telling them where and when to get the best value for money on a continental holiday.'[219] A more direct style, but similar discomfort with the concept of abroad, was apparent in 1956: 'It's easy when you know how ... foreign money is easy to understand.'[220]

In spite of its high pin-up content – one of the Labour complaints of 1955 was that an important announcement was deemed less important than 'Miss Lea Pericoli's petticoats', actress Cecile Aubry was captioned 'Paris sends a real honey' and by 1957 the paper was running an 'Ideal Holiday Girl' contest complete with swimsuit shots of entrants – it remained uncomfortable with any sense of permissiveness.[221] Marjorie Proops was famously told, 'You've got to watch it, you're a very sexy writer.'[222] Paul Holt, reviewing *From Here to Eternity*, felt the need to justify 'one of the frankest love scenes I have ever seen on screen', explaining that 'it wasn't unpleasant, because it seemed to be honest rather than provocative'.[223]

A poll of secondary school pupils' newspaper preferences in 1957 was damning evidence of the *Herald*'s utter failure to appeal to the young. Even the *Sketch*, fourth in secondary moderns, and the *News Chronicle*, fifth in public and grammar schools, crept into a couple of categories, but the *Herald* was nowhere in findings dominated by the *Mirror*.[224] Adrian Smith notes that:

During the Suez crisis, the enemy within was rock 'n' roll and above all the malevolent ghost of James Dean, busy subverting teenage girls and inciting teddy boys to trash milk bars; with *Hound Dog* at number three, and Bill Haley and Lonnie Donegan sharing three other Top 10 places, the *Herald* was preoccupied with Vera Lynn's winter tour and Ted Heath's new line up.[225]

He points ironically to 'a shocking four day exposé of teenage worship of Dean ... and a truly disturbing report on the insidious effects of rock 'n' roll ... five major features warning parents inside seven days'.[226]

Little had changed a year later as Elvis Presley dominated the charts with 'Hound Dog'. Stand-in music critic Michael Nevard devoted the bulk of his space to jazz and big band sounds, adding almost as a postscript: 'Vocal groups pour in from the rock garden. Weed out your own from this month's crop.'[227] Bandleader Geraldo opined that 'skiffle is bad music' while other interview subjects included the distinctly prewar duo of Tallulah Bankhead, billed as 'Dad's pin-up girl' and Boris Karloff, by now well into his parodic Ed Wood phase.[228]

A hankering for the past was perhaps natural. If freed circulations had produced little immediate effect on the *Herald*, the freeing of advertisers by the end of newsprint rationing certainly did. Surveys showed that, as well as declining year on year, *Herald* readers were less attractive to advertisers than any others in Fleet Street. They included the highest proportion of men (59 per cent in 1959–60) and, although no older than readers of the *Mail*, they were much the poorest readership.[229] D.J. Roe of advertising agents F.J. Roe told the 1961 Royal Commission on the Press: 'It is the sort of paper that you would see a manual worker pull out of his pocket during his tea break and have a look at the racing or the football.'[230] That the sports section, in particular football and racing, was the one part of the *Herald* generally conceded to be excellent was no consolation.[231]

Commercial television arrived in September 1955 to provide competition on two fronts – one reason perhaps why the *Herald* was always fiercely opposed to what it once termed a 'dangerous experiment'.[232] As former editor of *The Times*, Simon Jenkins, notes, broadsheet populars as a whole were vulnerable:

> Their emphasis on topical exposure in news coverage and vivid use of pictures made then particularly vulnerable to a medium which could produce coverage the night before and support it with pictures. Their nationwide circulations were unable to provide advertisers with the regional variations which the new commercial television could give, and they were less able to capitalise on the growth of classified advertising.[233]

The consequence, as *The Economist* was to point out in its oration over the *News Chronicle's* graveside in October 1960, was that 'now two million is not the ceiling, but the floor, below which popular newspapers have to struggle to survive'.[234] Falling well below this floor, the *Herald* was, in Curran's words: 'Progressively squeezed out of the advertising schedules.'[235] In 1955 advertising accounted for 46 per cent (£1.95m) of the *Herald's* total income.[236] By 1959 it was down to 35 per cent – the national press average in 1961 would be 45 per cent.[237] The *Herald's* losses in the first half of the 1950s were irritating but manageable.[238] As the implications of the new freedom to purchase advertising space worked their way through purchasing decisions, losses became insupportable, rising to £376,810 in 1957 and staying at similar levels for the rest of the 1950s.[239]

Closure was a distinct possibility as losses spiralled in 1957. Odhams chairman Arthur Duncan issued the less than totally reassuring statement that: 'All I can say at the moment is that we do not contemplate closing the paper down.'[240] Two possible escape routes faced Odhams, whose approach to the paper was summed up by *The Journalist* as 'no more money for *The Herald*'.[241] One was an approach from Walter Layton of the *News Chronicle*, which was in even deeper trouble than the *Herald*, about a merger to form an 'independent paper of the left', which if it had succeeded in retaining both readerships might have sold more than three million daily.[242] Several meetings were held in 1956 and 1957 but appear to have foundered on the TUC and Labour Party's reluctance to give up their hold on policy – which the *News Chronicle* would have regarded as a precondition – their suspicion of the *News Chronicle's* Liberal connections and traditions, and the inability of either set of proprietors to find the money necessary to promote a merged paper.[243]

Odhams, pointing to the Daily Herald (1929) Ltd's accumulated debts of over £2m and the paper's continuing circulation problems, instead opted to push the General Council for new publishing agreements, warning that 'if necessary they would have to take action to preserve the interests of stockholders'.[244] They asked for a 25-year licence to publish the paper, described by *The Economist* as 'a sensible tax dodge' allowing them to offset the *Herald*'s losses against the considerable profits made by their magazines and the *People,* and a loosening of policy controls, arguing that 'the paper is circumscribed by the control of policy ... [a] limitation on the minds of the staff, the advertisers and the freedom of expression'.[245] The licence was awarded, although not without dissent on the General Council.[246] The freeing of policy proved more contentious. The agreement eventually reached, by a happy coincidence Clause Four of the new publishing agreement, was very little different from the 1929 original: 'Whilst reserving the newspaper editorial freedom, the grantee [Odhams] shall maintain the political and industrial integrity of the paper and support the policies as from time to time approved by the Trades Union Congress and the Labour Party.'[247]

A new editor, Douglas Machray, succeeded Elliott in October 1957.[248] With Elliott went 12 members of staff including assistant editor Basil Denny, City editor V. Burtt, the contentious Davidson and such long-time stalwarts as sportswriter Clifford Webb and lobby correspondent Leslie Hunter, confidant of Herbert Morrison.[249] Six had been with the *Herald* since the 1930 relaunch, one since 1920, and three were within months of retirement age.[250] Francis Williams, writing in the *New Statesman*, said that the appointment of Machray, 46, a Scottish subeditor who had been production editor of the *Herald,* ended 'any further pretence that the *Herald* is primarily a political paper'.[251] He was as wrong as those who predicted a similar fate for the paper after his own replacement by Cudlipp in 1940. It all depends what one means by political. Machray has since been portrayed in some quarters as something of a political innocent who wandered into an almighty row by suddenly coming out in favour of nuclear disarmament, a direct challenge to Gaitskell's Labour Party policy.[252] Goodman disagrees completely:

> He was a very tough, individual character not disposed to blind obeisance to anybody and knew exactly what he was doing and what he was taking on. His view was that if you toed the line you not only emasculated the truth, but that readers would know that you were not telling them the truth, and that the *Herald* had to demonstrate its independence to prosper commercially and

politically. He wanted the *Herald* to be what the *News Chronicle* had once been.[253]

The front page leader of 26 February 1958 was headlined 'A policy for staying alive ... There's only one answer' and concluded: 'Britain is already naked. IT IS AN ILLUSION TO BELIEVE THAT OUR BOMBS CAN CLOTHE US IN THE GARMENTS OF EITHER SAFETY OR PRESTIGE. THEY CAN MERELY BANKRUPT US.' This appears to have fallen as a bombshell among the movement's leaders.[254] But a strong hint had been dropped the day before in a leader complaining about the delay in clarifying Labour's current defence policy:

What's the Labour Party doing? What is the TUC doing?
    Nothing has happened. The result so far is nil. The TUC is left waiting for the Labour Party to make up its mind how to do it.
    It is astonishing, it is appalling – that we are waiting for a committee when the world danger is so great. Labour should be at the head of the people, not trailing after them.[255]

It was also logical that a *Herald* display of independence would be to the left. This was the period of 'Butskellism' when the party policies converged, and for the *Herald* to dissent to the right of the current Labour line would have carried it into the already crowded centre-right ground. Goodman recalls that the bulk of the paper's staff were firmly behind Machray, with even a committed Gaitskellite like political reporter Harold Hutchinson 'coming close at one point to accepting the argument'.[256] The paper also reported an extraordinary response from readers, the vast majority in favour of its line.[257] Goodman recalls there being 13,000 letters on the subject. [258] Columnist Michael Foot said, 'At last the people are waking up.'[259] The Labour establishment were less impressed. Tewson was 'beside himself'.[260] Morgan Phillips, secretary of the Labour Party, was on the phone on the morning of the leader demanding a reply which was duly printed on the following day.[261] His attack focused on issues of protocol and procedure rather than the substantive issues. He was 'profoundly disturbed' at an 'ill-considered attempt, supported by misleading information, to interfere in the current private discussions between the Labour Party and the Trades Union Congress'. The paper's 'sensational front-page spread' was 'seriously in conflict with Labour Party policy'.[262]

Machray, who denied any intention to divide the party, launched a poll of readers asking four questions about disarmament policy.[263] Gaitskell rang Surrey Dane, chair of the *Herald*, to demand that it be stopped.[264] Machray, though under pressure from Ainsworth, refused.[265] The controversy culminated in a meeting at the St Ermin's

Hotel at which Gaitskell accused Machray of ignorance of party policy and being influence by 'irresponsible elements' before making the mistake of referring to 'thoughtless pacifist behaviour'. Machray, who had an impressive war record, exploded: 'Call me what you like Hugh, but don't call me a pacifist.'[266] Under immense pressure, Machray contemplated resignation but stayed on.[267] The *Herald* did not entirely neglect non-political interests during this period. The second day of the row also saw it launch the *'Daily Herald* "Anita Ekberg" lookalike', seeking out the British girl with the greatest resemblance to the rather top-heavy (39.5–23–37 according to the *Herald*) Swedish film star.[268] The endless search for more women readers continued with the launch of new columnist 'Jenny Gaye' billed as 'newly married and still a little dreamy', delivering a chatty, faux-naif stream of consciousness about her husband:

> Called Peter – big and ginger and perfect bliss to be married to. But husbands are funny sometimes, aren't they? I've found that out already although I've only been married for 11 days and one hour and 33 minutes.[269]

Goodman recalls that Machray handled an occasionally though not exclusively, politically contentious staff – 'It was one of the jokes of Fleet Street that there were more Socialists on the *Express* than the *Herald*' – with great skill and shrewdness.[270] But his independence did not halt the slide. Losses continued to run at more than £300,000 a year – the *Herald* would lose just over £1m in the last three years of the decade.[271] Nineteen fifty-eight was, with a decline of 97,000 in average sale, proportionately the paper's worst year since the late 1920s.[272] The frustration for the *Herald* was that they appear to have been performing the basic task of any newspaper, giving readers what they want. Research in the late 1950s shows that, even if journalists were inclined to dismiss it as a boring paper, readers of the *Herald* were happier than those of any paper, with the *News Chronicle* second.[273] But they were being steadily culled by nature, and not replaced.

By 1960 Machray was petitioning for a further loosening of the party tie.[274] His view was cited in support by Odhams as they again pressed the General Council and proved much more successful in rewriting the *Herald*'s Clause Four than Hugh Gaitskell would be with the Labour Party's.[275] The new version read: 'Whilst reserving to the newspaper editorial freedom, the grantee will maintain the political and industrial integrity of the paper as an independent newspaper of the left.'[276] Having helped break the tie, Machray was replaced by John Beavan, formerly London editor of the *Manchester Guardian*.[277] Advertising rates were slashed from £15 to £10 per column inch, briefly giving the paper, now selling just over 1.4 million, the lowest rate per 1,000 circulation in Fleet Street.[278] At the same time Beavan, who declared 'You can no more have a working class newspaper than a working class refrigerator' pushed the paper upmarket in search of a new, more prosperous, readership.[279]

Foreign coverage was rediscovered, occupying the whole of page two where, big stories apart, it had been lucky to get a column in the 1950s.[280] Books, similarly woefully neglected throughout the entire postwar period, finally reappeared with Malcolm Muggeridge as chief reviewer.[281] Ballet and opera joined cinema and popular music on the arts pages.[282] Politically, the paper was once more aligned behind Gaitskell and the bomb, declaring: 'If people have no confidence that Labour puts the country's safety first, they will have no confidence in Labour ... If Labour follows Mr Cousins, the country will not follow Labour' as Frank Cousins, leader of the Transport and General Workers Union and a director of the paper, led a successful challenge to Gaitskell's defence policy at the 1960 TUC.[283] When Gaitskell lost again at the party conference, the *Herald* called for 'the sensible, responsible people in the Party ... to reassert their strength. Public opinion will be behind them.'[284] His 'Fight-and-fight again' speech at that conference, headlined 'GREAT GAITSKELL' and hailed by long-time fan Harold Hutchinson as 'the greatest personal achievement I have ever seen in politics' was said in the accompanying news story to have 'out of defeat ... snatched victory, a Dunkirk style victory'.[285]

The reasoning was that the brilliance of his speech had left him unchallengeable as party leader. It was left to Michael Foot to point out in his next column that Gaitskell had actually lost and that the cry 'we wuz robbed comes particularly ill from those in the Labour Party who made – and so long accepted without question – the rules and procedure according to which the Party made its great decision this week'.[286]

The establishment bias of the paper may have been the same, but the reporting was now different. Goodman, who made a wider-ranging, freer style of reporting a condition of accepting the post of industrial editor from Machray in 1958, was allowed to frankly describe the 'bitter division of opinion' at the TUC. [287] Manoeuvrings before the party conference induced the headline 'Split wide open'.[288] Days of minimising divisions, however serious, had gone the way of Socialist Realist industrial reporting. So too had automatic deference to labour establishment figures and institutions. The Amalgamated Engineering Union, which contrived to commit itself to vote both ways on separate resolutions on the bomb, and union leaders spoiling for a compromise were in receipt of a stinging rebuke which would hardly have been delivered by a tied paper: 'It is time union leaders realised they are not playing a private game of chess with block votes as the pieces ... There

IS a division ... which must be resolved one way or the other.'[289] A decade earlier Low had found that 'His stock depiction of the TUC as "an honest but simple-minded draught horse" ruffled feathers.'[290] Now Donald Zec, famous for the cartoon that brought the *Mirror* close to suppression in 1942, could take an idea from the simultaneous Olympics in Rome to draw Gaitskell, Cousins and AEU boss Carron complete with suitable symbols – CND for Cousins, a bomb for Gaitskell and Carron on both sides at once – on a shambolic victory rostrum.[291]

Like any newspaper, the *Herald* was always delighted to mix two longstanding interests where the opportunity occurred. Politics and photogenicity combined in the shape of a House of Commons secretary – 'Attractive dark-haired Betty Boothroyd, twice a Labour candidate' – off to the United States to work on John Kennedy's presidential campaign.[292] But it remained shaky on youthful tastes. Bing Crosby, arriving in London and saying 'They still seem to want me – but not the teenagers' or the break-up of the Crazy Gang were still bigger news than anybody they might want.[293] The review of 'Chain Gang', released simultaneously by Sam Cooke and Ronnie Carroll, spoke about young people, using the tone of a somewhat patronising anthropologist confronted with a deeply puzzling primitive people: 'It has all the obvious gimmicks ... body-shaking grunts and rattling effects.Yet even today's happy-go-lucky youngsters should realise, as they jig around their jukeboxes, that there's nothing amusing about chain gangs.'[294]

Odhams had hoped that the new approach and more competitive advertising rates would take sales back over 1.5 million, and eventually to two million.[295] It worked insofar as 1961 was the only year between 1950 and 1964 when *Herald* sales rose.[296] But the addition was only 6,000, which brought the total to 1.418 million.[297] The *Herald* was in any case bound to have picked up some of the readers disenfranchised when the *News Chronicle* was abruptly sold to its political antonym, the *Daily Mail*. The slide resumed, with 69,000 sales lost, in 1962.[298] Losses continued to accelerate out of control – £648,540 in 1960 and £786,000 in the 12 months to February 1962.[299] Beavan's relations with his staff were also difficult, partly because of a personal manner that belied strongly working-class origins. Goodman recalls:

He was a strange chap, pompous to an almost intolerable degree, with strange orotund mannerisms of speech. To his credit he tried to inject some quality journalism into the paper, and to some extent succeeded, but his relations with his staff were appalling. There was terrible tension and almost daily rows between Beavan, some journalists and the back bench.[300]

He had only been in office a few months when the *Herald* changed hands. Odhams were taken over by the Mirror Group. In commercial terms the *Herald* was a minor factor in the deal – both the Mirror and the Thomson group, the first company involved in talks with Odhams, were interested in their highly profitable magazines – the group had made £4m in 1960.[301] Sir Christopher Chancellor, chair of Odhams, admitted that they would not have touched the *Herald* with a barge-pole if it had been somebody else's property.[302] But it was an inescapable part of the deal. Gaitskell, Cousins and other labour leaders were drawn into the debate and political priorities determined the outcome. Gaitskell, a friend of Chancellor's, was initially inclined to support Odhams's preference for a merger with Thomson, but the outcome was effectively settled by Hugh Cudlipp's promise that the Mirror would maintain the *Herald* for a minimum of seven years.[303] It was, Cudlipp said later, the only time 'on which the man about to be hanged was given the privilege of selecting his own rope and specifying the time he should spend in the death cell before the definitive act'.[304]

The broad Labour preference for the Mirror was unsurprising. The *Daily Mirror* and its Sunday counterpart had been consistently and effectively pro-Labour since 1945. There was a fair case that if Hugh Cudlipp, whose achievements on both papers had given him the reputation of a popular press magician, could not sort out the *Herald*'s problems, then nobody could. Lord Thomson, a Canadian with an apparently insatiable appetite for newspapers, was known to lean to the right, although also to give his editors freedom.[305] Charles Leatherland remembered: 'He was a stranger to us. We knew the Mirror people.'[306] But as Thomson argued during the takeover battle, Odhams and Thomson were complementary companies. They competed in very few markets – in particular Thomson, though already owner of the *Sunday Times*, did not have a national daily.[307] Aside from the difficulties inherent in running the *Herald*, the Mirror Group would also be reluctant to do anything that affected their flagship daily.

Cudlipp took over as chairman and, while he said that 'nobody sane in publishing would have paid a penny to acquire the *Herald*', did his best to save it.[308] Beavan was an old friend, but was replaced in 1962 by another, Sydney Jacobson, political editor of the *Mirror*.[309] Leatherland remembered him as 'possibly the best editor we had in my time at the *Herald*', which included everyone back to Mellor.[310] Goodman agrees, saying,

> If there was a man Cudlipp trusted and regarded as a friend, it was Jacobson. He had a free hand, but he knew what Cudlipp wanted. The paper produced under Jacobson was probably as near to the intelligent left-of-centre daily as the *Herald* got in the last few years, and if he'd been given a minimum of five years, a lot of money – in

particular more journalists – and some patience, he might have saved it.[311]

That remains, like the possibility that Thomson, unfettered by the constraints of in-house competition, could have revived the paper's fortunes, one of the tantalising might-have-beens of the *Herald*'s final years. Still fettered by relative poverty – to have what was generally acknowledged as the best cuttings library in Fleet Street, presided over by a survivor of the Lansbury *Herald*, was little compensation for an undersized paper and the knowledge that 'if you were on a good story, you knew that the *Herald* would put in as much as it could, but that with the *Express*, *Mail* and *Mirror* pouring in resources you'd be up against it' – Jacobson and his team did their best.[312] Though an enthusiastic Gaitskell supporter, Jacobson was prepared to take a robust attitude to party ties – when Gaitskell threatened to attack the *Herald* at party conference for refusing to accept his line on the Common Market, he urged the party leader to do so as nothing could be better for the paper's circulation.[313]

Older readers were perhaps reassured by the continuing presence of familiar names like Ewer, fashion writer and artist Phyllis Stroudley, cartoonist Gilbert Wilkinson and motoring correspondent Tom Wisdom – who had been singled out for criticism in Maurice Webb's poll of movement *prominente* in 1937 but was still a familiar, immaculately dressed, cigarette-ash speckled figure among the motoring press more than a quarter of a century later.[314] Youth and its interests were finally considered newsworthy rather than subject for disbelieving scrutiny. There were still oddities. The *Herald* considered the impeccably upper-class Lady Longford, wife of Labour peer Frank, as someone worth quoting on Bank Holiday rioters in Hastings on the grounds that she was 'a mother of 8 and not surprisingly an expert on youth'.[315] But both the Beatles and the Rolling Stones were given front-page coverage in the space of three days in July 1964 and reviewer Michael Wale's comment that the Kinks' 'You Really Got Me Going' [sic] was the 'most way-out' hit yet at least suggested a reviewer dealing with something he recognised and understood.[316]

But the slide continued inexorably. In 1961 the Mirror Group, still relatively new owners, had told the Royal Commission that the *Herald* could be made self-supporting at a sale of 1.7 million.[317] In 1963, the average sale was almost 400,000 below that figure.[318] Advertising was still weakening. Curran notes that in 1955 the *Herald*'s share of national newspaper circulation and advertising revenue had been the same, 10.8 per cent. In 1964 its sales were 8.1 per cent of the total, but advertising had crashed to 3.5 per cent.[319] By mid 1963 the Mirror Group – now operating under the portentous title of the International Publishing Corporation (IPC) – had concluded that there was no way of saving the *Herald*. Cudlipp described it as 'a bloated, listless boa constrictor suffering from fatty degeneration of the heart, displaying the vital statistics of death as they are known and feared by any student of newspaper mortality'.[320] The name, director Ellis Birk would argue, was part of the problem – even if the *Herald* was no longer a tied paper, people thought it was.[321] Goodman concedes that there was something of a 'psychological hangover' among staff who had grown accustomed to the tie.[322] It would be better, concluded the IPC board, to transfer the seven-year pledge to a new title and make a fresh start. They put the idea to a clearly reluctant General Council, which cast around for alternative publishers – Thomson, The *Sunday Citizen* (*Reynolds News* dressed as lamb), Robert Maxwell and an ill-defined 'group of wealthy socialists' were all considered – but found nothing better than IPC on offer.[323]

The IPC proposal was for a new 'independent paper devised for the 1960s'.[324] The General Council continued to express its reluctance and at one point pulled out of negotiations in a dispute over the amount they would receive for their *Herald* shares.[325] Cecil King, asked by TUC General Secretary George Woodcock, to value their 49 per cent holding, had said 'zero', but was prepared to make a payment.[326] At this point the possible outcome was that the *Herald* would continue on a 'care and maintenance basis' until the end of the seven-year pledge, at which point, said IPC director Gibson, it was unlikely it would be selling even 600,000 copies daily.[327] This may have been exaggeration for negotiation purposes, but the possibility of continuing helpless decline was certainly not lost on the *Herald*'s long-suffering journalists, a group who as *The Journalist* noted had 'for the best part of a decade ... had to cope in a paper uncertain about its "image" and repeatedly trying to change'.[328] They appealed to the General Council not to jeopardise the relaunch in a row over a difference of £25,000.[329] On January 29 1964 the TUC agreed to accept £75,000 and the copyright to the *Daily Herald* title, which they hold to this day.[330]

Based on extensive market research, the new IPC paper, called the *Sun*, was sold to the world as 'the only newspaper born of the age we live in'.[331] Simon Jenkins is probably nearer the mark in assigning parentage to 'wishful thinking out of market research'.[332] Tony Benn greeted the first issue as 'appalling ... basically the same minus the *Herald* political content'.[333] A.C.H. Smith argues that 'apart from the title, very little had changed'.[334] It failed to hang on to even the *Herald*'s final circulation, and was soon losing money in quantities the *Herald* had never dreamt of.[335] In 1969 it was sold to Rupert Murdoch, who, adopting a formula and eventually politics diametrically opposite to those of the old *Herald,* would transform it into the dominant popular newspaper in Britain.[336]

The one attempt since to launch a dedicated left-of-centre national paper, the Manchester-based *News on Sunday*, shared the *Daily Citizen*'s achievement of raising an amount of money – £6.5 million – which was impressive by the standards of the left, but hopelessly inadequate for the national press.[337] It collapsed after seven chaotic, contentious months in 1987.[338] This was all in the future as the *Herald* ran through its final weeks, enthusiastically plugging its successor. The final issue appeared on 14 September 1964, 52 years and five months after the first. The leader, headlined 'See you all tomorrow' said:

This is not a wake. Not an occasion for more than a quick glance at the past ... what matters is tomorrow. And tomorrow can be a very bright day.

No newspaper has won more affection from its readers than the *Herald*. No newspaper has had a greater role to play in national affairs.

Life does not stand still. The *Herald* came into existence half a century ago to do a job. The job has been done.[339]

Conclusion

The race is not always to the swift, or the battle to the strong. But that's the way to bet.

Damon Runyon

So did the *Daily Herald* fail? The political balance is hard to assess. We lack a definitive view of how much notice people take of political advice proferred by newspapers. Martin Linton of the *Guardian*[1] and John Curtice of Strathclyde University, impeccably reputable commentators, have reached almost diametrically differing conclusions about the accuracy of the *Sun*'s notorious claim, after the 1992 General Election, that 'It was the Sun wot won it'.[2] Colin Seymour-Ure has noted that the bulk of media studies conventional wisdom has pointed to 'reinforcement and not change'.[3]

Hugh Dalton, who had no particular reason to commend the *Herald*, and Hannen Swaffer, both believed that by providing a reliable, trusted means of communication between leaders and rank-and-file it helped save Labour from total disintegration in 1931.[4] Wilfred Fienburgh argued a 'reinforcement' case for its contribution to the eventual triumph of 1945.[5] On the other hand it is worth noting the extent to which the *Herald* and Labour's fortunes were apparently inversely related. The paper struggled against the Liberal press while Labour was making huge electoral headway in the 1920s, and enjoyed its greatest circulation triumphs in the years immediately before and after the disastrous election of 1931; it was clearly outperformed by the *Mirror* in the lead up to the triumph of 1945 and forced into closure only weeks before the party returned to power in 1964. Only in the 1950s, when both Labour and the *Herald* struggled, did their fortunes run in parallel. With evidence so inconclusive, it is again worth noting Alan Lee's comment, related to the nineteenth-century press, but evidently applicable to this century, that: 'There are serious methodological ... problems involved in getting to know how communicated ideas and information affect their recipients, particularly if a problem is given a historical dimension.'[6]

The commercial and financial record is clearer. The *Herald*'s resounding failure is underlined by the sale to Odhams in 1929 and its eventual closure in 1964. Successful newspapers are neither sold, particularly when the vendors are the TUC and the sale is for practical purposes a commercial privatisation, nor closed. Both actions came after all the possibilities of the previous model of production had been progressively exhausted. The circulation history is one of almost ceaseless decline. Only times of peak political excitement in the 1920s and the spectacular circulation wars of 1931–33 saw *Herald* sales rising. It was a remarkably consistent loss-maker, profitable only under the abnormal conditions of the Second World War.

There is little doubt that the *Guardian* was right when in 1964 it described the *Herald* as a victim of poverty – 'Its own and that of its readers'.[7] The problems described by Fyfe in his 'Ragged man' speech to the 1924 Labour conference recurred alarmingly during the 1950s.[8] His complaints that the paper was undersized and staffed by journalists on lower wages working with more limited resources than those on rival papers, were echoed by his successors in the last decade of the *Herald*'s existence. Underfunding presents newspapers with almost insuperable problems. It subjects them to day-to-day crisis management, with decisions dictated by immediate survival needs. Strategic thinking goes out of the window. Employees live with permanent insecurity knowing, in a labour-intensive industry, that cost cuts are likely to mean jobs lost. Where cuts may be essential in the short-term, their long-term impact on competitive prospects can be extremely damaging. The late 1923 economies that kept the *Herald* in being, but ended a short-lived attempt to match competitors' news services, exemplify this. Less acute, but ultimately as harmful is the problem of knowing, or at least suspecting, what the paper should do and being unable to afford it. The paper may not be in immediate danger of closure, but operating at subsistence level leaves it unable to raise its sights from survival to real progress, incapable of funding the improvements necessary to competitive success. This affliction finished movement ownership in the late 1920s, only to reassert itself in the 1950s with Odhams disinclined to pour magazine profits into their highly unprofitable daily paper.

The *Guardian*'s point about readers' poverty is equally significant. Here again the 1950s echoed the 1920s. In the earlier decade the problem was subjective analysis by advertisers, excluding the paper from the schedules. By the 1950s quantitative analysis was firmly dominant, but the *Herald*'s declining, ageing and heavily working-class readership – *Guardian* television columnist Nancy Banks-Smith, once a *Herald* journalist, has recalled being told that the paper was written for 'the Durham miner' – lost its attraction for advertisers once the abolition of newspaper rationing allowed them to advertise where they wished and commercial television had opened up new possibilities.[9] Proof of the importance of readership profile in the highly polarised British market is that the *Herald* closed with a readership double that of *The Times, Financial Times* and *Guardian* combined.[10] The argument that the successive loss of the two left-of-centre popular dailies, the *News Chronicle* and *Herald* is proof of advertising industry bias is, however, made less convincing by the similar fate in 1971 of the the ultra-Tory *Daily Sketch.*

Commercial television, which also induced livelier news coverage by the BBC, hit the *Herald* journalistically. Television news was less of a worry for the heavy papers – which provide more detailed reporting than television can possibly match – or the tabloids, with their entertainment and human interest agendas. Broadsheet popular papers faced a competitor which reported news in very much the same way as themselves – brightly and concisely, but with serious matters treated seriously – with the addition of moving pictures within hours rather than stills the next day. Once so dominant, the broadsheet popular sector no longer exists. The *Herald* and *News Chronicle* are dead while the *Express* and, to a slightly lesser extent, the *Mail* have been forced downmarket and into tabloidisation.

The *Herald* was to a great extent the victim of circumstances, not so much the Miracle as the Ragged Man of Fleet Street, but the question asked of any ragged man is how far he is responsible for his own plight. The most successful national dailies have been run by proprietors and managements whose overriding priority is the paper. For the TUC and Labour Party the *Herald* was a means to an end, its fortunes subordinate to political and industrial objectives. For Odhams it appears first to have been a means of keeping their printing presses at full capacity, then a drain on profits from their magazines and the *People.* Deeply unimaginative publishers, they never outgrew their roots in printing. They could innovate on the production side, to briefly stunning effect in 1930 with the relaunched *Herald.* In 1960 when it was the first paper to run a full editorial page in colour, on Princess Margaret's wedding.[11] But once shorn of the insurance and free gifts of the 1930s, they had no editorial idea how to revitalise the *Herald.* The word which recurs in descriptions of their approach is 'imitative'. Whether it was Southwood hankering after the *Express* approach in the 1930s, his successors seeking posthumous guidance from their dead leader at seances after 1946, or the *Herald* attempting to adapt *Mirror* design to its broadsheet format after 1951, Odhams looked to imitate others rather than develop ideas of their own.

The question of what makes a successful paper is a difficult one, but the historic evidence is that papers which do well competitively invariably have a distinctive self-confident editorial identity. Contrast the apparent omnipotence of the postwar *Daily Mirror,* with the same title under the onslaught of the *Sun* in the 1970s and after. The *Mirror* was, in Colin Seymour-Ure's wonderfully apt phrase, 'literally outstripped by the *Sun'*.[12] While not wanting to follow its rival downmarket, it was fearful of the consequences of not doing so. Inevitably it did so half-heartedly and with little conviction. There are strong elements both of chicken-and-egg and of retrospection in this. A strong identity is of little use if it repels rather than attracts readers, while success breeds confidence and failure has the opposite effect. But there are no prizes for equivocation. A strong and distinctive identity can counterbalance apparent competitive disadvantage. Both the *Financial Times* and the *Guardian* have been confident enough of their distinctive appeal to stay out of the price wars initiated by *The Times* in the mid 1990s and appear to have been justified in their faith. Though less successful, the *Herald's* 'Miracle of Fleet Street' survival when it went to 2d in 1920 has something of this quality.

It is doubtful whether the *Herald* really possessed such an identity after the Lansbury years. While moving away from the exclusively political preoccupations of the Lansbury *Herald*, the later versions showed a marked lack of adaptability, whether to the human interest story in the 1920s or the music trends of the 1950s. While it adopted many of the norms of popular press reporting after 1930, these cohabited with rather than being integrated with serious political and industrial coverage, giving it a peculiar hybrid quality epitomised by covers juxtaposing Arthur Henderson with Carole Lombard or Pierre Laval with kidnapped dancers. Content surveys show that the *Herald* was always more serious-minded than its popular competitors, but it is a mistake to automatically conflate 'serious' with 'quality'. The *Herald* should have been strongest on political and industrial coverage, but there is evidence of besetting weakness. Lloyd George was being politically malicious when he jibed that 'Bevin controlled the *Herald*, so to know what was going on in the Labour Party you had to read the *News Chronicle*', but he had a point.[13] Official status compromised the *Herald's* political journalism. It might lead to the suppression of stories of serious interest, such as Morrison's London Transport plans in 1931 or Attlee's intention to retire and back Hugh Gaitskell in 1955. It led to the passive, initiativeless reporting of General Elections noted in the Nuffield election surveys.

Geoffrey Goodman points to a tradition of dully unimaginative industrial coverage – invariably quoting officials uncritically, reporting the president's speech at every conference and failing to make anything of background or colour. This officially-derived one-dimensional picture of the world of labour ironically contrasted with consistently good coverage of capitalism in its financial columns.[14] It is also a mistake to conflate 'political' merely with reports of speeches, resolutions, votes and legislation. As former *Herald* foreign correspondent Roger Matthews noted in 1956, and many commentators –

most recently John Pilger – have pointed out since, there was plenty of politics in the *Mirror*.[15] So too the *Sun* in the 1980s and 1990s, but these papers expressed politics in personal, human interest, terms. As Swaffer argued in his early 1930s critique of the *Herald's* journalism: 'We must dig down and extract the fundamental issue from every story ... There is a basis of drama, colour and movement in every wage-fight, in every political issue. The invention is always much easier to describe than the inventor. But the world wants the invention told and explained in terms of the inventor; the war in terms of the soldier.'[16]

The *Herald* was rarely good at this. And being tied to an official policy deprived it of what Francis Williams termed 'the priceless journalistic gift of surprise'.[17] Yet predictability can be leavened with passion. When former editor of *The Times* Wickham Steed mused: 'What does the public want ... as a rule it wants emotions', he was thinking of human interest stories, but his view can apply equally to political coverage.[18] The Lansbury *Herald's* Poplar coverage abounds in excitement, engagement and commitment – in short in emotions – that can reach and exhilarate the reader of microfilm copies three-quarters of a century later. Just as Poplar councillor John Scurr's political trajectory parallels the paper's in the 1920s, so does the longest *Herald* career of all, W.N. Ewer's half-century of service, follow its political development with striking precision. Once a fervent communist, he moved through disillusionment to rigidly orthodox labourism. As Goodman remembers: 'He was in no way a figure of fun. His views were pretty rigid by then, but you had to remember that this was a chap that had interviewed Trotsky on the steps of the Smolny Institute. You had to regard that with respect.'[19]

The *Herald* could probably have done with a little less respectability. It had, as A.C.H. Smith noted, an establishment voice.[20] This is hardly surprising. The Labour elite were a kind of establishment. But the most successful popular papers have been members of the awkward squad, vocally conveying popular grievance but combining this with an ability to both excite and entertain readers – it is no fluke that 'It's just a laugh' is the classic *Sun* reader's response to the paper's excesses. The *Herald* counselled respectability, restraint and discipline. This may, perhaps, be the way to win elections, but it is no way to sell newspapers. The *Herald* was rarely likely to make anyone laugh and the excitement that once animated men like Scurr and Ewer was rarely recaptured after 1922. By defining itself in political terms, and defining 'politics' in terms of direct electoral or industrial activity, the *Herald* undoubtedly limited its appeal. John Benson and other historians have argued that, while the politically active and the industrially militant have commanded historians' attention, they were always a minority.[21]

As ever, the *Herald* was reflecting the movement it served. Geoff Mulgan of the Demos think-tank has noted that 'It is a shame that British politics is so weak on culture. In almost every other European country politics and culture are interwoven ... Every political movement needs a soundtrack.'[22] The most acute atomisation of the consequences of this for labour, and by implication the *Herald,* was offered in the late 1920s by Egon Wertheimer, London correspondent of *Vorwarts,* the German Social Democratic Party's equivalent of the *Herald.* He contrasted the countercultural SPD, where membership implied significant personal commitment and admission to a network of leisure, cultural and sporting bodies linked to the party, with Labour's absence of any such extra-political culture.[23] He argued: 'Separated by no class barriers from the mental and spiritual concepts of capitalism which would otherwise have given birth to an exclusively proleterian way of life and morality, and deep-rooted in natural religious tradition, the Labour Party has never been able to make a clean breakaway from the capitalist culture.'[24] This limited the *Herald*'s ability to offer much that was really distinctive, outside the narrowly-defined area of politics. It ensured that labour supporters and members felt few inhibitions about buying capitalist newspapers, if these served their needs better. It is worth noting the movement leaders who in the 1950s were loudest in their condemnation of the 'disloyalty' of the rank and file to the paper were Vincent Tewson and Tom O'Brien, who were so little rooted in counterculture that they had accepted knighthoods.[25]

There may have been opportunities to avert the fate of 1964. While the possibility of Thomson beating the Mirror in 1961 and offering the *Herald* resources later put into *The Times* and *Sunday Times* tantalises, the real missed chance was 1957. It is possible that the lack of imagination that characterised both sets of proprietors – Cadbury's, Odhams and the TUC – would have destroyed the prospects of a merged *Chronicle–Herald.* Cadbury's were as cheapskate in their management style as Odhams. Labour and the TUC were still determined to hang on to the party tie. Both groups quite reasonably shied away from the unpleasant choices, the rationalisation and the job losses that follow when two papers merge into one. But a merged paper with an initial sale of close to three million could not have been squeezed out of the advertising market in the same way that the *Herald,* a little above one and a half million and the *News Chronicle,* somewhere below, were. It might have developed into a left-of-centre daily occupying much the same space in the popular market as the *Guardian* now does in the quality press, where it commands the allegiance, one suspects, of numerous children and grandchildren of *Herald* and *News Chronicle* readers made upwardly mobile by higher education and the expansion of the liberal professions. Instead both papers were dead within seven years, permanently skewing the balance of the national press.

It is easy to deride the *Herald*. The values it espoused are now deeply unfashionable, even within the party it was created to support. There was a rather earnest decency about it, epitomised in the way the 'Traveller' went around the country collecting political opinions at the same time as its competitors were handing out money. It was commercially unsuccessful and its political effect unmeasurable. It was too often dull and constrained by the limitations of the movement it supported. So was it all a 52-year waste of time, money and energy? Yes, provided one is convinced that the labour movement's parallel struggles have been futile, that political activity is pointless and that the current structure of the British national press represents the ideal. But on any broader view, the balance sheet looks much better. Labour has aimed to create a better world founded on decent, humane values. The *Herald* sustained it in that attempt. Within the national press it was a countervailing force, offering an alternative to the know-nothingism, authoritarianism, crude social Darwinism and xenophobia which have pervaded the bulk of the popular press throughout this century. It was not the only paper to do so. The *News Chronicle* and, before it was overtaken by the twin traumas of *Sun* competition and Robert Maxwell, the *Mirror,* also fought these battles.

No paper, however, was more consistent than the *Herald* in offering a voice to those who are excluded, derided or both by the bulk of the mass-circulation press. Strikers, the Invergordon mutineers, foreigners whose viewpoints and interests did not necessarily coincide with those of British policy or capital – all were assured of fair treatment in at least one paper. Had the *Herald* survived until the late 1990s, its ingrained officialism might have limited the enthusiasm of its response to the long unofficial battle by sacked Liverpool dockers. But it would not, unlike today's popular press, have allowed their struggle to go unreported. Its values and aspirations were those historian Kenneth Morgan ascribed to Swansea, the city which in 1936 had the highest concentration of *Herald* readers in the country: 'A tolerant and sophisticated people ... using political power to create a decent and durable community'.[26]

Graham Cleverly's contention that the British popular press has yet to find a successful alternative to the entrepreneurial-capitalist model holds as true today as when he first wrote it in the mid 1970s.[27] But that does not mean that there is no alternative. Have we to assume that a national press which an Irish observer once defined as 'four of the best papers in the world, and five of the worst', and excludes all but the ultra-rich, is both inevitable and immutable?[28] If nothing else, the years since the *Herald*'s demise should have induced a healthy distrust of anyone who proclaims in any field, that 'there is no alternative'.

The *Herald* made a lot of mistakes. It was often confused in its journalistic purposes. In the 1950s its unique selling point was politics, and in the absence of a mass counterculture that was never going to be enough. It could never make up its mind whether it was a hard-nosed popular paper or a serious political daily. As both Swaffer and Goodman noted, it failed to find a way of linking the two approaches in a coherent whole. It often fell, in Maxton's terms, between horses – between commercial and political objectives. But the one mistake it never made was to assume that the world is unchangeable. The *Herald*'s struggle was to ensure that change should make it fairer, more equal and more humane. It lost more battles than it won, but the struggle was, and is, well worth it.

Notes

KEY TO NOTES

AM rep: Advertising Manager's report.
CM rep: Circulation Manager's report.
DH: *Daily Herald*.
DH dir: *Daily Herald* directors.
DLB: *Dictionary of Labour Biography*.
DNB: *Dictionary of National Biography*.
EBDH: Ernest Bevin papers, Warwick University: *Daily Herald* file.
Ed rep: Editor's report.
GM rep: General Manager's report.
JRMPRO: James Ramsay MacDonald papers, Public Record Office, Kew.
LPDH: Labour Party *Daily Herald* files, National Museum of Labour History, Manchester. Number refers to number of item in file.
LPEC: Labour Party, Executive Committee.
LPRAC: Labour Party, Report of the Annual Conference.
NPD: Newspaper Press Directory.
NUJ: National Union of Journalists.
NW: *Newspaper World*.
RCP: Royal Commission on the Press.
RPTUC: Report of the proceedings of the Trades Union Congress.
TUC: Trades Union Congress files, Modern Records Centre, Warwick University. Number refers to number of file.
TUCFC/FGPC: Trades Union Congress, Finance/Finance and General Purposes Committee.
TUCGC: Trades Union Congress, General Council.
UP: University Press.
VHPCo dir: Victoria House Printing Company directors.
WPN: *World's Press News*.

All books published in London unless otherwise specified.

INTRODUCTION

1. A.J.P. Taylor, *English History 1914–45*, Penguin 1970, p 191.
2. Justin Wintle and Richard Kenin, *The Penguin Concise Dictionary of Biographical Quotation*, Penguin 1981, p 399.
3. Francis Williams, *Nothing So Strange*, Cassell 1970.

4. Matthew Engel, *Tickle the Public*, Gollancz 1996, p 59.
5. Royal Commission on the Press 1947–49, Minutes of evidence 26th day, 18.3.48, HMSO, Cmnd 7416, paragraph 8660.
6. Ibid.
7. David Ayerst, *The Manchester Guardian: Biography of a Newspaper*, Cornell UP, Ithaca, New York 1971, pp 627–9.
8. DH 2.7.57; Peter Chippindale and Chris Horrie, *Stick It Up Your Punter!*, Mandarin 1992, p 12.
9. Ivon Asquith, 'The Structure, Ownership and Control of the Press, 1780–1855', in George Boyce, James Curran and Pauline Wingate (eds) *Newspaper History: From the 17th Century to the Present Day*, Constable 1978, p 109.
10. James Curran and Jean Seaton, *Power Without Responsibility*, Fontana 1981, p 47.
11. Ibid, p 47; David Goodhart and Patrick Wintour, *Eddie Shah and the Newspaper Revolution*, Coronet 1986, p 145.
12. Arthur Schlesinger Jr, *Robert Kennedy and His Times*, Futura 1979, p 952.
13. Philip Snowden 'Why Labour Papers Fail', *Sell's World Press* 1919, pp 23–4.
14. Ethel Bentham, 'Memorandum on the *Daily Herald*', 17.9.25, TUC files ref 789.1; LPDH 462.
15. Curran and Seaton, *Power*, p 79.
16. Francis Williams, *Dangerous Estate*, Longman 1957, p 182.
17. K. Hudgell (*Daily Mirror* company secretary) to author, 12.5.81.
18. Joel Wiener, 'Sources for the Study of Newspapers' in Laurel Brake, Aled Jones and Lionel Madden (eds) *Investigating Victorian Journalism*, Macmillan 1990, p 162.

CHAPTER 1: THE FIRST *DAILY HERALD*, 1912–21

1. W.N. Ewer, *The Miracle of Fleet Street*, syndicated (unpublished?) feature in *Daily Mirror* library, 1949, p 1.
2. Reginald Pound and Geoffrey Harmsworth, *Northcliffe*, Cassell 1959, p 196.
3. James A. Epstein, 'Feargus O'Connor and the *Northern Star*', *International Review of Social History*, vol 21, no 1, 1976, pp 80, 86–7.
4. Curran and Seaton, *Power*, p 53.
5. Stanley Harrison, *Poor Men's Guardians*, Lawrence and Wishart 1974, pp 141–9.
6. Curran and Seaton, *Power*, pp 53–4.
7. James Curran, 'Capitalism and Control of the Press 1800–1975', in James Curran, Michael Gurevitch and Janet Woollacott (eds) *Mass Communication and Society*, Edward Arnold 1977, pp 196–213.
8. Deian Hopkin, 'The Left-Wing Press and the New Journalism', in Joel H Wiener (ed.) *Papers for the Millions: The New Journalism in Britain 1850–1914*, Greenwood, Westport, Connecticut 1988, pp 226–30.

9. Alan Lee, *Origins of the Popular Press in England 1855–1914*, Croom Helm 1976, p 115.
10. Harrison, *Poor Men's Guardians*, p 168.
11. Edward Mortimer, *The Rise of the French Communist Party*, Faber and Faber 1974, p 21; Dafin Todorov, *Freedom Press: The Development of the Progressive Press in Western Europe and the USA*, International Organisation of Journalists, Prague 1980, pp 63–7; Elliott Shore, 'Selling Socialism: *The Appeal to Reason* and the Radical Press in Turn of the Century America', in *Media, Culture and Society*, vol 7, no 2, 1985, pp 167–8.
12. Vernon Lidke, *The Alternative Culture: Socialist Labour in Imperial Germany*, Oxford UP 1985, p 141; W.L. Guttsman, *The German Social Democratic Party 1875–1933*, George Allen and Unwin 1981, pp 131,172–3; Alex Hall, *Scandal, Sensation and Social Democracy: The SPD Press and Wilhelmine Germany 1890–1914*, Cambridge UP 1977, pp 31–9.
13. Ibid.
14. Colin Seymour-Ure 'The Press and the Party System Between the Wars', in Gillian Peele and Chris Cook (eds) *The Politics of Reappraisal*, Macmillan 1975, p 244 .
15. Ibid, p 236.
16. Ibid, p 232.
17. D.L. LeMahieu, *A Culture for Democracy*, Clarendon, Oxford 1975, p 111.
18. Ibid, p 23.
19. Ibid, p 25.
20. James Curran, Angus Douglas and Gary Whannell, 'The Political Economy of the Human Interest Story', in Anthony Smith (ed.) *Newspapers and Democracy*, MIT Press, Cambridge, Massachusetts 1980, pp 288–316.
21. LeMahieu, *A Culture*, pp 27, 69.
22. Ibid, pp 28–9.
23. Ibid, p 18.
24. DH 1.12.19.
25. Stephen Koss, *The Rise and Fall of the Popular Press in Britain: Volume 2: The Twentieth Century*, Hamish Hamilton 1984, pp 155–6.
26. Bob Holton, '*Daily Herald* v *Daily Citizen* 1912–15', *International Review of Social History*, vol 19, 1974, p 349; RPTUC (1907) pp 162–3, (1908) p 86–9.
27. Adrian Smith, *The New Statesman: Portrait of a Political Weekly 1913–31*, Frank Cass 1996, pp 39–43.
28. Henry Pelling, *A Short History of the Labour Party*, Macmillan 1961, pp 18–19.
29. Ibid, p 18.
30. Tomichi Ichikawa, *The Daily Citizen 1912–15: A Study of the First Labour Daily Newspaper in Britain*, M Phil thesis, University of Wales, Aberystwyth 1985 (unpublished) pp 11–19.
31. John Saville, 'C.W. Bowerman', DLB vol 5, p 31.

32. George Lansbury, *The Miracle of Fleet Street*, Victoria House 1925, p 44; Raymond Postgate, *Daily Herald: Analysis*, unpublished (1923?), in G.D.H. Cole papers, Nuffield College, Oxford, 1911 section, pp 1, 3.

33. Lansbury, *Miracle*, pp 44–5; Postgate, *Analysis*, 1911, pp 1, 3.

34. Lansbury, *Miracle*, p 47; Raymond Postgate, *A Life of George Lansbury*, Longman 1951, p 136.

35. Circular to party secretaries from *Daily Herald* Management Committee 22.7.11, Bryan papers, London School of Economics, vol 2b (ii) item 4.

36. Prospectus from *Daily Herald* Printing and Publishing Company 4.7.11, Bryan papers, vol 2b (ii) item 5.

37. Prospectus, 4.7.11; Postgate, *Lansbury*, p 136.

38. Postgate, *Lansbury*, p 136.

39. Smith, *New Statesman*, p 39.

40. Lansbury, *Miracle*, p 10.

41. Postgate, *Analysis*, 1912–14, p 3.

42. George Slocombe, *The Tumult and the Shouting*, Heinemann 1936, p 32.

43. Rowland Kenney, *Westering*, Dent 1939, pp 174–5.

44. Ibid, p 175.

45. Ibid, p 179.

46. Slocombe, *Tumult*, p 30.

47. Kenney, *Westering*, pp 179–80; Lansbury, *Miracle*, pp 31–2; Frank Harris, *My Life and Loves*, W.H. Allen 1925.

48. Kenney, *Westering*, p 180; Lansbury, *Miracle*, pp 31, 35; *The Labour Who's Who 1927*, Labour Publishing Company, p 190; WPN 25.1.32.

49. Slocombe, *Tumult*, pp 32–3; Kenney, *Westering*, p 190–1.

50. George Lansbury, *My Life*, Constable 1928, p 142; *Miracle*, pp 13–16; Buxton to Lansbury 28.5.13, Lansbury Papers, London School of Economics, vol 7, item 50; Holton, 'Herald v Citizen', p 367.

51. Slocombe, *Tumult*, p 32.

52. Lansbury, *Miracle*, pp 11, 157–8.

53. Postgate, *Analysis*, 1912–14, pp 3, 4.

54. Lansbury, *Miracle*, pp 12–13.

55. Ibid, p 14.

56. Kenney, *Westering*, pp 179–80.

57. Postgate, *Analysis*, 1912–14, p 3.

58. Ibid, p 6.

59. Postgate, *Lansbury*, p 138.

60. Lansbury, *Miracle*, p 38.

61. Ibid, p 33; Postgate, *Analysis*, 1912–14, pp 5–17; *Lansbury*, p 138.

62. Lansbury, *My Life*, p 175.

63. Postgate, *Analysis*, 1912–14, p 14.

64. Lansbury, *Miracle*, p 34.

65. Postgate, *Analysis*, 1912–14, p 6.

66. Ibid, p 1; Lansbury, *Miracle*, pp 89–90.

67. Kenney, *Westering*, pp 181, 190; *Labour Who's Who 1927*, p 65, Francis Meynell, *My Lives*, Random House, New York 1971, p 112.

68. Postgate, *Analysis*, 1912–14, pp 3–4.
69. Kenney, *Westering*, p 192.
70. Ibid, p 191; Lansbury, *Miracle*, p 33; Postgate, *Analysis*, 1912–14, p 4; Martin Walker, *Daily Sketches: A Cartoon History of Twentieth Century Britain*, Frederick Muller 1978, p 12.
71. Postgate, *Analysis*, 1912–14, p 4; Walker, *Sketches*, p 7; Colin Seymour-Ure and Jim Schoff, *David Low*, Secker and Warburg 1985, p 148.
72. John Jensen, *A Sort of Bird of Freedom: Will Dyson 1880–1938*, University of Kent 1996, pp 9–12.
73. Walker, *Sketches*, p 7.
74. Lansbury, *Miracle*, pp 32–35, 75–85; *My Life*, p 141; Slocombe, *Tumult*, p 36; Postgate, *Analysis*, 1912–14, p 17.
75. Ewer, *Miracle*, p 2.
76. Postgate, *Lansbury*, p 141.
77. Lansbury, *Miracle*, p 87 (House of pretence); Postgate, *Lansbury*, p 140 (War that matters).
78. Lansbury, *Miracle*, p 55.
79. Postgate, *Analysis*, 1912–14, p 7.
80. Lansbury, *Miracle*, p 34; *My Life*, p 178.
81. Slocombe, *Tumult*, p 37.
82. John Saville, 'Gould, Gerard (1885–1936)', DLB vol 7, pp 96–7.
83. Slocombe, *Tumult*, p 37; Margaret Cole (ed.), *Beatrice Webb Diaries 1912–24*, Longmans 1952, entries for 8.3.14 (p 21), 3.5.14 (p 24).
84. Margaret Cole, 'Mellor, William 1888–1942', DLB vol 4, pp 123–6.
85. Kenney, *Westering*, p 11; Ewer, *Miracle*, p 2.
86. Postgate, *Analysis*, p 7; Lansbury, *Miracle*, p 14.
87. Lansbury, *Miracle*, p 35.
88. Slocombe, *Tumult*, p 36.
89. Cole, *Webb Diaries 1912–24*, entry for 3.5.14 (p 24).
90. Keith Harding, 'The Co-Operative Commonwealth: Ireland, Larkin and the *Daily Herald*' in S. Yeo (ed.) *New Views of Co-Operation*, Routledge 1988, pp 91–2; Ichikawa, *Daily Citizen*, p 30.
91. Ichikawa, *Daily Citizen*, p 11.
92. Ibid, pp 21–3.
93. Hopkin, 'Left-Wing Press' pp 236–7.
94. Ichikawa, *Daily Citizen*, pp 47–9, 54; *Sell's World Press*, 1919, pp 84–5.
95. Holton, '*Herald* v *Citizen*', p 363.
96. Kenney, *Westering*, p 190.
97. Cole, *Webb Diaries 1912–24*, entry for 22.4.14 (p 23).
98. Holton, '*Herald* v *Citizen*', p 361.
99. Ibid, p 362.
100. Ibid, p 362.
101. Ibid, p 362.
102. Lansbury, *Miracle*, p 96.
103. Postgate, *Lansbury*, p 149.
104. Postgate, *Analysis*, 1912–14, p 13.
105. Holton, '*Herald* v *Citizen*', pp 374–5.

106. Postgate, *Analysis*, 1912–14, p 5; Cole, *Webb Diaries 1912–24*, entry for 22.4.14 (p 23).
107. Ewer, *Miracle*, p 2.
108. Ibid, p 2.
109. Holton, '*Herald* v *Citizen*', p 370.
110. Ibid, p 372.
111. Postgate, *Analysis*, 1914–16, p 20.
112. Henderson to Allen 11.6.15, quoted in Martin Gilbert, *Plough My Own Furrow: The Story of Lord Allen of Hurtwood as Told Through His Writings and Correspondence*, Longman 1965, p 33.
113. Postgate, *Analysis*, 1912–14, p 5.
114. Ibid, p 5; Lansbury, *Miracle*, p 16.
115. Postgate, *Analysis*, 1914–16, pp 21–3.
116. Ibid, 1917–19, p 28; Meynell, *My Lives*, pp 107–8.
117. Lansbury, *Miracle*, pp 102–56.
118. F.M. Leventhal, *The Last Dissenter: H.N. Brailsford and His World*, Clarendon, Oxford 1985, p 142.
119. Lansbury, *Miracle*, p 16.
120. Ibid, pp 58–64, 113–5.
121. Postgate, *Analysis*, 1917–19, p 29; LeMahieu, *A Culture*, p 208.
122. Circular from DH Trade Union Committee to executive officers and members of the trade union movement 29.11.19, LPDH 1.
123. Lansbury to Bevin 5.11.19, Ernest Bevin papers, Warwick University EBDH 5.
124. Ernest Bevin, 'The Written Word: Ways and Means', manuscript of article for DH, n.d., EBDH 1.
125. Lansbury, *Miracle*, p 37; Postgate, *Lansbury*, p 186–7.
126. WPN 1.8.29; Lansbury to Hodges 11.3.21, Miners Federation of Great Britain, *Annual Volume of Proceedings*, 1921. MFGB executive 17.3.21, item no 4.
127. WPN 5.9, 14.11.29. *Labour Who's Who*, 1927, p 24.
128. John and Mary Postgate, *A Stomach for Dissent: The Life of Raymond Postgate 1896–1971*, Keele University Press 1994, p 107.
129. Ibid, pp 110–11.
130. 'Felix Boyne' (W.J. Ryan), *Fleet Street in Twilight*, Selwyn and Blount 1923, p 48.
131. Postgate, *Analysis*, 1919–23, pp 13–25, 40–44.
132. Jensen, *Dyson*, p 23; Walker, *Sketches*, p 84–5.
133. Postgate, *Lansbury*, p 188.
134. Tom Driberg, '*Swaff*': *The Life and Times of Hannen Swaffer*, MacDonald and Jane's 1974, pp 130–2.
135. Lansbury, *My Life*, pp 223–64; Cole, *Webb Diaries 1912–24*, entry for 28.3.20 (p 177).
136. Lansbury, *Miracle*, pp 121–6; Postgate, *Lansbury*, p 187.
137. DH 19.2.21.
138. Lansbury, *Miracle*, pp 65–6.
139. Henry Pelling, *A History of British Trade Unionism*, Pelican 1965, p 262.
140. Henry Hamilton Fyfe, *Sixty Years of Fleet Street*, W.H. Allen 1949, p 192.

141. Evelyn Sharp, *Unfinished Adventure*, Bodley Head 1933, p 176.
142. Christopher Andrew, *Secret Service*, Sceptre 1986, pp 385–8.
143. Postgate, *Lansbury*, p 196.
144. Maurice Cowling, *The Impact of Labour*, Cambridge UP 1971, p 35; Bill Schwarz, *Constitutionalism and Extra-Parliamentary Action*, Centre for Contemporary Studies, Birmingham University, occasional paper no 75, 1984, p 55.
145. Gerry W. Reynolds and Tony Judge, *The Night the Police Went on Strike*, Weidenfeld and Nicolson 1968, pp 137, 149–50.
146. Hugh Clegg, *A History of British Trade Unions Since 1889: Vol II, 1911–33*, Oxford UP 1985, p 292.
147. Postgate, *Lansbury*, p 209.
148. Andrew Williams, *Labour and Russia*, Manchester UP 1989, p 8.
149. Postgate, *Analysis*, 1919–23, p 2.
150. Cowling, *Impact of Labour*, pp 30–44.
151. DH 16.4.20; Lansbury, *Miracle*, pp 67–9.
152. Postgate, *Analysis*, 1919–23, p 3.
153. Statement to TUC Parliamentary Committee Jan 1920, LPDH 6.
154. Lansbury, *Miracle*, p 4.
155. Ibid, p 18.
156. LPRAC 1920, p 175.
157. Circular from *Daily Herald* Trade Union Committee 29.11.19, LPDH 1.
158. Briefing document for Bevin for 1920 TUC, EBDH 14.
159. Postgate, *Lansbury*, p 221.
160. Ibid; Postgate, *Analysis*, 1919–23, p 4.
161. Seymour-Ure, *Press and Party System*, p 237.
162. Postgate, *Lansbury*, p 211.
163. James Curran, 'Advertising as a Patronage System', in H. Christian (ed.) *Sociology of Journalism and the Press*, Sociological Review monograph no 29, University of Keele 1980, p 76.
164. Ibid, p 75.
165. Ibid, p 75.
166. Ibid, pp 76–81.
167. Postgate, *Analysis*, 1919–23, p 5.
168. NW 23.9.22.
169. NW 23.9.22.
170. NW 18.3.22.
171. Postgate, *Lansbury*, p 185.
172. Memo from DH Trade Union Committee 29.11.19, LPDH 1; Report of finance sub-committee to DH board 2.6.27, TUC 788.5.
173. Postgate, *Lansbury*, p 210.
174. Ibid, p 211.
175. Ibid, p 211.
176. Ibid p 212; Meynell, *My Lives*, pp 120–2; Lansbury, *Miracle*, pp 140–50.
177. Postgate, *Lansbury*, p 213; Meynell, *My Lives*, pp 121–2.
178. Postgate, *Lansbury*, p 213; Meynell, *My Lives*, p 122.
179. Postgate, *Lansbury*, p 213.
180. Ibid, p 213; Meynell, *My Lives*, p 123.

181. Meynell, *My Lives*, p 123–4.
182. Postgate, *Lansbury*, p 213; Ewer, *Miracle*, p 4.
183. Ewer, *Miracle*, p 4.
184. Ibid, p 4.
185. DH Board Statement 6.9.21, LPDH 17.
186. NW 22.10.21.
187. Seymour-Ure, 'Press and Party', p 248.
188. NW 25.3, 23.4.22.
189. NW 2.9.22.
190. NW 12.11.21, 23.12.22.
191. NW 11.2, 15.7.22.
192. NW 24.6, 15.8.22 (News), 29.7. 22 (Chronicle).
193. Report on DH financial position 4.1.22 LPDH 47.
194. DH Board 6.9.21 LPDH 17.
195. DH Board 6.9.21 LPDH 17.
196. DH 17.10.21.
197. DH 19.11.21.
198. DH 2.1.22, Lansbury, *Miracle*, pp 2–3.
199. Lansbury, *Miracle*, p 162.

CHAPTER 2: THE FIRST TRANSITION, 1921–22

1. Noreen Branson, *Poplarism 1919–25: George Lansbury and the Councillors' Revolt,* Lawrence and Wishart 1979, pp 9–52.
2. James Gillespie, 'Poplarism and Proletarianism: Unemployment and Labour Politics in London 1918–34', in David Feldman and Gareth Stedman-Jones (eds) *Metropolis – London: Histories and Representation Since 1880*, Routledge 1989, p 174.
3. DH 2, 3, 5.9.21.
4. DH 30.8–9.9.21.
5. DH 30.8–9.9.21.
6. DH 3, 5.9.21.
7. DH 1.9.21.
8. DH 1.9.21.
9. DH 1.9.21.
10. DH 3.9.21.
11. DH 1, 2, 3.9.21.
12. DH 5.9.21.
13. DH 7.9, 13.10.21.
14. Branson, *Poplarism*, pp 83–103.
15. DH 13.10.21.
16. Francis Williams, *Press, Parliament and People*, Heinemann 1946, p 152.
17. Arthur Christiansen, *Headlines All My Life*, Heinemann 1956, pp 160 9.
18. George Orwell, 'Decline of the English Murder', in *Collected Essays, Journalism and Letters Vol 4: In Front of Your Nose 1945–50*, Penguin 1970, pp 124–8.

19. DH 18.3.22 (Tipton), 27.5.22 (Bottomley).
20. DH 16.6.22.
21. DH 2, 3, 4.1.22.
22. DH 2.1.22 (children), 12.4.22 (Skeggs).
23. DH 7.1.22.
24. DH 13.10.21, *Labour Who's Who 1927*, p 101.
25. DH 13.10.21 (Krassin, Nansen), 16.6.22 (Henderson, Thomas).
26. DH 7.9.22.
27. DH 2.1.22.
28. DH 8.3.22.
29. Clifford Allen: memo on editorial policy 11.5.27, TUC 788.5; memo on DH staff reorganisation 11.3.29, TUC 788.8.
30. Lansbury to Bramley 3.10.23, LPDH 245, LPRAC 1924, p 178.
31. DH 2.1.22.
32. DH 8.3.22.
33. DH 19.2.21.
34. DH 28.9.21.
35. DH 19.2.21.
36. DH 22.10.21.
37. DH 19.12.21.
38. DH 31.3.22.
39. DH 1.9.21 (busmen), 31.3.22 (Liberals).
40. DH 16.6.21.
41. DH 2.1.22.
42. DH 11.2, 17.8.22.
43. DH 2.1.22.
44. Richard Price, *Labour in British Society*, Routledge 1990, p 155.
45. DH 11.2.22.
46. DH 8.3.22.
47. DH 11.2.22.
48. Williams, *Labour and Russia*, pp 8–24.
49. Allen, Memorandum on the *Daily Herald* 17.9.25, LPDH 464, Citrine to Mellor 31.10.28, TUC 788.61; Henry Hamilton Fyfe, *My Seven Selves*, Allen and Unwin 1935, p 254.
50. Lansbury, *My Life*, pp 235–6.
51. DH 3.1.22.
52. DH 19.1.22.
53. DH 1.5.22.
54. DH 25.4.22.
55. DH 15.1, 25.4, 3.5.22.
56. DH 16.6.22.
57. DH 1.9.21.
58. DH 13.10.21.
59. Ross McKibbin, *The Ideologies of Class: Social Relations in Britain 1880–1950*, Oxford UP 1990, p 34.
60. DH 12.4.22.
61. DH 3.5.22.
62. *Independent* 21.9.95; *Morning Star* 21.12.95.

63. Independent Labour Party statement to members on 'The Daily Paper' July 1911, Bryan Papers, LSE Library, vol 2b (ii), item 7; Holton, '*Herald* v *Citizen*', p 364; Ichikawa, *Daily Citizen*, p 18.
64. Lansbury, *My Life*, p 176; Postgate, *Lansbury*, p 142.
65. Postgate, *Lansbury*, p 143.
66. DH 5.9.22.
67. Ross McKibbin, *The Evolution of the Labour Party 1910–24*, Clarendon, Oxford 1974, p 224.
68. Memo from *Herald* General Manager on the Financial Relationship between DH, Victoria House, TUC and Labour Party, n.d. TUC 789.01; *Herald* circular to debenture holders n.d., (late Nov 1921), LPDH 21; LPEC 7.12.21; TUCGC 7.12.21; *Miners Federation Proceedings* 1921, executive 8–9.12.21, item 9, p 529; NW 24.12.21.
69. TUCGC 14.12.21; Joint meeting of LP and TUC 14.12.21, TUCGC and LPEC minutes.
70. Joint meeting 14.12.21.
71. Report of joint sub-committee, n.d., LPDH 24.
72. McKibbin, *Evolution*, p 222.
73. Henderson to Whitehead 17.1.22, LPDH 35.
74. DH sub-committee to LPEC and TUCGC members 10.1.22, LPDH 26.
75. Circular to affiliated bodies 14.1.22, LPDH 32.
76. Circular 14.1.22.
77. DH 24.1.22.
78. DH directors report 17.2.22, LPDH 53.
79. Directors 17.2.22; Report of joint sub-committee n.d., LPDH 97.
80. TUCGC 1.3.22.
81. Lansbury to Henderson 11.1.22, LPDH 28.
82. Lansbury to Henderson 2.3.22, LPDH 63.
83. Henderson to Lansbury 3.3.22, LPDH 64.
84. DH 18.3.22.
85. DH 12.4.22.
86. Summary of levy results to 12.5.22, LPDH 98.
87. Lansbury, *Miracle*, p 162.
88. Minutes of joint meeting 9.5.22, LPDH 90.
89. DH 10.5.22.
90. *Daily Herald* financial history 2.6.27.
91. Minutes of joint meeting of LPEC, TUCGC 21.5.22.
92. NW 2.9.22; *The Journalist*, 1922–3 seriatim.
93. *Miners Federation Proceedings* 1922, Annual Conference 18.7.22, p 474.
94. NW 10.6.22.
95. TUCGC 31.5.22.
96. Lansbury, *Miracle*, p 36.
97. DH 29.7.22.
98. Fyfe, *Seven Selves*, pp 78–101, 106ff, 233–4; NW 9.9.22.
99. Fyfe, *Sixty Years*, p 193; Fyfe to Lansbury 31.7.22, Lansbury Papers, LSE, Box 28a, item 155.
100. NW 2.9.22.
101. DH 4.9.22; *Herald* financial history 2.6.27.

102. RPTUC 1922, pp 91–7; DH 6.9.22.
103. DH 6.9.22.
104. RPTUC 1922, pp 316–7.
105. Ibid, p 317.

CHAPTER 3: THE SECOND *DAILY HERALD*: ON THE EDGE 1922–23

1. *Herald* Accountant to joint bodies 4.12.22, TUC 789.01; *Herald* financial history 2.6.27.
2. DH 23.11.22.
3. Wake and Henderson to affiliated bodies 8.12.22, LPDH 154; TUCGC min 27.11.22.
4. Lansbury and Henderson appeal n.d., LPDH 159.
5. DH 22.1.23.
6. Pugh report on position of the *Daily Herald* newspaper 24.1.23, TUC 788.
7. Report of joint committee 14.2.23, TUC 788.
8. Sir Norman Angell, *After All*, Hamish Hamilton 1951, pp 110–33; Marwick, *Clifford Allen*, pp 11–19.
9. Report to joint committee 1.3.23, LPDH 181, TUC 788.
10. Minutes of joint committee 2.3.23, LPDH 182; LPRAC 1923, p 208.
11. Report of circulation sub-commitee 13.2.23, TUC 788.
12. Joint committee 1.3.23.
13. DH 19.4.23. Report to finance committee 16.4.23, TUC 788.
14. DH 2.5.23.
15. Fyfe, *Sixty Years*, p 193; NW 16.12.22.
16. McKibbin, *Evolution*, p 229; Postgate, *Lansbury*, p 221.
17. DH 23.10.22.
18. DH 23.11.22.
19. DH 27.11.22.
20. Lord Citrine, *Two Careers*, Hutchinson 1967, p 349.
21. DH 26.1.23.
22. DH 7.12.22.
23. DH 29.8.23.
24. DH 21.11.22.
25. David Marquand, *Ramsay MacDonald*, Jonathan Cape 1977, p 282.
26. Postgate, *Analysis*, 1919–23, p 6.
27. DH 19.12.22.
28. Fyfe reply to directors' memos 19.11.25, LPDH 481, TUC 789.1.
29. NW 22.9.23.
30. DH 10.3.23.
31. DH 9, 10.1.23.
32. DH 10.1.23.
33. DH 7.2.23.
34. DH 7.8.23.
35. DH 9.11.22.
36. Postgate, *Analysis*, 1919–23, p 8.
37. DH 15.2.23.

38. DH 10.3.23.
39. DH 17.2.23 (Jones), 10.3.23 (MacDonald); 21.3.23 (Snowden).
40. Editor's report 19.1.28, TUC 788.24.
41. DH 14.2.23 (NUWM), Postgate, *Analysis*, 1919–23, p 6.
42. Postgate, *Lansbury*, p 149.
43. Gillespie, 'Poplarism and Proleterianism', p 173.
44. DH 10.8.23.
45. DH 5.7.23.
46. DH 5, 7.7.23.
47. DH 5.7.23.
48. DH 7.7.23.
49. DH 10.7.23.
50. DH 16.7.23.
51. DH 10.7.23.
52. DH 11.7.23.
53. DH 19.7.23.
54. DH 20.8.23.
55. DH 10.8.23.
56. Postgate, *Analysis*, 1919–23, p 14.
57. DH 31.10.22.
58. DH 11.12.22.
59. DH 1, 3.9.23.
60. DH 22.1.28.
61. Angus MacIntyre, *A Proleterian Science*, Cambridge UP 1980, p 205.
62. Ibid, p 206.
63. *Tribune*, 10.1.97.
64. DH 26.1.23.
65. DH 20.2.23.
66. DH 5.3.23.
67. DH 12.4.23.
68. DH 9.4.23.
69. MacIntyre, *Proleterian Science*, p 206.
70. DH 11.6.23.
71. DH 25, 30.8.23.
72. Allen memo on *Herald* 17.9.25, LPDH 464; McKibbin, *Ideologies*, pp 34–5.
73. DH 1.5.23.
74. DH 7, 14.23.
75. DH 29.8.23.
76. DH 9.4.23.
77. DH directors minutes 22.5.23, LPDH 788.
78. DH directors 22.5.23, RPTUC 1923, pp 65–73, 224; Draft Supplementary Report of General Council on the *Daily Herald* to the 1923 Trades Union Congress, p 8; DH 27.8.23.
79. Fyfe, *Seven Selves*, p 257.
80. Financial sub-committee report to TUCGC 23.5.23, TUC 788.
81. DH 27.8.23.
82. RPTUC 1923, p 365.

83. LPRAC 1923, pp 207–8.
84. Report to joint meeting 23.8.23, LPDH 223; Report of joint meeting 23.8.23, TUCGC minutes.
85. Joint meeting report 23.8.23.
86. Joint meeting report 23.8.23.
87. DH 24.8.23.
88. DH 24.8.23.
89. DH 25, 29, 30, 31.8.23.
90. DH 30.8.23.
91. DH 24.8.23.
92. DH 30.8.23.
93. Joint meeting report 23.8.23.
94. TUCGC 30, 31.8, 4.9.23.
95. TUCGC 4.9.23.
96. DH 6.9.23.
97. RPTUC 1923, pp 352–5.
98. RPTUC 1923, pp 355–8.
99. Ibid, pp 359–63.
100. Ibid, p 363.
101. Ibid, p 359.
102. RPTUC 1923, p 358; DH 7.9.23.
103. Fyfe, *Seven Selves*, p 251.
104. RPTUC 1923, pp 363–70; DH 8.9.23.
105. General Manager's Report 12.9.23, TUC 788.1; Joint council minutes 27.9.23, LPDH 226; Millwood to Henderson 28.9.23, LPDH 227; *Herald* assistant GM to Holmes (PKTF secretary) 19.9.23, LPDH 242.
106. GM rep 25.9.23, LPDH 244; TUCGC 27.9.23.
107. Staff proposals n.d. (Sep 1923), LPDH 228.
108. Day staff to Pugh n.d. (Oct 1923), LPDH 241; Barrow to Lansbury 1.10.23, LPDH 234.
109. PKTF proposals 8.10.23, LPDH 248.
110. PKTF 8.10.23.
111. Fyfe reply 15.10.23, LPDH 264.
112. Heads of department responses 11.10.23, LPDH 255–7, 260; Barrow to Inquiry Committee 16.10.23, LPDH 265; Inquiry Committee minutes 24.10.23, LPDH 273.
113. Inquiry Committee minutes 29.10.23, LPDH 275; TUC 789.5; Lansbury memo n.d. (Nov 1923) LPDH 298.
114. Inquiry Committee minutes 7.11.23, LPDH 287; TUC 789.5.
115. Bramley to members of Inquiry Committee 16.11.23, LPDH 292.

CHAPTER 4: THE SECOND *DAILY HERALD*: NOT AT ALL SATISFIED 1923–26

1. Ewer, *Miracle*, p 4.
2. RPTUC 1924, p 256.
3. DH 9.2.24.

4. NW 15.12.23.
5. Lansbury memo to TUC 18.7.24, LPDH 358.
6. DH 14.12.23; GM reps 25.11.23, LPDH 244, 15.4.24 LPDH 311.
7. RPTUC 1924, p 267.
8. DH 9.2.24.
9. GM rep 19.9.24, LPDH 367.
10. Allen memo 17.9.25.
11. Circulation Manager's report 21.5.25, LPDH 435; GM rep 22.4.26, LPDH 497.
12. RPTUC 1924, p 266.
13. LPRAC 1924, p 177.
14. *Herald* profit and loss accounts to 31.12.24, LPDH 436, TUC 788.21, to 30.6.25, LPDH 480, to 31.12.25, LPDH 498.
15. GM rep 2.1.25, LPDH 390.
16. Fyfe, Lansbury memo to DH directors, TUCGC, LPEC 8.8.24, TUC 788.12.
17. Millwood to Henderson 6.11.24, LPDH 370; Lansbury estimates n.d., LPDH 372; TUCFC 2.1.25 item 22.
18. Bramley to Millwood 7.11.24, TUC 788.01.
19. TUCFC 2.1.25.
20. TUCFC 2.1.25.
21. Millwood to Bramley draft letter 4.4.24, TUC 788; NW 14.6.24.
22. Curran, 'Advertising as a patronage system', pp 76–81.
23. AM rep 16.7.25, LPDH 453; AM rep 22.4.26, LPDH 497.
24. AM rep 16.2.26, LPDH 493.
25. AM rep 2.12.24, LPDH 374.
26. GM rep to LPEC, 7.11.24.
27. AM rep 10.12.25, LPDH 488.
28. AM rep 21.1.26, LPDH 490.
29. AM rep 22.4.26, LPDH 497.
30. RPTUC 1925, p 496.
31. Wilsdon (Upholsterers) to DH 10.4.25, Williams to Bramley 18.6.25, Citrine to Williams 14.12.25, Williams to Citrine 15.12.25, TUC 788.04.
32. Citrine to Williams 19.12.25, Wilsdon to Citrine 16.4, 12.8, 17.8, 10.9, 30.12.26, 2.8.27, TUC 788.04.
33. Lansbury to Millwood 3.1.25, LPDH 391; Fyfe to sub-committee 19.11.25, LPDH 481, TUC 789.1; NW 7.2.25.
34. DH 30.1.25.
35. Lansbury, *My Life*, p 195.
36. DH special committee 11.2.25, TUC 788, 15.4.25, LPDH 430; Millwood to Turner 31.3.25, LPDH 428 TUC 788.
37. TUCFC 2.1.25.
38. Special committee 19, 24.2.25, TUC 789.1.
39. Fyfe, *Sixty Years*, p 193.
40. Ibid, p 193; Special committee 11.3.25, LPDH 408.
41. French (Typographical Association) to Bramley 23.3.25, TUC 788.

42. TUCGC 25.3.25; Allan Bullock, *The Life and Times of Ernest Bevin, Vol I, Trade Union Leader 1881–1940*, Heinemann 1960, pp 222–3.
43. Fyfe, *Seven Selves*, p 277.
44. Bevin, 'Memorandum on the *Daily Herald*' 15–25.9.25, LPDH 461, TUC 789.1.
45. Fyfe to sub-committee 19.11.25, LPDH 481, TUC 789.1; GM rep 2.1.26, LPDH 490.
46. Fyfe to Hicks 30.4.25, NUJ chapel to Fyfe 18.5.25, to VHPCo board 18.5.25 TUC 788.
47. VHPCo sub-committee 3.6.25, TUC 788.11.
48. Fyfe, *Sixty Years*, p 194.
49. Ibid, pp 194–5; VHPCo sub-committee 16.3, 19.4.26 TUC 789.1; Citrine to Williams 16.3.26, TUC 789.1.
50. RPTUC 1926, p 494.
51. Ibid, 1926 pp 492–3.
52. Allen memo 17.9.25.
53. Fyfe to sub-committee 19.11.25.
54. MacDonald to Allen 27.11.25, MacDonald papers, John Rylands Library, Manchester, folder no 5; 'Ours is not an ordinary parliamentary movement 1922–26', in Alan McKinlay and R.J. Morris, (ed.) *The ILP on Clydeside: From Foundation to Disintegration* 1893–1932, Manchester UP, pp 167–9.
55. MacDonald to Allen 9.11.25.
56. MacDonald to Turner 3.3.25, JRMPRO File 1170.1 Item 801.
57. DH 23.1.24.
58. Fyfe to sub-committee 19.11.25.
59. DH 26.1.25.
60. GM rep 14.7.24, LPDH 355.
61. RB Walker 'Memo on the *Daily Herald*', 22.9.25, LPDH 464, TUC 789.1.
62. Brodzky to Bramley 29.12.23, 1.1.24, TUC 788.
63. Bramley to Brodzky 3.1.24, TUC 788.
64. DH 22.11.23.
65. DH 13.10.24.
66. DH 24.10.24.
67. DH 3.12.23.
68. DH 26.10.23.
69. DH 26.11.23.
70. DH 3.4.24.
71. DH 22.11.23.
72. Egon Wertheimer, *Portrait of the Labour Party*, Putnam's 1928, p 177.
73. McKibbin, *Evolution*, p 130.
74. DH 18.10.24.
75. DH 25.10.24.
76. Fyfe, *Seven Selves*, p 262.
77. DH 26.11.23.
78. DH 8.8.24, 23.12.25.
79. DH 19.3.25.

80. DH 10, 11.12.23.
81. DH 8.1.24.
82. DH 19.12.23, 5.1.24.
83. DH 23.1.24.
84. DH 24.1.24.
85. DH 12.2.24.
86. DH 8.3.24.
87. DH 28.2.24 (Wheatley), 12.3.24 (Bondfield).
88. DH 28.2.24 (Olivier), 12.3.24 (Shaw), 4.4.24 (Clynes).
89. DH 22.2.24.
90. Fyfe, *Seven Selves*, pp 258–60.
91. DH 23.1.24.
92. DH 21.2.24.
93. DH 19.3.24.
94. DH 15.8.24.
95. Fyfe, *Seven Selves*, p 258.
96. Ibid, p 262; DH 10, 13, 28.5.24.
97. DH 29.5, 3.6.24.
98. DH 15.7.24.
99. DH 15.7.24.
100. DH 16.7.24.
101. Fyfe, *Seven Selves*, chap 5; NW 9.9.22.
102. DH 11.8.24.
103. DH 22, 23.8.24.
104. Margaret Cole (ed.), *The Beatrice Webb Diaries 1924–32*, entry for 24.9.24, p 43.
105. Fyfe, *Seven Selves*, p 258.
106. Ibid, pp 258–60.
107. Ibid, p 261.
108. Trevor Wilson (ed.), *The Political Diaries of C. P. Scott 1911–28*, Collins 1970, entries for 27–30.11.24.
109. DH 14.8.24.
110. DH 4.11.24.
111. DH 4.12.24.
112. DH 4.12.24.
113. DH 22.8.25ff (happiness), 18.9.25ff (Ten Commandments), 3.4.26ff (gambling).
114. DH 3.11.24ff.
115. DH 13, 14, 17.2.25.
116. DH 7.3.25.
117. DH 13.4.25, 1.1.26; Marquand, *MacDonald*, pp 452–5.
118. DH 7.3.25.
119. DH 7.3.25; Fyfe to MacDonald 23.3.25, JRMPRO File 1170:1 Item 438.
120. DH 30.1, 1, 2, 2.26.
121. DH 22,24.1.24.
122. DH 27, 28.3.24; Ken Fuller, *Radical Aristocrats*, Lawrence and Wishart 1985, pp 71–6.

123. DH 1.4.24.
124. DH 22.2.24; Bramley to Thomas 5.3.24, TUC 788.
125. DH 26.4.24.
126. DH 16, 18, 19.2.24.
127. DH 18,26.2.24.
128. DH 26.2.24.
129. TUCGC 4.9.24, RPTUC 1925, p 492.
130. Allen memo 17.9.25.
131. DH 29.11.23.
132. DH 26.1.25.
133. DH 3, 21.9.25.
134. DH 26.9.24.
135. DH 29, 30.9, 3.10.25.
136. DH 30.9.25.
137. DH 30.9.25.
138. Fyfe, *Seven Selves*, p 254; Fyfe to MacDonald 5.4.24, JRMPRO File 2, Item 62.
139. A. Williams, *Labour and Russia*, p 24 .
140. Ibid, p 24; DH 22.12.24.
141. DH 11.9.25.
142. DH 9.6.25 (Humber towns), 19.8.25 (credits).
143. DH 30.1.25 (only system), 14.4.25 (working-class governments).
144. DH 28.2.25 (fantastic fictions), 6.10.25 (strange confusions).
145. DH 23.1.24.
146. DH 23.1.24.
147. DH 24.1.24.
148. DH 18.8.24.
149. DH 3.7.24 (Morel), 28.8.24 (Noel-Baker).
150. DH 5.1.25.
151. DH 19.3.26.
152. Bentham, memo on DH 17.9.25.
153. Bevin, memo 15–25.9.25.
154. Allen, memo 17.9.25.
155. Fyfe, to sub-committee 19.11.25.
156. Marwick, *Clifford Allen*, p 193.
157. DH 4.2.26.
158. DH 24.4.26.
159. DH 13.2.26.
160. DH 3.4.24 (Curzon), 7.4.24 (Boat Race).
161. DH 26.7, 1.8.24.
162. DH 30.7.24.
163. DH 5, 7, 8, 16, 18, 21, 24.5.24.
164. DH 30.7–9.8.24.
165. DH 1.8.24 (Appeals), 2.8.24 (All Classes), 4.8.24 (Public Feeling).
166. DH 5, 7.8.24.
167. DH 9.8.24 (Henderson/Vaquier), 9.12.24 (Smith).
168. DH 13.5.24.
169. DH 5.5.24, Teashop slavery campaign, DH 12.9.23ff.

170. DH 13.5.24.
171. DH 11.7.24.
172. DH 19.5.24 (ban on DH), 27.6.24 (letters).
173. DH 19.5.24 (cartoon), 12.6.24 (profits).
174. DH 26, 28, 29.5.24.
175. DH 6.5.24.
176. DH 27.12.24.
177. DH 12.10.25.
178. DH 3.7.25.
179. DH 19.3.24.
180. DH 9.7.24.
181. DH 22, 23, 24.1.25 (Hawke), 23.5.25 (Scorecards).
182. DH 18.8.25; Tony Mason, 'Local Heroes', paper given at the Sport, Literature and National Identity conference, Swansea, 30 April 1995.
183. DH 26.1.25.
184. DH 3.1.25 (Swastika), 26.2.25 (Esperanto).
185. DH 21.10.25.
186. TUCGC 27–28.10.25, Sub-committee 27, 29.10.25, LPDH 475/6.
187. DH 9.2.26.
188. DH 25.2.26.
189. DH 30.8.26.
190. Allen memo 17.9.25.
191. R.K. Middlemass, *Politics in Industrial Society*, Andre Deutsch 1979, p 194.
192. DH 4.7.25.
193. DH 26.2.26.
194. DH 21, 24, 25, 29, 31.7.25.
195. DH 3.4.26.
196. DH 15.1.26 (General Strike), 29.4.26 (Minority Movement).
197. DII 31.7.25.
198. DH 31.7.25.
199. DH 3.5.26.
200. DH 4.5.26; Henry Hamilton Fyfe, *Behind the Scenes of the Great Strike*, Labour Publishing Company 1926, pp 34–5.
201. DH 4.4.26.
202. DH 1.8.25.
203. Fyfe, *Behind the Scenes*, pp 25–6, *Sixty Years*, p 198; TUCGC 3.5.26 minute 31, 4.5.26 min 36.
204. Fyfe, *Behind the Scenes*, p 26; Tracey to Fyfe 6.5.26, TUC (General Strike files) 252.62 (12).
205. BW 10.5.26.
206. BW 12.5.26.
207. Fyfe, *Sixty Years*, p 199.
208. GM rep 28.5.26, LPDH 504.
209. GM rep 28.5.26.
210. CM rep 17.6.26, LPDH 505.
211. AM rep 16.6.26, LPDII 505, 21.7.26, LPDII 512.
212. Fyfe, *Seven Selves*, pp 275–6.

213. Ibid, pp 276–7.
214. Memo (unsigned) n.d. (late July 1926?), TUC 788.01.
215. Unsigned memo.
216. Fyfe, *Seven Selves*, p 278.
217. Ibid, p 279.
218. VHPCo directors 27.7.26, LPDH 788.11.
219. DH 30.8.29.
220. RPTUC 1926, pp 455–6.
221. DH 30.8.26; Clegg, *British Trade Unionism*, pp 414–5, 419.
222. DH 25.5.26; Clegg, *British Trade Unionism*, pp 419–20; Paul Davies, *A.J. Cook*, Manchester UP 1987, pp 136–7.
223. DH 25.5.26.
224. DH 18.5–19.6.26.
225. DH 26.6.26.
226. DH 1.6.26.
227. DH 5.6.26.
228. DH 24.7.26.
229. DH 12.8.26.
230. DH 29.5, 18.8.26.
231. DH 26.7.26.
232. DH 19.8.26; Davies, *Cook*, pp 109, 177.
233. DH 9.8.26.

CHAPTER 5: THE SECOND *DAILY HERALD:* A DECLINE WHICH IS LAMENTABLE, 1926–28

1. NW 7.8.26.
2. VHPCo dir min 26.8.26, TUC 788.11.
3. Margaret Cole, 'Mellor', DLB vol 4, pp 123, 6.
4. Mervyn Jones, *Michael Foot*, Gollancz 1994, p 60; Michael Foot in conversation with author 23.7.92.
5. Cole, 'Mellor', p 123.
6. Ibid, pp 123–6; Douglas Hill (ed.), *Tribune 40*, Quartet 1977, pp 2–6.
7. VHPCo dir 26.8.26.
8. Fyfe, *Behind the Scenes*, pp 26, 54.
9. Fyfe, *Seven Selves*, p 254.
10. Unsigned memo.
11. Cole, 'Mellor', pp 123–4.
12. John Saville, 'Clifford Allen 1889–1939', DLB vol 2, pp 2–3; Postgate and Postgate, *A Stomach*, p 41; NW 18.9.26; 'Iconoclast' [M.A. Hamilton], *Man of Tomorrow: J. Ramsay MacDonald,* Leonard Parsons, Newcastle on Tyne, 1923, pp 87–8.
13. RPTUC 1926, pp 363–4.
14. RPTUC 1927, p 401.
15. Clegg, *British Trade Unions 1911–33*, p 426.
16. Unsigned memo.
17. WPN 10.3.32.

18. Unsigned memo.
19. GM rep 19.11.26; TUC 788.21.
20. VHPCo dir 18.1.27, 27.3.28, TUC 788.11; GM rep 1.9.27, LPDH 533, 26.9.27; TUC 788.21, Editor's report 19.1.28, 16.2.28, 22.3.28, TUC 788.24.
21. Ed rep 22.3.28; VHPCo dir 22.9.27, TUC 789.1.
22. Ed rep 22.3.28.
23. DH 7.9.26 (Pugh), 15.9.26 (Basic Industry).
24. DH 3.9.26.
25. DH 8.11.26.
26. DH 30.10.26.
27. DH 6, 7.11.26.
28. DH 25.11.28.
29. Fyfe, *Sixty Years*, p 199.
30. Cole (ed.), *Webb Diaries 1924–32*, entry for 22.8.27, p 151.
31. DH 31.3–5.4.27.
32. DH 2.10.26 (MacDonald), 24.11.26 (Cotton).
33. DH 22.9.26.
34. DH 28.5.28.
35. DH 6.10.26.
36. RPTUC 1928, p 500.
37. DH 21.5.28.
38. DH 4.10.28.
39. DH 4.10.28.
40. DH 4.10.28.
41. DH 7.7.28.
42. DH 1.7.27.
43. RPTUC, pp 455–6.
44. DH 15.10.26.
45. DH 15.10.26.
46. RPTUC 1928, p 499.
47. DH 21.1.27.
48. DH 17.1.27.
49. DH 22.1.27.
50. DH 11.4.28.
51. DH 30.7.28.
52. DH 29.8.27.
53. DH 5–9.4.27 (denunciation), 18.4.27 (Maxton).
54. DH 14.5.27; TUCGC 27.4.27 min 204.
55. DH 6.10.26.
56. DH 12.10.26.
57. DH 12.10.26.
58. DH 4.2.27.
59. DH 19.10.27.
60. DH 21.12.27.
61. DH 22.12.27.
62. DH 13, 23.1.28.
63. Citrine to Turner 24.8.28, TUC 788.62.

64. DH 21.6.28.
65. DH 21.6.28.
66. DH 25.6.28.
67. DH 25,27.6,2.7.28.
68. Belt (secretary of Herald League) to VHPCo dir 18.11.26, TUC 788.01.
69. Rudland to Citrine 9.11.26, Citrine to Williams 13.11.26, TUC 788.
70. VHPCo dir min 23.11.26; LPDH 514, 6.12.26, LPDH 523.
71. DH 29.8.27.
72. DH 27.2.28 .
73. DH 13.8.28.
74. DH 27.8.28.
75. DH 5.9.28.
76. DH 10.9.26.
77. A Williams, *Labour and Russia*, p 41.
79. DH 13.5.27.
80. DH 25, 26.5.27.
81. DH 13.5.27.
82. DH 7.1.27 (Lozovsky), 9.9.27 (break).
83. DH 10.9.27.
84. NW 3.3.28.
85. VHPCo dir 27.3.28, LPDH 543.
86. DH 2.8.27.
87. DH 7.11.27.
88. DH 7.11.27.
89. DH 7.12.26, 5, 24.1.27.
90. DH 24.1–7.2.27.
91. DH 3.5.27.
92. DH 5.1.27.
93. McKibbin, *Ideologies*, p 1.
94. DH 3.1.28.
95: DH 20.2.28.
96. DH 16.8.28.
97. DH 24.8.27.
98. DH 25.8.27.
99. DH 10.1.28.
100. DH 10.1.28.
101. DH 14.2.28.
102. GM rep 15.12.27.
103. Allen memo for Finance Committee 11.5.27, TUC 788.5.
104. CM rep 15.12.27, TUC 788.22.
105. Ed rep 19.1.28, TUC 788.24.
106. DH 9.6.28.
107. DH 9, 15.6.28.
108. DH 2.12.27.
109. DH 15.10.27, 10.4.28.
110. DH 10, 13.8.28.
111. DH 13, 18, 22–5.8.28.

112. Miles Kington, 'You Are Mr Lobby Lud', BBC Radio 4, December 1983.
113. DH 16.8.27.
114. DH 16.8.27.
115. DH 17.8.27.
116. DH 19.8.27 (Canadian, teacher), 29.8.27 (farmworkers).
117. DH 3.9.27.
118. DH 30, 31.12.27.
119. DH 13.9.27.
120. DH 27.9.27.
121. DH 11.6, 13.7.28.
122. DH 20.6.28.
123. DH 7.2.27 (Welsh rugby), 27.8.28 (football).
124. DH 25.10, 3.11.27.
125. DH 10.8, 21.11.27 (Stag hunting), 26.4.27 (greyhounds).
126. DH 26.4.27.
127. DH 21.6.27.
128. DH 22.8.27.
129. DH 17.9.27.
130. DH 15.3.28.
131. DH 5.6.28.
132. RPTUC 1928, p 497.
133. Ad Man 19.1, 16.2, 22.3, 24.4, 21.5.28, TUC 788.23.
134. Ad Man 21.5.28, TUC 788.23; Reports to VHPCo dir 24.5.28, LPDH 544.
135. Curran, *Advertising*, p 79.
136. Unsigned, undated memo (Dec 1926?) on advertising, LPDH 521.
137. CM rep 15.12.27.
138. VHPCo dir 18.2.28; TUC 788.26.
139. VHPCo dir 18.2.28.
140. GM rep 29.8.28, TUC 788.21.
141. GM rep 29.8.28.
142. GM rep 26.9.27, TUC 788.21.
143. RPTUC 1928, p 495.
144. CM rep 21.7.27, 19.1.28, TUC 788.22.
145. NW 12.3, 13.8.27, 20.10.28 (*Express*), 23.7.27, 13.10.28 (*Mail*); CM rep 17.1.29, LPDH 558, TUC 788.22.
146. NW 23.7.27, 28.7.28 (*News*), 4.2.28 (*Gazette*), 10.3, 21.7.28 (*Chronicle*), 16.6.28 (*Sketch*), 23.6.28 (*Mirror*); CM rep 17.1.29.
147. DH 1.2.28, CM rep 16.2.28, TUC 788.23.
148. RPTUC 1927, p 401; Ben Turner, *About Myself*, Humphrey Toulmin 1930, p 352.
149. VHPCo dir rep 18.1.27, TUC 788.
150. VHPCo dir rep 22.2.27, TUC 788.
151. VHPCo dir 22.2.27.
152. Agenda, minutes Finance Committee meeting 10.3.27, TUC 789.1.
153. Williams report n.d. (Feb/Mar 1927), TUC 788.01.
154. GM rep 29.8.28.

155. CM rep 21.6.28, TUC 788.22.
156. Allen and Williams memo 11.4.27, TUC 789.01.
157. Turner memo to FC 13.5.27, TUC 788.5.
158. FC rep 2.6.27, TUC 788.5, VHPCo dir special meeting 14.6.27, TUC 788.11, ordinary meeting 22.6.27, TUC 788.26.
159. RPTUC 1927, pp 397–403.
160. RPTUC 1927, p 401.
161. Publication Fund Summary 27.10.28, TUC 789.01.
162. Consultation meeting min 21.12.27, TUC 788.1.
163. Middleton to Citrine 24.1.28, Citrine to Henderson 27.1.28, TUC 789.7.
164. VHPCo FC report 26.9.27, TUC 788.5.
165. VHPCo dir special memorandum 18.11.27, TUC 788.5.
166. VHPCo dir special memo, 18.11.27.
167. Joint meeting min 15.2.28, TUC 789.81.
168. TUCFC 7.5.28, item 47.
169. Citrine memo to GC 21.6.28, TUC 789.01.
170. Note on Citrine memo 21.6.28.
171. RPTUC 1928, p 504.
172. Ibid, p 505.
173. Ibid, p 496.
174. Ibid, p 507.

CHAPTER 6: THE SECOND TRANSITION, 1928–30

1. Marwick, *Allen*, p 107.
2. CM rep 22.11.28, LPDH 551.
3. CM rep 13.10.28, LPDH 550.
4. AM rep 18.11, 13.12.28, LPDH 551, 554.
5. Allen to Williams 9.11.28, TUC 788.5. .
6. Memo for joint meeting of Finance Sub Committees 29.11.28, TUC 789.82.
7. Report of joint meeting 12.12.28, LPDH 554.
8. Meeting between DH deputation and McLannan (National Provincial Bank) 21.1.28, TUC 789.8.
9. Prudential to Citrine 24.1.29, undated handwritten note (late Jan), Firth (TUC) to Prudential 1.2.29, TUC 789.821.
10. Report of meeting 5.2.28, TUC 789.8; TUCFGPC 18.3.29, min no 117.
11. Firth to May 11.2.29; Shaen, Roscoe to Citrine 8.3.29, TUC 789.821; Report of meeting 13.2.29; Firth to Citrine 16.3.29; Memo for TUCFGPC 7.3.29; Firth to Citrine 16.3.29, TUC 789.8.
12. Geilinger memo n.d. (Mar 1928), TUC 789.821.
13. Allen memo 25.2.29, TUC 789.8; GM rep 21.2.29, LPDH 562.
14. Allen memo 25.2.29.
15. Allen memo re staffing n.d. (11–19.3.29), TUC 789.821.
16. Turner to Allen 21.3.29, TUC 789.7.
17. Allen to Turner, Citrine 29.3.39, TUC 789.8.

18. Handwritten note on memo re future of DH 7.3.29, TUC 789.8; Report of call from Evans (CIS) to Citrine 14.3.29, TUC 789.821.
19. Turner to Citrine 17.3.29, TUC 789.821.
20. RPTUC 1927, p 401.
21. John Saville, 'Sir Ben Turner 1863–1942', DLB vol 8, pp 253–5.
22. Shaen, Roscoe to Citrine 18.3.29, TUC 789.821.
23. TUCGC 27.3.29, min no 142.
24. Citrine to May 28.3.29, TUC 789.7.
25. TUC circular no 60 (1928–29) to affiliated organisations 28.3.29, TUC 789.8; Citrine to Williams 28.3.29, TUC 789.7.
26. Henderson to Citrine 26.3.29, TUC 789.7.
27. DH 25.4.29.
28. GM rep 21.2.29, LPDH 562.
29. DH 22.3.29.
30. DH 31.1.29.
31. DH 13.4.29.
32. DH 4.10.28.
33. DH 4.10.28.
34. DH 8.4.29.
35. DH 22.3.29 (MacDonald), 27.3.29 (Lloyd George).
36. DH 22.4 – 30.5.29 (leader features), 13.5.29ff (little letters), 4.3.29–1.5.29 (boxes).
37. DH 23.5.29.
38. DH 25.5.29.
39. DH 21.5.29.
40. DH 17.5.29 (Sweeping), 22.5.29 (Whirlwind).
41. DH 10.5.29.
42. DH 30.5.29.
43. DH 1.6.29.
44. DH 31.5.29.
45. DH 6.6.29.
46. Williams to Citrine 8.6.29, Citrine to Williams 10.6.29, TUC 788.
47. Ed rep 2.7.29, TUC 788.24.
48. DH 6, 7, 8, 11, 12.6.29.
49. DH 7–29.8.29 (Hague conference), 21.8.29 (Slocombe).
50. DH 14.9.29.
51. TUC 1929 Private Session transcript, TUC 788.51.
52. DH 8.6.29.
53. DH 19.7.29.
54. DH 19.7.29.
55. DH 10.9.26.
56. DH 22.7.29 (Trotsky), 26.7.29 (GBS).
57. DH 24.8.29 (Buchanan), 3.12.29 (Wheatley).
58. DH 24.8.29.
59. DH 24.8.29 (Buchanan), 6.12.29 (Wheatley).
60. DH 6.12.29.
61. DH 20.11.29 (Brown), 22.11.29 (Clarke).
62. DH 21, 22.12.29, 21.1.30.

63. DH 19.10.29 (Seeking work), 13.12.29 (Mines).
64. DH 25.10.29, 13.12.29.
65. Robert Skidelsky, *Politicians and the Slump*, Pelican 1970, pp 387, 401.
66. DH 10.2.30.
67. Skidelsky, *Politicians*, pp 192–214.
68. DH 9.9.29.
69. DH 14, 27.2.29.
70. DH 13.3.29.
71. DH 26.11.28.
72. DH 28.12.28.
73. DH 11.10.28 (Mostly 16–21), 13.10.28 (Cheery mood).
74. Clegg, *British Trade Unionism 1911–33*, p 453.
75. DH 25.10.28.
76. DH 27.10.28 (claims), 5, 6.11.28 (denials).
77. DH 7.10.29.
78. DH 11.10.29.
79. Citrine to Mellor 31.10.28, TUC 788.61.
80. A. Williams, *Labour and Russia*, pp 90, 139–40.
81. DH 24.9.29.
82. DH 2.1.30.
83. DH 2.1.30.
84. DH 25.10.29 (Crash), 26.10.29 (leader).
85. DH 30.11.29.
86. DH 27.11.28ff.
87. DH 2.10.28.
88. DH 22.3.29.
89. DH 24.10.29, Chippindale and Horrie, *Stick It Up*, p 79.
90. DH 6–9, 16.3.29.
91. DH 4.3.30.
92. DH 15.9.28.
93. Wertheimer, *Portrait*, p 80.
94. DH 31.1.29.
95. DH 19.9.28.
96. DH 31.10.28.
97. WPN 28.11.29.
98. DH 20, 24.8.28.
99. DH 22.8.28 (Bible), 22.11.28 (45 lit figures), 15.12.28 (policeman).
100. DH 18, 19, 21, 23.11.29.
101. DH 6.1, 22.2.30.
102. DH 6.1.30.
103. DH 22.2.30.
104. DH 25.2.30.
105. 1929 Private session transcript.
106. CM rep 3.6.29, TUC 788.22; Ed rep 2.7.29, TUC 788.24.
107. VHPCo dir min 5.7.29, TUC 788.11.
108. CM rep 3.6.29.
109. CM rep 1.7, 2.8.29.

110. W.J.B. Odhams, *The Business and I*, Martin Secker 1935, pp 74–5; R.J. Minney, *Viscount Southwood*, Odhams 1954, p 220.
111. Minney, *Southwood*, pp 102, 177–83.
112. Charles Wintour, *The Rise and Fall of Fleet Street*, Hutchinson 1989, pp 49–50.
113. Minney, *Southwood*, pp 118–19, 186–91; F Williams, *Dangerous*, p 186.
114. Minney, *Southwood*, pp 186–92; F. Williams, *Dangerous*, pp 186–7.
115. Minney, *Southwood*, p 220.
116. Ibid, p 217–21; Williams, *Dangerous*, p 187.
117. Minney, *Southwood*, pp 217–21; Fyfe, *Sixty Years*, pp 188–91.
118. GM rep 12.9.23 TUC 788.1.
119. Minney, *Southwood*, p 228; Williams, *Dangerous*, p 157.
120. TUCGC 23.7.29 min no 243, transcript of discussion, TUC 788.51.
121. Transcript of discussion on DH and Victoria House n.d., TUC 788.51.
122. Minney, *Southwood*, p 226.
123. TUCGC 23.7.29 transcript.
124. Bullock, *Bevin*, p 422.
125. Minney, *Southwood*, pp 92, 220–2.
126. VHPCo dir min 19.7.29, TUC 788.11.
127. TUCGC 23.7.29 transcript.
128. Shaen, Roscoe to Citrine 27.8.29, TUC 788.51; TUCGC 23.7.29 transcript.
129. Articles of Agreement for *Daily Herald* 1929 Ltd, paras 94–7, TUC Library.
130. VHPCo dir min 21.8.29; TUC GC 23.7.29 transcript.
131. VHPCo dir min 30.8.29.
132. TUCGC 2.9.29 min no 296.
133. Chris Cunneen, 'McIntosh, Hugh Donald (1876–1942)', *Australian Dictionary of Biography, vol 10,* Melbourne UP 1986, pp 284–5; Denzil Batchelor, *Jack Johnson and His Times,* Sportsman's Book Club 1957, pp 61–73.
134. McIntosh to Citrine 26.8.29, TUC 788.51.
135. Citrine to McIntosh 30.8.29, TUC 788.51.
136. Cunneen, 'McIntosh', p 286.
137. TUCGC 2.9.29 min no 296.
138. 1929 private session transcript.
139. WPN 8.8.29.
140. Rudland (Birmingham TC) to Citrine 26.9.29, TUC 788.51; Elisabeth Williamson (South Marylebone ILP) to Middleton 7, 24.10.29; Middleton to Williamson 8, 25.10.29, LPDH 570–3.
141. Derby and District Trades Council to Citrine 22.9.29, Citrine reply 25.9.29, TUC 788.51.
142. DH 12, 14, 15.11.29.
143. VHPCo Board min 22.10.29 TUC 788.11; Williams to Citrine 7.10.29; Bevin to Citrine 7, 14.10.29; Citrine to Bevin 8, 9, 22.10.29, TUC 789.2.
144. GM rep 19.9, 17.10.29, TUC 788.22.
145. AM rep 20.11.29, TUC 788.23.

146. DH 12.11.29; WPN 14.11.29; DH headed notepaper used for letter 20.12.29, LPDH 661.
147. VHP Codir min 24.9.29, TUC 788.11.
148. WPN 14.11.29.
149. WPN 14.11.29.
150. WPN 23.1.30.
151. Willie Thompson, *The Good Old Cause: British Communism 1920–1991*, Pluto 1992, p 225.
152. WPN 23.1.30.
153. VHPCo dir min 26.11.29, TUC 788.11.
154. VHPCo dir min 21.1.30, TUC 788.11, WPN 14.4.32.
155. Minney, *Southwood*, p 232.
156. TUC circular no 17 (1929–30) 19.11.29, TUC 788.8, LPDH 603; DH 'A' directors report to TUC 12.5.30, TUC 790.01; Ticket for Cardiff conference 7.12.29, LPDH 605; TUC/Labour Party joint letter to Trades Councils/Labour Parties in Cardiff area n.d. (Nov 1929), LPDH 606.
157. Bullock, *Bevin*, p 474.
158. Middleton to Joseph Jones (Yorkshire Miners) 8.1.30, LPDH 705.
159. Speech outline (n.d.), TUC 790.
160. Draft resolution (n.d.), TUC 788.89.
161. 'How the Scheme Works' draft leaflet (n.d.), TUC 788.89.
162. Bevin to Citrine 18.11.29, LPDH 584; DH 19.12.29.
163. GM rep 1.7.29, LPDH 788.22.
164. 'How the Scheme Works'.
165. Dane to Middleton 20.12.29, LPDH 661.
166. DH 'A' dir 12.5.30, Helper kit LPDH 643–4, TUC 790.
167. Helper kit.
168. *The Helper* no 1, 23.1.30.
169. *The Helper* nos 1–4.
170. *The Helper* nos 2, 3, 4.
171. *The Helper* no 4.
172. *The Helper* no 5.
173. *The Helper* no 6; Middleton to Labour Party secretaries 20.2.30, LPDH 748, to local parties 11.3.30, LPDH 774.
174. Middleton and Shepherd to local parties 26.2.30, LPDH 770.
175. *The Helper* no 6.
176. DH 'A' dir 12.5.30.
177. Ibid.
178. Bevin to VHPCo dir 25.3.30, TUC 788.22.
179. Ibid.
180. DH 15.3.30.
181. Barbara Neild and John Saville, 'Scurr, John (1876–1932)', DLB vol 4, pp 154–5.

CHAPTER 7: THE THIRD *DAILY HERALD* 1930–64

1. DH 17.3.30.

2. Minney, *Southwood*, p 237.
3. Bullock, *Bevin*, p 457.
4. Minney, *Southwood*, p 292.
5. DH 17.3.30; James Jarche, *People I Have Shot*, Methuen 1934, p 115.
6. LeMahieu, *A Culture*, pp 252–9.
7. Allen Hutt, *Newspaper Design*, Oxford UP 1960, p 36.
8. *Labour Magazine*, April 1930, p 550.
9. DH 17.3.30.
10. DH 17.3.30.
11. DH 8.4.30.
12. DH 17.3.30.
13. DH 12.3.30, 1.4.30.
14. Wilfred Fienburgh, *1930–55: 25 Momentous Years – A 25th Anniversary in the History of the Daily Herald*, Odhams 1955, p 19.
15. William Rust, *The Story of the 'Daily Worker'*, People's Press 1949, p 2; Seymour-Ure, 'Press and Party System', p 243; Harrison, *Poor Men's Guardians*, p 200.
16. DH 8.4.30.
17. DH 30.6.30; Kneeshaw to Middleton n.d. (Aug 1930), LPDH 902.
18. Seymour-Ure, 'Press and Party System', p 248; Minney, *Southwood*, p 240.
19. F. Williams, *Dangerous*, p 170; Tom Clarke, *My Lloyd George Diary*, Methuen 1939, pp 78–80.
20. F. Williams, *Dangerous*, p 173; *The Helper* (2nd series) no 2, 18.6.30 .
21. WPN 21.3.32. .
22. *The Economist* 15.7.33.
23. NPD 1936, p 311.
24. Tom Jeffrey and Keith McLelland, 'A World Fit To Live In: The *Daily Mail* and the Middle Class 1918–39', in James Curran, Anthony Smith and Pauline Wingate (eds) *Impacts and Influences*, Methuen 1987, p 33.
25. David and Gareth Butler, *British Political Facts 1990–94*, Macmillan 1994, p 215.
26. Bullock, *Bevin*, p 491.
27. Written evidence to RCP, 3rd day, 15.10.47, HMSO Cmd 7318, p 20.
28. LPRAC, p 82.
29. Webb memo 22.11.37, TUC 790.01.
30. F. Williams, *Dangerous*, p 198.
31. *The Journalist*, April, July, August 1938. Driberg, *Swaff*, p 202.
32. Jeremy Tunstall 'The British Press in the Age of Television', in H Christian (ed.) *Sociology of Journalism and the Press*, Sociological Review monograph 29, Keele University 1980, p 25.
33. F. Williams, *Dangerous*, pp 175–7; Fyfe, *Sixty Years*, p 171.
34. Author's personal recollection.
35. *The Economist*, 15.7.33.
36. DH balance sheets 1930 9, TUC files box 1532.
37. Ibid.

38. DH balance sheet 1938; DH sales figures 1930–49 (found in *The Times* archive by then archivist, Melanie Aspey).
39. Fyfe, *Press Parade*, p 108.
40. Curran, *Advertising*, p 80.
41. Ibid, p 80.
42. Ibid, p 83.
43. Incorporated Society of British Advertisers, *The Readership of Newspapers and Periodicals in Great Britain*, ISBA 1936.
44. WPN 28.4, 30.6.38.
45. DH balance sheet 1937; AM rep 18.11.26, TUC 788.22.
46. Curran, *Advertising*, p 73.
47. DH sales figures 1930–49.
48. DH balance sheets 1935–7.
49. DH sales figures 1930–49.
50. DH 26.11.36; WPN 12.10, 19.11.33; NPD 1940, p 312.
51. Interview with Sir Tom Hopkinson, 25.6.82.
52. Hutt, *Newspaper Design*, p 37.
53. F. Williams, *Nothing So Strange*, p 131.
54. Driberg, *Swaff*, pp 173–7, 255.
55. Christiansen, *Headlines*, p 91; M. Bryant and S. Heneage, *Dictionary of British Cartoonists and Caricaturists*, Scolar, Aldershot 1994, p 210.
56. Jensen, *Dyson*, pp 38–9.
57. Russell Davies and Liz Ottaway, *Vicky*, Secker and Warburg 1987, pp 31–3.
58. Ibid, p 33.
59. Webb to George Woodcock 28.9.63, TUC 790.7.
60. Driberg, *Swaff*, p 197.
61. Herald NUJ chapel report 27.7.31; Dunbar to Citrine 1.6.32, TUC 790.2.
62. Dunbar to Citrine 1.6.32.
63. Oral evidence to RCP, 3rd day 15.10.47, para 436.
64. Wintour, *Fleet Street*, p 58.
65. Derek Jameson, *Last of the Hot Metal Men*, Penguin 1991, p 54.
66. Webb to Woodcock 28.9.63.
67. Driberg, *Swaff*, p 198.
68. Ibid, p 202.
69. Ibid, pp 188–9.
70. Curran and Seaton, *Power*, pp 126–7.
71. Webb memo 22.11.37.
72. Analysis of coverage July 1938, TUC 790.01.
73. Douglas Jay, *Change and Fortune*, Hutchinson 1980, p 66.
74. DH 25.8.31; F. Williams, *Nothing So Strange*, p 101.
75. DH 22.10.31 (Swaffer), 28.10.31 (leader).
76. DH 29.10.31.
77. DH 1, 2.10.35.
78. DH 3.12.36.
79. F. Williams, *Nothing So Strange*, p 141; Minney, *Southwood*, pp 292–3.

80. Bernard Donoghue and George Jones, *Herbert Morrison: Portrait of a Politician*, Weidenfeld and Nicolson 1973, p 143.
81. Michael Foot, *Aneurin Bevan: Vol 1 1897–1945*, Paladin 1975, p 308.
82. George Orwell, 'Boy's Weeklies', in *Collected Essays, Journalism and Letters, Vol 1, An Age Like This 1920–40*, Penguin 1970, p 529.
83. Fyfe, *Press Parade*, p 106.
84. Feinburgh, *25 Momentous Years*, pp 81–2; D. Griffiths (ed.), *Encyclopedia of the British Press 1422–1992*, Macmillan 1992, p 139.
85. DH 3.10.35.
86. F. Williams, *Nothing So Strange*, pp 95, 113.
87. Ibid, p 114–15; Interview with Lord Jay 21.6.81.
88. Curran and Seaton, *Power*, p 71.
89. Driberg, *Swaff*, p 180.
90. WPN 30.6.38.
91. DH 29.8.31, 14.9.35.
92. DH 30, 31.10.31.
93. DH 1.5.30, 15–16.5.30 (debutantes), 11.6.30 (nephew).
94. DH 27.7.31.
95. WPN 8.2.40.
96. F. Williams, *Dangerous Estate*, p 198.
97. F. Williams, *Nothing So Strange*, p 131.
98. F. Williams, *Press, Parliament and People*, p 155–6; Minney, *Southwood*, p 286.
99. Hugh Cudlipp, *At Your Peril*, Weidenfeld and Nicolson 1962, p 272.
100. Ben Pimlott (ed.), *The Political Diaries of Hugh Dalton 1918–40, 1945–60*, Cape 1986, entry of 5.6.38, p 233.
101. Richard Cockett, *Twilight of Truth*, Weidenfeld and Nicolson 1989, pp 43–5.
102. F. Williams, *Nothing So Strange*, p 134; Jay, *Change and Fortune*, pp 66–72.
103. F. Williams, *Nothing So Strange*, p 132.
104. Jay, *Change and Fortune*, p 66; Interview with Lord Leatherland 4.6.81.
105. Cudlipp, *At Your Peril*, p 273.
106. DH 15.9.38.
107. DH 22, 26.9.38.
108. DH 27.9.38.
109. DH 29.9.38.
110. DH 1.10.38.
111. DH 25.5.30; A.J.P. Taylor, *Beaverbrook*, Penguin 1974, p 499.
112. F. Williams, *Nothing So Strange*, p 150.
113. *The Economist* 3.1.40; DH balance sheets 1938–9.
114. DH balance sheets 1938, 1939, 1942.
115. DH 30.8.23.
116. Curran and Seaton, *Power*, p 99.
117. DH statistics for 5-week periods ending 31.8.40, 30.8.41, TUC box 1532.
118. DH sales figures 1930–49.
119. DH balance sheets 1941–5.

120. Curran and Seaton, *Power*, p 126.
121. DH 5.1.43 (Webb), 11.4.43 (Bray).
122. NPD 1946 p 59.
123. Ibid.
124. Griffiths, *Press Encyclopedia*, p 600.
125. Ibid, p 82; Suzanne Bardgett, 'No braver companion ... no finer reporter: The writings of AB Austin, *Daily Herald* War Correspondent 1940–43', *Imperial War Museum Review no 6*, 1991, p 17.
126. Bardgett, 'No braver companion', pp 17–25.
127. F. Williams, *Nothing So Strange*, p 154; WPN 8.2.40.
128. F. Williams, *Nothing So Strange*, pp 150, 154.
129. Ibid, p 155.
130. Ibid, p 155; TUCGC 28.2.40 min no 121, 24.4.40 min no 166.
131. Griffiths, *Press Encyclopedia*, p 179; G.M. Thomson, 'Percy Cudlipp (1905–62)', E.T. Williams and C.S. Nicholls (eds) *Dictionary of National Biography 1961–70*, Oxford UP 1981, p 251; Jay, *Change and Fortune*, p 82.
132. Thomson, 'Cudlipp', DNB 1961–70, p 251; WPN 15, 22.2.40; David Low, *Low's Autobiography*, Michael Joseph 1956, p 287; D.Griffiths, *Plant Here the Standard*, Macmillan 1996, pp 253–5.
133. Griffiths, *Standard*, p 254, *Encyclopedia*, p 179.
134. Griffiths, *Encyclopedia*, p 179.
135. Jay, *Change and Fortune*, pp 110–1.
136. DH 4.4.40.
137. Cockett, *Twilight of Truth*, p 178.
138. DH 5.1.40.
139. DH 2.7.42.
140. DH 1.7.42.
141. DH 3.7.42.
142. DH 2.12.42.
143. DH 3.12.42.
144. DH 16.2.43.
145. DH 19.2.43.
146. DH 20.2.43.
147. Oral evidence to RCP, 27th day 31.3.48, HMSO Cmd 7432, para 9164; Cecil King, *With Malice Toward None*, Sidgwick and Jackson 1970, pp 312–3.
148. Oral evidence 31.3.48, para 9081.
149. Christiansen, *Headlines*, p 221.
150. Citrine to Cudlipp 31.5.44, Cudlipp to Citrine 7.6.44, TUC 790.07.
151. Jones, *Foot*, p 118.
152. Mass Observation Report no 1420 'Daily Herald Readers', Sep 1942, Mass Observation Archive, Sussex University.
153. Interview with Sir Tom Hopkinson 25.6.82.
154. Curran and Seaton, *Power*, pp 84–7.
155. A.C.H. Smith, *Paper Voices*, Chatto 1975, p 72.
156. T. Matthews, *The Sugar Pill*, Gollancz 1957, p 88.

157. Adrian Smith, 'The Fall and Fall of the Third *Daily Herald* 1930–64', paper delivered at Institute for Contemporary British History conference 10.9.96, p 9.

158. Minutes of conference on *Daily Herald* 7.3.46, TUC 790.01.

159. A. Smith, 'Third *Daily Herald*', p 12.

160. Maurice Edelman, *The Mirror: A Political History,* Hamish Hamilton 1966, p 149.

161. R.B. McCallum and Alison Readman, *The British General Election of 1945*, Frank Cass 1964, p 190.

162. Fienburgh, *25 Momentous Years*, p 149.

163. Edelman, *The Mirror*, p 149–50.

164. Minney, *Southwood*, p 351; DH sales figures 1930–49.

165. DH sales 1930–49.

166. NPD 1951, p 11.

167. DH 5.7.48.

168. DH 8.7.48.

169. DH 28.10.48.

170. DH 29.10.48.

171. Marjorie Proops obituary, *Guardian* 11.11.96.

172. DH 28.7.48.

173. Koss, *Rise and Fall*, p 644.

174. DH sales figures 1930–49.

175. *Daily Mirror* documentary evidence to RCP 1961–62, HMSO cmd 1812, vol 1, p 103.

176. Ibid, p 103.

177. Seymour-Ure and Schoff, *David Low*, pp 107–9; Bryant and Heneage, *Dictionary of British Cartoonists*, pp 17–18.

178. *Mirror* evidence to RCP 1961–62, p 102.

179. Lord Ardwick, 'W.N. Ewer 1885–1977', in Lord Blake and C.S. Nicholls (eds) *Dictionary of National Biography 1971–80*, pp 320–1; Interview with Geoffrey Goodman 6.11.86.

180. Hutt, *Newspaper Design*, p 47 .

181. Ibid p 264; *Printer's World* 18.4.57.

182. Jay, *Change and Fortune*, p 229.

183. WPN 27.11, 4.12.53.

184. WPN 4.12.53.

185. WPN 4.12.53.

186. WPN 4.12.53; Gordon Shaffer, *Baby in the Bathwater*, Book Guild, Lewes 1996, p 104; Leatherland interview 4.6.81.

187. Jay, *Change and Fortune*, p 229.

188. Philip Williams (ed.), *The Diaries of Hugh Gaitskell 1945–58*, Cape 1983, p 420.

189. Philip Williams, *Hugh Gaitskell,* Cape 1979, p 667.

190. P. Williams, *Gaitskell Diaries*, p 420.

191. Colin Seymour-Ure, *The Political Impact of the Mass Media,* Constable 1974, p 228.

192. Goodman interview 6.11.96.

193. Leslie Hunter, *The Road to Brighton Pier*, Arthur Barker 1959, p 34.

194. Ibid, pp 162–70.
195. Brian Brivati, *Hugh Gaitskell*, Richard Cohen 1996, p 171.
196. DH 11.4.51.
197. DH 23.4.51.
198. DH 24.4.51.
199. DH 20, 24.4.51.
200. Pimlott (ed.), *Dalton Diaries*, entry of 27.2.53, p 604; Janet Morgan (ed.), *The Backbench Diaries of Richard Crossman*, Cape 1981, entries of 10.3.52 (p 87), 24.9.52 (p 138), 14.10.52 (p 158), 23.10.52 (p 165), 26.2.53 (p 205); Jay, *Change and Fortune*, pp 225, 227.
201. DH 2–6.1.56.
202. DH 6.1.56.
203. DH 1, 3, 5.11.56.
204. P. Williams, *Gaitskell Diaries*, p 420.
205. Ibid, WPN 4.10.57.
206. Tewson to Dunbar 23.9.52, TUC 790.63.
207. *Keesing's Contemporary Archives*, Aug 17–24, 1951, para 15716A.
208. DH 'A directors' memo 29.4.57, TUC 790.7.
209. *Mirror* evidence to RCP 1961–62, p 102.
210. TUCGC min 21.12.55, TUC 790.37.
211. TUCGC min 3, 21.10.55, TUC 790.37; Chairman's reports to annual meeting of Odhams Press 1953, 1955, TUC 790.
212. Tewson memo 28.7.54, TUC 790.
213. Goodman interview 6.11.96.
214. A.Smith, 'Third *Daily Herald*', p 14.
215. Goodman interview 6.11.96.
216. DH 9.7.57.
217. A.J.P. Taylor, *A Personal History*, Coronet 1984, p 262; DH 31.10.53 (Independent mind), 4.1.56 (I say what I please).
218. Taylor, *Personal History*, p 275; Adam Sisman, *A.J.P. Taylor: A Biography*, Mandarin 1995, p 237.
219. DH 27.11.53.
220. DH 14.1.56.
221. Labour Party NEC minutes 22.6.55, TUC 790.37; DH 31.10.53 (Aubry), 20.7.57 (Holiday Girl).
222. Engel, *Tickle the Public*, p 187.
223. DH 7.1.53.
224. WPN 24.5.57.
225. A. Smith, 'Third *Daily Herald*', p 14 .
226. Ibid, p 34.
227. DH 25.7.57.
228. DH 27.5.57 (Geraldo), 13.7.57 (Karloff), 15.7.57 (Bankhead).
229. Hulton Readership Surveys, 1956–60.
230. F.J. Roe Ltd oral evidence to RCP 13.11.61, HMSO cmd 1812, vol 2, p 313, para 12883.
231. Goodman interview 6.11.96.
232. DH 14.11.53.

233. Simon Jenkins, *Newspapers: The Power and the Money*, Faber 1979, pp 32–3.
234. *The Economist* 27.11.60.
235. Curran and Seaton, *Power*, p 118.
236. DH balance sheet 1956, TUC 1532.
237. DH statistics 1.1–31.12.59, TUC 1532, Curran and Seaton, *Power*, p 73.
238. DH balance sheets 1951–56, TUC 1532.
239. DH balance sheets 1957–57, TUC 1532.
240. WPN 14.6.57.
241. *The Journalist*, July 1957.
242. Lord Layton, oral evidence to RCP 27.7.61, vol 2, p 465, para 6272; WPN 10.5.57; Duncan to Tewson 29.5.57, TUC 790.7.
243. Layton evidence to RCP 27.7.61, para 6274; Goodman interview 6.11.96.
244. 'A' directors memo 29.4.57, memo for TUCGC 26.6.57, TUC 790.7.
245. 'A' directors 29.4.57, *The Economist* 29.4.57.
246. TUCGC 29.5.57 min no 140.
247. Financial agreement 20.8.57, TUC 790.7, TUCGC 24.7.57 min no 154.
248. WPN 20.9, 4.10.57; *The Journalist* Sep/Oct 1957.
249. WPN 4.10.57.
250. H.J. Bradley (NUS) to Tewson 1.10.57, TUC 790.2.
251. *New Statesman* 21.9.57, quoted in *The Journalist* Sep/Oct 1957.
252. Jay, *Change and Fortune*, p 252.
253. Goodman interview 6.11.96.
254. DH 26.2.58; Jay, *Change and Fortune*, p 252; Geoffrey Goodman, *The Awkward Warrior: Frank Cousins, His Life and Times*, Davis-Poynter 1979, pp 208–9.
255. DH 25.2.58.
256. Goodman, *Frank Cousins*, p 208.
257. DH 1.3, 17.3.58.
258. Goodman interview 6.11.96.
259. DH 28.2.58.
260. Goodman, *Frank Cousins*, p 208.
261. Ibid, p 208.
262. DH 27.2.58.
263. DH 27.2.58.
264. Goodman, *Frank Cousins*, p 209.
265. Ibid, p 209.
266. Ibid, p 209.
267. Ibid, pp 209–10.
268. DH 27.2.58.
269. DH 11.3.58.
270. Goodman interview 6.11.96.
271. DH balance sheets 1958–60, TUC 1532.
272. Mirror evidence to RCP 1961–62, p 103.
273. James Curran, 'Advertising and the Press', in James Curran (ed.) *The British Press: A Manifesto*, Macmillan 1978, p 251.
274. Gibson (Odhams) to Tewson 3.6.60, TUC 790.7.

275. TUCGC 24.8.60; *Keesing's* 10–17.12.60, Para 17806.
276. RPTUC 1960, p 499.
277. WPN 2.9.60; David Ayerst, *The Manchester Guardian: Biography of a Newspaper*, Cornell UP, USA 1971, pp 570, 600–1.
278. WPN 2.9.60.
279. NPD 1961, p 16.
280. DH 1.9.60.
281. Curran and Seaton, *Power*, p 118.
282. Ibid, p 118.
283. DH 7.9.60.
284. DH 6.10.60.
285. DH 6.10.60.
286. DH 7.10.60.
287. DH 3.9.60; Goodman interview 6.11.96.
288. DH 3.10.60.
289. DH 5.9.60.
290. Seymour-Ure and Schoff, *David Low*, p 110.
291. DH 8.9.60.
292. DH 14.9.60.
293. DH 1.9.60 (Bing), 12.9.60 (Crazy Gang).
294. DH 22.9.60.
295. WPN 2.9.60.
296. *Mirror* evidence RCP 1961–62, p 103.
297. Ibid, p 103.
298. Ibid, p 103.
299. Ibid, p 72; De Launay (Odhams) to Woodcock 18.7.63, TUC 790.7.
300. Goodman interview 6.11.96.
301. Odhams oral evidence to RCP 4.5.61, vol 1, para 334, p 34; *Keesing's* 2–9.9.61, paras 18303A, 18304; TUCGC 22.2.61; Hugh Cudlipp, *Walking on the Water*, Bodley Head 1976, pp 246–8; Lord Thomson, *After I Was Sixty*, Hamish Hamilton 1975, pp 95–8.
302. Odhams evidence to RCP 1961–62, para 338, p 35.
303. P. Williams, *Hugh Gaitskell*, p 669.
304. Cudlipp, *Walking*, p 247.
305. Goodman interview 6.11.96.
306. Leatherland interview 4.6.81.
307. Thomson, *After Sixty*, p 98.
308. Hugh Cudlipp, *Walking*, p 248.
309. Ibid, p 249.
310. Leatherland interview 4.6.81.
311. Goodman interview 6.11.96.
312. Ibid.
313. P. Williams, *Hugh Gaitskell*, p 669.
314. DH 1.7, 8.9.64; Webb memo 22.11.37; Description of Wisdom by Stuart Marshall (*Financial Times*) to author 9.12.96.
315. DH 4.8.64.
316. DH 4.7.64 (Stones), 7.7.64 (Beatles), 8.9.64 (Kinks).
317. *Daily Mirror* oral evidence to RCP 26.6.61, para 2395, p 197.

318. RPTUC 1964, p 339.
319. Curran, 'Advertising and the Press', p 251.
320. Cudlipp, *Walking*, p 249.
321. Ibid p 249. TUCGCFGP 15.8.63, TUC 790.7.
322. Goodman interview 6.11.96.
323. Memo to TUCGCFGP 7.10.63, TUCGCFGP 7.10.63, TUC 790.7.
324. Account of meetings between TUC and IPC 15.8.63, TUC 790.7.
325. TUCGCFGP 9.1.64, TUC 790.7.
326. TUCGCFGP meeting with IPC 10.12.63, TUC 790.7.
327. Ibid.
328. *The Journalist*, Jan 1964.
329. DH NUJ chapel resolution Jan 1964, TUC 790.7.
330. Meeting between TUCGC and IPC 29.1.64, TUC 790.7.
331. DH 14.9.64.
332. Jenkins, *Newspapers*, p 37.
333. Tony Benn, *Out of the Wilderness: Diaries1963–7*, Hutchinson 1987, entry of 15.9.64, p 141.
334. Smith, *Paper Voices*, p 328.
335. Cudlipp, *Walking*, p 250.
336. Ibid, p 252; Chippindale and Horrie, *Stick It Up*, p 8.
337. Peter Chippindale and Chris Horrie, *Disaster: The Rise and Fall of the News on Sunday*, Sphere 1988, pp 51–68.
338. Ibid, pp 149–232.
339. DH 14.9.64.

CONCLUSION

1. *Guardian* 30.10.95 (Linton); John Curtice, 'Does *The Sun* Shine on Tony Blair?: Evidence From the British Election Panel Study', paper delivered at American Political Science Association conference, San Francisco 31.8.96; *Independent* 26.9.96.
2. *Times Higher Education Supplement* 9.2.96.
3. Bullock, *Bevin*, p 491 (Dalton); RCP 1947 3rd day 15.10.47, written evidence, p 20, para 50 (Swaffer).
4. Fienburgh, *25 Momentous Years*, pp 159–161.
5. Alan Lee, *Origins of the Popular Press in Britain 1855–1914*, Croom Helm 1976, p 18.
6. *Guardian* 14.9.64.
7. LPRAC 1924 p 177.
8. *Guardian* 23.8.90.
9. Curran and Seaton, *Power*, p 119.
10. Chairman's speech to 1960 AGM TUC 790.
11. Colin Seymour-Ure 'Fleet Street', in David Butler and Michael Pinto-Duschinsky (eds) *The British General Election of 1970*, Macmillan 1971, p 235.
12. Cudlipp, *At Your Peril*, pp 274–5.
13. Koss, *Rise and Fall*, pp 555–6.

14. Goodman interview 16.11.96.
15. Matthews to Tewson 25.8.60, TUC 790.7; *Observer* 16.1.97.
16. Driberg, *Swaff,* p 180.
17. F. Williams, *Dangerous,* p 182.
18. LeMahieu, *A Culture,* p 111.
19. Goodman interview 19.11.96.
20. A.C.H. Smith, *Paper Voices,* p 72.
21. John Benson, *The Working Class in Britain 1850–1939,* Longman 1989, pp 1, 174–201.
22. *New Statesman,* 20.12.96 .
23. Wertheimer, *Portrait,* p 113.
24. Ibid p 91.
25. Tewson to Dunbar 23.9.52, TUC 790.63; *Keesing's Contemporary Archives,* Aug 17–24, 1951, para 15716A.
26. Kenneth Morgan, *Modern Wales: Politics, Places and People,* University of Wales Press, Cardiff 1995, p 319.
27. Graham Cleverley, *The Fleet Street Disaster,* Constable 1976, p 155.
28. Remark made to author while in Ireland, February 1986.

Bibliography

PRIMARY SOURCES

Manuscript
Ernest Bevin papers, Modern Records Centre, Warwick.
Walter Citrine papers, London School of Economics.
G.D.H. Cole papers, Nuffield College, Oxford.
Daily Herald file, Daily Mirror Library.
Labour Party (*Daily Herald*) files, Labour Party Headquarters, Walworth Road, London, (now at the National Museum of Labour History, Manchester).
Labour Party Executive minutes. Harvester microfilm.
George Lansbury papers, London School of Economics.
Ramsay MacDonald papers: (i) Public Record Office, Kew; (ii) John Rylands Library, Manchester.
Mass Observation Archive, University of Sussex.
Miners Federation of Great Britain executive minutes, South Wales Miners Library, University of Wales, Swansea.
Trades Union Congress (*Daily Herald*) Files, Congress House, London, (now at the Modern Records Centre, Warwick University).
Trades Union Congress, General Council and Finance and General Purposes Committee minutes, General Strike files, Modern Records Centre, Warwick.

Printed
British Worker.
Daily Herald.
The Economist.
The Journalist.
Keesing's Contemporary Archives.
Labour Magazine, 1930.
Labour Party, *Report of the Annual Conference.*
Labour Who's Who 1927, Labour Publishing Company.
The Newspaper Press Directory, Mitchell and Co.
Newspaper World.
Royal Commissions on the Press, 1947–49, 1961–62, 1974–77.
Sell's World Press, 1919, 1921.
Report of the Proceedings of the Trades Union Congress.
World's Press News.

Interviews
Geoffrey Goodman, 6 November 1996.
Sir Tom Hopkinson, 25 June 1982.
Lord (Douglas) Jay, 21 June 1981.
Lord (Charles) Leatherland, 4 June 1981.

SECONDARY SOURCES

Books

Works on the Daily Herald its staff and directors.
Angell, Sir Norman, *After All*, Hamish Hamilton 1951.
—— *The Press and the Organisation of Society*, Gordon Fraser 1933.
Lord Ardwick, 'W.N. Ewer (1885–1977)', in Lord Blake and C.S. Nicholls (eds)
    Dictionary of National Biography 1971–80, Oxford UP 1986.
Boyne, Felix [W.P. Ryan], *Fleet Street in Starlight*, Selwyn and Blount 1923.
Branson, Noreen, *Poplarism 1919–25: George Lansbury and the Councillors'
    Revolt*, Lawrence and Wishart 1979.
Bullock, Alan, *The Life and Times of Ernest Bevin: Vol 1, Trade Union Leader
    1881–1940*, Heinemann 1960.
Calder, Ritchie, 'Lord Francis-Williams (1903–70)', in E.T. Williams and C.S.
    Nicholls (eds) *Dictionary of National Biography 1961–70*, Oxford UP 1981.
Lord Citrine, *Men and Work*, Hutchison 1964.
—— *Two Careers*, Hutchinson 1967.
Cole, Margaret, 'William Mellor (1888–1942),' DLB vol 4, 1977.
'Daily Herald', *Ten Thousandth Issue Celebration Souvenir*, Odhams 1948.
Driberg, Tom, *'Swaff': The Life and Times of Hannen Swaffer*, MacDonald and
    Jane's 1974.
Dutt, R. Palme, *The Rise and Fall of the 'Daily Herald'*, Labour Monthly/Daily
    Worker 1964.
Fienbergh, Wilfred, *1930–55: 25 Momentous Years: A 25th Anniversary in the
    History of the Daily Herald*, Odhams 1955.
Fyfe, Henry Hamilton, *Behind the Scenes of the Great Strike*, Labour Publishing
    Company 1926.
—— *My Seven Selves*, Allen and Unwin 1935.
—— *Press Parade*, Watts and Co 1936.
—— *Sixty Years of Fleet Street*, W.H. Allen 1949.
Gilbert, Martin, *Plough My Own Furrow: The Story of Lord Allen of Hurtwood as
    Told Through His Writings and Correspondence*, Longman 1965.
Harding, Keith, 'The "Co-operative Commonwealth": Ireland, Larkin and the
    Daily Herald', in S. Yeo (ed.) *New Views of Co-operation*, Routledge 1988.
Holman, Bob, *Good Old George*, Lion, Oxford 1990.
Hopkinson, Tom, *Of This Our Time*, Hutchinson 1982.
Hunter, Leslie, *The Road to Brighton Pier*, Arthur Barker 1959.
Jarche, James, *People I Have Shot*, Methuen 1934.
Jay, Douglas, *Change and Fortune*, Hutchinson 1980.

Jensen, John, *'A Sort of Bird of Freedom': Will Dyson 1880–1938*, University of Kent 1996.

Jones, Mervyn, *Michael Foot*, Gollancz 1994.

Kenney, Rowland, *Westering*, Dent 1939.

Lansbury, Edgar, *George Lansbury: My Father*, Sampson Low and Marston 1935.

Lansbury, George, *The Miracle of Fleet Street*, Victoria House 1925.

—— *My Life*, Constable 1935.

—— *Looking Backwards and Forwards*, Blackie 1935.

Leventhal, F.M. *Arthur Henderson*, Manchester UP 1989.

—— *The Last Dissenter: H.N. Brailsford and His Times*, Oxford UP 1985.

Low, David, *Low's Autobiography*, Michael Joseph 1956.

Marwick, Arthur, *Clifford Allen: The Open Conspirator*, Oliver and Boyd 1964.

Mason, Keith, *Front Seat*, self-published, Nottingham 1987.

Meynell, Francis, *My Lives*, Random House, New York 1971.

Minney, R.J., *Viscount Southwood*, Odhams 1954.

Neild, Barbara, and John Saville, 'John Scurr (1876–1932)', DLB vol 4, 1977.

Odhams, W.J.B., *The Business and I*, Martin Secker 1935.

Postgate, John and Mary, *A Stomach for Dissent: The Life of Raymond Postgate*, Keele UP 1994.

Postgate, Raymond, *A Life of George Lansbury*, Longman 1951.

Saville, John, 'Clifford Allen (1885–1939)', DLB vol 2, 1974.

—— 'C.W. Bowerman (1851–1947)', DLB vol 5, 1979.

—— 'Gerald Gould (1885–1936)', DLB vol 7, 1984.

—— 'Sir Ben Turner (1863–1942)', DLB vol 8, 1987.

Schneer, Jonathan, *Ben Tillett*, Croom Helm 1982.

—— *George Lansbury*, Manchester UP 1990.

Seymour-Ure Colin, and Jim Schoff, *David Low*, Secker and Warburg 1985.

Sharp, Evelyn, *Unfinished Adventure*, Bodley Head 1933.

Sisman, Adam, *A.J.P. Taylor: A Biography*, Mandarin 1995.

Slocombe, George, *The Tumult and the Shouting*, Heinemann 1936.

Taylor, A.J.P., *Personal History*, Coronet 1984.

Thomson, G.M., 'Percy Cudlipp (1905–62)', in DNB 1961–70.

Turner, Ben, *About Myself*, Humphrey Toulmin 1930.

Williams, Francis, *Press, Parliament and People*, Heinemann 1946.

—— *Dangerous Estate*, Longman 1957.

—— *A Pattern of Rulers*, Longman 1965.

—— *Nothing So Strange*, Cassell 1970.

Works on the Press

Allen, Robert, *Voice of Britain: The Inside Story of the Daily Express*, Patrick Stephens, Cambridge 1983.

Andrews Linton, and H.A. Taylor, *Lords and Laborers of the Press*, Southern Illinois UP 1970.

Armstrong, W. (ed.), *With Malice Toward None, A War Diary by Cecil King*, Sidgwick and Jackson 1970.

Asquith, Ivon, 'The Structure, Control and Ownership of the Press 1780–1855', in George Boyce, James Curran and Pauline Wingate (eds)

Newspaper History: From the 17th Century to the Present Day, Constable 1978.

Ayerst, David, *The Manchester Guardian: Biography of a Newspaper*, Cornell UP, Ithaca, New York 1971.

Boyce, George, James Curran and Pauline Wingate (eds), *Newspaper History: From the 17th Century to the Present Day*, Constable 1978.

Brodzky, Vivian (ed.), *Fleet Street: The Inside Story*, MacDonald 1966.

Bryant, M. and S. Heneage, *Dictionary of British Cartoonists and Caricturists, 1730–1980*, Scolar, Aldershot 1994.

Lord Camrose, *Newspapers and Their Controllers*, Cassell 1947.

Chippindale, Peter and Chris Horrie, *Disaster! The Rise and Fall of the News on Sunday*, Sphere 1988.

—— *Stick It Up Your Punter!*, Mandarin 1992.

Christiansen, Arthur, *Headlines All My Life*, Heinemann 1956.

Clarke, Tom, *My Lloyd George Diary*, Methuen 1939.

Cleverley, Graham, *The Fleet Street Disaster*, Constable 1976.

Cockett, Richard, *Twilight of Truth: Chamberlain, Appeasement and the Manipulation of the Press*, Weidenfeld 1989.

Cudlipp, Hugh, *Publish and Be Damned*, Andrew Dakers 1953.

—— *At Your Peril*, Weidenfeld and Nicolson 1962.

—— *Walking on the Water*, Bodley Head 1976.

Curran, James (ed.), *The British Press: A Manifesto*, Macmillan 1978.

Curran, James, 'Advertising as a Patronage System', in H. Christian (ed.) *Sociology of Journalism and the Press*, Sociological Review monograph no 29, Keele University 1980.

Curran, James, Angus Douglas and Gary Whannell, 'The Political Economy of the Human Interest Story', in Anthony Smith (ed.) *Newspapers and Democracy*, MIT Press, Cambridge, Mass 1980.

Curran, James, and Jean Seaton, *Power Without Responsibility*, Fontana 1981.

Davies, Russell, and Liz Ottaway, *Vicky*, Secker and Warburg 1987.

Edelman, Maurice, *The Mirror: A Political History*, Hamish Hamilton 1966.

Evans, Trevor (ed.), *The Great Bohunkus*, W.H. Allen 1953.

Gannon, Franklin L., *The British Press and Germany 1936–1939*, Oxford UP 1971.

Goodhart, David and Patrick Wintour, *Eddie Shah and the Newspaper Revolution*, Coronet 1986.

Griffiths, Denis, *Plant High the Standard*, Macmillan 1996.

(ed.), *Encyclopaedia of the British Press*, Macmillan 1992.

Grundy, Bill, *The Press Inside Out*, W.H. Allen 1976.

Hall, Alex, *Scandal, Sensation and Social Democracy: The SPD Press and Wilhelmine Germany 1890–1914*, Cambridge UP 1977.

Hansard, B.M., *In and Out of Fleet Street*, Hansard Publishing, Gosport 1935.

Herd, Harold, *The March of Journalism*, Allen and Unwin 1972.

Hill, Douglas (ed.), *Tribune 40*, Quartet 1977.

Harrison, Stanley, *Poor Men's Guardians*, Lawrence and Wishart 1974.

Hopkin, Deian, 'The Socialist Press in Britain 1890–1910', in George Boyce, James Curran and Pauline Wingate (eds) *Newspaper History: From the 17th Century to the Present Day*, Constable 1978.

—— 'The Left-wing Press and the New Journalism', in Joel H. Wiener (ed.), *Papers for the Millions: The New Journalism in Britain 1850–1914*, Greenwood, Westport, Connecticut 1988.

Hutt, Allen, *Newspaper Design*, Oxford UP 1960.

Incorporated Society of British Advertisers, *The Readership of Newspapers and Periodicals in Great Britain*, ISBA 1936.

Jameson, Derek, *Touched by Angels*, Ebury Press 1988.

—— *Last of the Hot Metal Men*, Penguin 1991.

Jenkins, Simon, *Newspapers: The Power and the Money*, George Allen and Unwin 1979.

—— *The Market for Glory*, Faber and Faber 1986.

King, Cecil, *The Future of the Press*, MacGibbon and Kee 1967.

—— *Strictly Personal*, Weidenfeld and Nicolson 1969.

Koss, Stephen, *Fleet Street Radical: A.G. Gardiner and the Daily News*, Allen Lane 1973.

—— *The Rise and Fall of the Political Press in Britain, Volume 2: The Twentieth Century*, Hamish Hamilton 1984.

Kynaston, David, *The Financial Times: A Centenary History*, Viking 1988.

Lee, Alan, *Origins of the Popular Press in Britain 1855–1914*, Croom Helm 1976.

LeMahieu, D.L., *A Culture for Democracy*, Clarendon, Oxford 1988.

Linton, David and Ray Boston, *The Newspaper Press in Britain: An Annotated Bibliography*, Mansell 1987.

Mathews, T.S., *The Sugar Pill*, Gollancz 1957.

Negrine, Ralph, *Politics and the Mass Media in Britain*, Routledge, 1994.

Orwell, George, 'Boy's Stories', in *Collected Essays, Journalism and Letters, Vol One: An Age Like This 1920–40*, Penguin 1970.

Political and Economic Planning, *Report on the British Press*, PEP 1938.

Pound, Reginald and Geoffrey Harmsworth, *Northcliffe*, Cassell 1959.

Rust, William, *The Story of the Daily Worker*, People's Press 1949.

Schaffer, Gordon, *Baby in the Bathwater*, Book Guild, Lewes 1996.

Seymour-Ure, Colin, *The Political Impact of the Mass Media*, Constable 1974.

—— 'The Press and the Party System between the Wars', in Gillian Peele and Chris Cook (eds) *The Politics of Reappraisal 1918–39*, Macmillan 1975.

Smith, A.C.H., *Paper Voices*, Chatto and Windus 1975.

Smith, Adrian, *The New Statesman: Portrait of a Political Weekly 1913–1931*, Frank Cass 1996.

Smith, Anthony, *The Newspaper: an International History*, Thames and Hudson 1979.

Snowden, Philip, 'Why Labour Papers Fail', in *Sell's World Press* 1919.

Steed, Henry Wickham, *The Press*, Penguin 1938.

Taylor, A.J.P., *Beaverbrook*, Penguin 1974.

Todorov, Dafin, *Freedom Press: The Development of the Progressive Press in Western Europe and the USA*, International Organisation of Journalists, Prague 1980.

Lord Thomson, *After I Was Sixty*, Hamish Hamilton 1975.

Tunstall, Jeremy, *The Media in Britain*, Constable 1983.

——'The British Press in the Age of Television', in H. Christian (ed.) *Sociology of Journalism and the Press*, Sociological Review Monograph 29, Keele University 1980.

Walker, Martin, *Daily Sketches: A Cartoon History of Twentieth Century Britain*, Frederick Muller 1978.

Whale, John, *The Politics of the Media*, Fontana 1977.

Wiener, Joel, 'Sources for the Study of Newspapers', in Laurel Brake, Aled Jones and Lionel Madden (eds) *Investigating Victorian Journalism*, Macmillan 1990.

Wilson, Trevor (ed.), *The Political Diaries of C.P. Scott 1911–28*, William Collins 1970.

Williams, Raymond, *Culture and Society 1780–1950*, Chatto and Windus 1958.

—— *The Long Revolution*, Chatto and Windus 1961.

Wintour, Charles, *The Rise and Fall of Fleet Street*, Hutchinson 1989.

Works on the Labour Movement

Bellamy, Joyce and John Saville (eds), *Dictionary of Labour Biography, vols 1–8*, Macmillan 1973–87.

Benson, John, *The Working Class in Britain 1850–1939*, Longman 1989.

Birch, Lionel (ed.), *A History of the TUC 1868–1968*, TUC 1968.

Brand, Carl F., *The British Labour Party*, Oxford UP 1965.

Brivati, Brian, *Hugh Gaitskell*, Richard Cohen 1996.

Brown, George, *In My Way*, Gollancz 1971.

Callaghan, John, *Socialism in Britain*, Blackwell, Oxford 1990.

Castle, Barbara, *Fighting All the Way*, Macmillan 1993.

Clegg, Hugh, *A History of British Trade Unions Since 1889, vol II 1911–33*, Clarendon, Oxford 1985.

Cole, G.D.H., *A History of the Labour Party from 1914*, Macmillan 1968.

Cole, Margaret (ed.), *The Beatrice Webb Diaries 1912–24*, Longman 1952.

—— *The Beatrice Webb Diaries 1924–32*, Longman 1956.

Cowling, Maurice, *The Impact of Labour 1920–24*, Cambridge UP 1971.

Cross, Colin, *Philip Snowden*, Barrie and Rockcliff 1966.

Davies, Paul, *A.J. Cook*, Manchester UP 1987.

Donoghue, Bernard and George Jones, *Herbert Morrison: Portrait of a Politician*, Weidenfeld and Nicolson 1973.

Foot, Michael, *Aneurin Bevan: Volume One 1897–1945*, Paladin 1975.

—— *Aneurin Bevan: Volume Two 1945–1960*, Davis-Poynter 1973.

Gillespie, James, 'Poplarism and Proletarianism: Unemployment and Labour Politics in London 1918–34', in David Feldman and Gareth Stedman-Jones (eds) *Metropolis: London: Histories and Representation Since 1880*, Routledge 1989.

Goodman, Geoffrey, *The Awkward Warrior: Frank Cousins, His Life and Times*, Davis Poynter 1979.

Griffiths, Robert, *S.O. Davies: A Socialist Faith*, Gomer Press, Llandyssul 1983.

Gupta, Partha Sarathi, *Imperialism and the British Labour Movement*, Macmillan 1975.

Hannington, Wal, *Unemployed Struggles 1919–36*, Lawrence and Wishart 1936.

Hinton, James, *Labour and Socialism*, Wheatsheaf, Brighton 1983.

Howell, David, *British Social Democracy*, Croom Helm 1976.

Hutt, Allen, *British Trade Unionism*, Lawrence and Wishart 1941.

'Iconoclast' [M.A. Hamilton], *The Man of Tomorrow: J. Ramsay MacDonald*, Leonard Parsons, Newcastle on Tyne 1923.

Knox, William, *James Maxton*, Manchester UP 1987.

Lee, Jennie, *My Life with Nye*, Jonathan Cape 1980.

McHenry, Dean, *The Labour Party in Transition 1931–1938*, George Routledge 1938.

MacIntyre, Angus, *A Proletarian Science*, Cambridge UP 1980.

McKibbin, Ross, *The Evolution of the Labour Party 1910–24*, Clarendon, Oxford 1974.

—— *The Ideologies of Class: Social Relations in Britain 1880–1950*, Oxford UP 1990.

McKinley, Alan, and R.J. Morris, *The ILP on Clydeside: From Foundation to Disintegration 1893–1932*, Manchester UP 1991.

Mahon, John, *Harry Pollitt: A Biography*, Lawrence and Wishart 1976.

Marquand, David, *Ramsay MacDonald*, Jonathan Cape 1977.

—— *The Progressive Dilemma*, Heinemann 1991.

Middlemas, Robert Keith, *The Clydesiders*, Hutchinson 1965.

—— *Politics in Industrial Society*, Andre Deutsch 1979.

Miliband, Ralph, *Parliamentary Socialism*, Allen and Unwin 1961.

Morgan, Janet (ed.), *The Backbench Diaries of Richard Crossman*, Jonathan Cape 1981.

Morgan, Kenneth, *Labour People*, Oxford UP 1987.

Morris, Margaret, *The General Strike*, Penguin 1976.

Pelling, Henry, *A History of British Trade Unionism*, Pelican 1963.

—— *A Short History of the Labour Party*, Macmillan 1961.

Phelps-Brown, Henry, *The Origins of Trade Union Power*, Oxford UP 1983.

Pimlott, Ben (ed.), *The Political Diaries of Hugh Dalton 1918–40, 1945–60*, Jonathan Cape 1986.

Price, Richard, *Labour in British Society*, Routledge 1990.

Renshaw, Patrick, 'The Depression Years', in B. Pimlott and C. Cook (eds) *Trade Unions in British Politics*, Longman 1982.

Reynolds, Gerry W. and Tony Judge, *The Night the Police Went on Strike*, Weidenfeld and Nicolson 1968.

Saville, John, *The Labour Movement in Britain*, Faber and Faber 1988.

Schwarz, Bill, *Constitutionalism and Extra-Parliamentary Action*, Centre for Contemporary Cultural Studies, University of Birmingham, occasional paper no 75 1984.

—— and Martin Durham, 'A Safe and Sane Labourism', in Mary Langan and Bill Schwarz (eds) *Crises in the British State*, Hutchinson 1985.

Shaw, Eric, *Discipline and Discord in the Labour Party*, Manchester UP 1988.

Skidelsky, Robert, *Politicians and the Slump*, Pelican 1970.

Thompson, Willie, *The Good Old Cause: British Communism 1920–1991*, Pluto Press 1992.

Thurtle, Ernest, *Time's Winged Chariot*, Chaterson 1945.
Tracey, Herbert, *The Book of the Labour Party (3 vols)* Books for Libraries Press, Freeport, NY 1971.
Wertheimer, Egon, *Portrait of the Labour Party*, Putnam 1929.
White, Joseph, *Tom Mann*, Manchester UP 1991.
Williams, Philip, *Hugh Gaitskell*, Jonathan Cape 1979.
—— (ed.), *The Diaries of Hugh Gaitskell 1945–58*, Jonathan Cape 1983.
Williams, Andrew, *Labour and Russia*, Manchester 1989.
Winstone, Ruth (ed.), *Years of Hope: Papers and Letters of Tony Benn 1940–62*, Hutchinson 1994.
Wrigley, Chris, *Lloyd George and the Challenge of Labour*, Harvester, Hemel Hempstead 1990.

Historical Background
Addison, Paul, *The Road to 1945*, Jonathan Cape 1975.
Andrew, Christopher, *Secret Service*, Sceptre 1986.
Ball, Stuart, *Baldwin and the Conservative Party*, Yale UP, New Haven 1988.
Batchelor, Denzil, *Jack Johnson and His Times*, Sportsman's Book Club 1957.
Blythe, Ronald, *The Age of Illusion*, Hamish Hamilton 1963.
Butler, David and Gareth Butler, *British Political Facts 1900–1994*, Macmillan 1994.
Cunneen, Chris, 'Hugh Donald McIntosh (1876–1942)' in J Ritchie, (ed.) *Australian Dictionary of Biography Vol 10*, Melbourne UP 1986.
Dangerfield, George, *The Strange Death of Liberal England*, MacGibbon and Kee 1966.
Gilbert, Martin, *Winston S Churchill, Volume VI, Finest Hour 1939–41*, Heinemann 1983.
Halsey, A.H. (ed.), *Trends in British Society Since 1900*, Macmillan 1972.
Hennessy, Peter, *Never Again: Britain 1945–51*, Jonathan Cape 1992.
Kinnear, Michael, *The Fall of Lloyd George*, Macmillan 1973.
Lidke, Vernon, *The Alternative Culture: Socialist Labour in Imperial Germany*, Oxford UP 1985.
McCallum, R.B. and Alison Readman, *The British General Election of 1945*, Oxford UP 1947.
Mansfield, Peter, *The British in Egypt*, Weidenfeld and Nicolson 1971.
Morgan, Kenneth O., *Modern Wales: Politics, Places and People*, University of Wales Press, Cardiff 1995.
Mortimer, Edward, *The Rise of the French Communist Party*, Faber and Faber 1974.
Mowat, C.L., *Britain Between the Wars 1918–40*, Methuen 1955.
Orwell, George, 'Decline of the English Murder', in *Collected Essays, Journalism and Letters: Vol 4: In Front of Your Nose 1945–50*, Secker and Warburg 1970.
Schlesinger Jr, Arthur M., *Robert Kennedy and His Times*, Andre Deutsch 1978.
Stevenson, John, *British Society 1914–45*, Penguin 1984.
Symons, Julian, *Horatio Bottomley*, Cresset 1955.
Taylor, A.J.P., *The Trouble Makers*, Hamish Hamilton 1957.
—— *English History 1914–45*, Penguin 1970.

Whittington-Egan, Richard, *The Ordeal of Philip Yale Drew*, Harrap 1972.
Wintle, Justin, and Richard Kenin, *The Penguin Concise Dictionary of Biographical Quotation*, Penguin 1981.

Fiction
Gibbs, Philip, *The Street of Adventure*, Heinemann 1919.
Thomas, Gwyn, *Sorrow for Thy Sons*, Lawrence and Wishart 1986.
Tressell, Robert, *The Ragged Trousered Philanthropists*, Lawrence and Wishart 1955.
Wodehouse, P.G., *Ukridge*, Herbert Jenkins 1924.

Articles
Bardgett, Suzanne, 'No Braver Companion ... No Finer Reporter: The writings of A.B. Austin, *Daily Herald* War Correspondent 1940–43', *Imperial War Museum Review*, no 6, 1991.
Chalaby, Jean, '20 Years of Contrast: The French and British Press in the Interwar Period', *European Journal of Sociology*, vol XXXVII, 1996.
Deli, Peter, 'The Image of the Russian Purges in the *Daily Herald* and the *New Statesman*', *Journal of Contemporary History*, vol 20, 1985.
Epstein, James A., 'Feargus O'Connor and the Northern Star', *International Review of Social History*, vol 21, no 1, 1976.
Holton, Robert, '*Daily Herald* v *Daily Citizen* 1912–15', *International Review of Social History*, vol 19, 1974.
Richards, Huw, 'The *Daily Herald* 1912–64', *History Today*, December 1981.
—— 'The *Daily Herald* 1919–40', *Bulletin of the Society for the Study of Labour History* 1982.
—— 'News Coverage or Bingo?', *Journalism Studies Review*, July 1983.
—— 'Mourned but Not Missed by the Masses', *Times Higher Education Supplement*, 14.9.89.
—— '"The Ragged Man of Fleet Street": The *Daily Herald* in the 1920s', *Contemporary Record*, vol 8, 1994.
—— '"Selling the Pass": The *Daily Herald* and the 1923 Docks Strike', *Studies in Newspaper and Periodical History*, 1994 Annual.
Shore, Elliott, 'Selling Socialism: *The Appeal to Reason* and the Radical Press in Turn of the Century America', *Media, Culture and Society*, vol 7, no 2, 1985.

Unpublished Material
Curtice, John, 'Does the *Sun* shine on Tony Blair?: Evidence from the British Election Panel Study', paper given at the American Political Studies Association, San Francisco, 31 August 1996.
Ewer, W.N., 'The Miracle of Fleet Street', syndicated(?) feature 1949, *Daily Mirror* library.
Ichikawa, Tomoko, 'The *Daily Citizen* 1912–15: A Study of the First Labour Daily Newspaper in Britain', MPhil thesis, University College of Wales, Aberystwyth 1985.
Mason, Tony, 'Local Heroes', paper given at the Sport, Literature and National Identity conference, Swansea, 30 April 1995.

Postgate, Raymond, '*Daily Herald* analysis', G.D.H. Cole Papers, Nuffield College, Oxford.

Richards, Huw, 'The *Daily Herald* 1919–40', Society for the Study of Labour History conference, Birkbeck College November 1980.

—— 'Between Two Stools?', *New Socialist*, 1982.

—— '"Constriction, Conformity and Control": The Taming of the *Daily Herald* 1921–30', Open University PhD thesis, 1993.

Smith, A.C.H., Elizabeth Immirzi, Trevor Blackwell, 'The Popular Press and Social Change 1935-65', Centre for Contemporary Cultural Studies, University of Birmingham 1970.

Smith, Adrian, 'The Fall and Fall of the Third *Daily Herald* 1930–64', paper at Institute for Contemporary British History conference, 10 September 1996.

Todd, Sue, 'The *Daily Herald*', draft script for audio-visual display at National Museum of Film, Television and Photography, Bradford June 1985.

Broadcast Material

Kington, Miles, 'You Are Mr Lobby Lud', BBC Radio 4, December 1983.

Index

Index by Auriol Griffith-Jones